The Social Thought of
Émile Durkheim

Social Thinkers Series

Series Editor
A. Javier Treviño
Wheaton College, Norton, MA

Published

The Social Thought of Georg Simmel
By Horst J. Helle

The Social Thought of Émile Durkheim
By Alexander Riley

The Social Thought of C. Wright Mills
By A. Javier Treviño

Forthcoming

The Social Thought of Karl Marx
By Justin P. Holt

The Social Thought of Erving Goffman
By Michael Hviid Jacobsen and Søren Kristiansen

The Social Thought of Talcott Parsons
By Helmut Staubmann

The Social Thought of
Émile Durkheim

Alexander Riley
Bucknell University

Los Angeles | London | New Delhi
Singapore | Washington DC

Los Angeles | London | New Delhi
Singapore | Washington DC

FOR INFORMATION:

SAGE Publications, Inc.
2455 Teller Road
Thousand Oaks, California 91320
E-mail: order@sagepub.com

SAGE Publications Ltd.
1 Oliver's Yard
55 City Road
London EC1Y 1SP
United Kingdom

SAGE Publications India Pvt. Ltd.
B 1/I 1 Mohan Cooperative Industrial Area
Mathura Road, New Delhi 110 044
India

SAGE Publications Asia-Pacific Pte. Ltd.
3 Church Street
#10-04 Samsung Hub
Singapore 049483

Copyright © 2015 by SAGE Publications, Inc.

Printed in the United States of America.

Library of Congress Cataloging-in-Publication Data

Riley, Alexander.
The social thought of Émile Durkheim /
Alexander Riley, Bucknell University.

pages cm.—(Social thinkers series)
Includes bibliographical references and index.

ISBN 978-1-4522-0263-1 (alk. paper)

1. Durkheim, Émile, 1858–1917.
2. Sociology—Philosophy. I. Title.

HM479.D87R56 2013
301.01—dc23   2013037525

Acquisitions Editor: Jeff Lasser
Editorial Assistant: Lauren Johnson
Production Editor: David C. Felts
Copy Editor: Kim Husband
Typesetter: C&M Digitals (P) Ltd.
Proofreader: Talia Greenberg
Cover Designer: Gail Buschman
Marketing Manager: Erica DeLuca

14 15 16 17 18 10 9 8 7 6 5 4 3 2 1

To the memory of Robert Bellah, perhaps the greatest scholar of religion and culture since Durkheim, who died on July 30, 2013, as I was finishing the final draft of the manuscript

Contents

Series Editor's Foreword

The SAGE Social Thinkers series is dedicated to making available compact, reader-friendly paperbacks that examine the thought of major figures from within and beyond sociology. The books in this series provide concise introductions to the work, life, and influences of the most prominent social thinkers. Written in an accessible and provocative prose, these books are designed for advanced undergraduate and graduate students of sociology, politics, economics, and social philosophy, as well as for scholars and socially curious general readers.

The first few volumes in the series are devoted to the "classical" thinkers—Karl Marx, Émile Durkheim, Max Weber, Georg Simmel, George Hebert Mead, Talcott Parsons, and C. Wright Mills—who, through their seminal writings, laid the foundation for much of current social thought. Subsequent books will feature more "contemporary" scholars as well as those not yet adequately represented in the canon: Jane Addams, Charlotte Perkins Gilman, Harold Garfinkel, Norbert Elias, Jean Baudrillard, and Pierre Bourdieu. Particular attention is paid to those aspects of the social thinker's personal background and intellectual influences that most impacted his or her approach in better understanding individuals and society.

Consistent with SAGE's distinguished track record of publishing high-quality textbooks in sociology, the carefully assembled volumes in the Social Thinkers series are authored by respected scholars committed to disseminating the discipline's rich heritage of social thought and to helping students comprehend key concepts. The information offered in these books will be invaluable for making sense of the complexities of contemporary social life and various issues that have become central concerns of the human condition: inequality, social order, social control, deviance, the social self, rationality, reflexivity, and so on.

These books in the series can be used as self-contained volumes or in conjunction with textbooks in sociological theory. Each volume concludes with a Further Readings chapter intended to facilitate additional study and research. As a collection, the Social Thinkers series will stand as a testament to the robustness of contemporary social thought. Our hope is that these books on the great social thinkers will give students a deeper understanding of modern and postmodern Western social thought and encourage them to engage in sociological dialogue.

Premised on Newton's aphorism, "If I have seen farther, it is by standing on the shoulders of giants" (an aphorism, incidentally, that was introduced into sociology by Robert K. Merton, himself a towering figure in the discipline), the Social Thinkers series aims to place its readers on the shoulders of the giants of 19th- and 20th-century social thought.

Acknowledgments

My thanks to A. Javier Treviño for the invitation to write this book, which gave me a wonderful opportunity to summarize and put into order material I have been thinking with and teaching for the past decade and a half. I am profoundly indebted to the many colleagues and friends whose writing on Durkheim has influenced me in one way or another over the years. Far too numerous to attempt to name exhaustively, the most important among these scholars include Jeffrey Alexander, Robert Bellah, Philippe Besnard, Marcel Fournier, Mike Gane, Victor Karady, Steven Lukes, William Watts Miller, W. S. F. Pickering, and Edward Tiryakian. Readers of this book who wish to deepen their knowledge of Durkheim and the contemporary application of Durkheimian thought are strongly encouraged to consult their work.

Introduction

É mile Durkheim is universally recognized as one of the founders of the discipline of sociology, but he may well also be the member of the central trio of the founding generation (Max Weber and Karl Marx are its other two members) whose reputation is lowest among contemporary sociologists. He is not infrequently accused of seeing society as static and unchanging, and liking things that way, and of totally rejecting problems of interpretation and meaning. It is claimed by some that he is at his core an apolitical, or perhaps even reactionary, positivist who thinks sociology is or should be a kind of approximation of a laboratory science, and that he envisions the morally healthy society as a quasi-totalitarian entity that forcibly compels the individual to its collective will. A brief consultation of American and British introductory texts reveals a depressing scenario in which this caricature is drawn and redrawn, usually with little or no consultation of original sources and a mere glance at the already existing "common sense" about Durkheim in the discipline. Recently, in June 2012, a sociologist-blogger writing in the *Chronicle of Higher Education* online provided something of an ideal typical example of this kind of derisive and uninformed dismissal of Durkheim. In an entry titled "Flawed Sociology on Gay Parenting," Laurie Essig denounced a study on homosexual parenting that produced results with which she was dissatisfied by comparing the author of the study to the purportedly "deeply conservative" Durkheim. The questionable evidence submitted in defense of this claim was the fact that Durkheim believed the conjugal family is a particularly effective moral institution that should be preserved and strengthened. Alas, Essig lamented, it may unfortunately be the case that "every generation of sociology is doomed to have its Durkheim."

This may well be a particularly benighted example, but others could easily be mustered. The reasons for this state of affairs, in which people with Ph.D.s in sociology can come to believe things about one of the founders of the discipline (e.g., that Durkheim can be adequately considered a "conservative") that are wholly inconsistent with the content of his writings, are complex, but at least two central factors can be indicated: the political drift of much contemporary sociology to a position on the far cultural left where certain ideological commitments serve as a kind of *a priori* recognition of what is and what is not acceptable in sociological theory and research and a long and well-established tradition, especially in English-speaking sociology, of interpretation of the meaning of Durkheim's work that is based largely on significant misreading. One insightful recent commentator on Durkheim sums up the matter with acuity: "*It has rightly been observed that Durkheim is well-known but not known well*" (Jones, 2001, p. 1, emphasis added). The problem is not limited to the English-speaking academic world. One of the greatest French scholars of Durkheim's work remarked once in an interview that his interest in the founder of French sociology was stimulated initially by his "surprise" at the discovery of "the complexity of a body of thought . . . that had been presented to me in my previous studies as consisting of a great simplicity" (Besnard, 2004, p. 389).

Even foundational thinkers can be greatly or even completely misunderstood, especially by audiences who do not speak their native tongue. Unreliable translations emerge and circulate; important work is never translated and therefore seldom read or considered in summaries of the thinker's work; inaccurate or ideologically biased secondary interpretations by influential English-language scholars proliferate and become gospel; and formulaic and incorrect summaries of the work become omnipresent in textbooks, which cannibalistically sustain themselves on one another. Few ever go back to the original sources to see if the image created by all these distorting prisms is even close to the truth. Mary Pickering's recent work on Auguste Comte (2006, 2009) offers a troubling example of this phenomenon. She shows us, in an exhaustive multivolume intellectual biography of one of the founding figures of sociology, who is today almost never read, that a great deal and some of the most basic material that English-speaking sociologists have been taught about Comte's thought is wrong, often egregiously so.

In Durkheim's case, it is fairly clear that a small number of commentators have had a disproportionate impact on the way his thought is understood. In France, the reception of his work was fundamentally influenced for at least a generation after his death by the mercilessly antagonistic and careless reading of Marxists and other radical leftists such as Paul Nizan and Jean-Paul Sartre. In the United States, Talcott Parsons, in his well-known introduction to Durkheim's work, claimed that he should be viewed fundamentally as a student of the positivist Comte, whom Parsons named "Durkheim's acknowledged master" (Parsons, 1937, p. 307). Yet, as will become clear in this book, Durkheim criticized Comte relentlessly and explicitly denied the appellation "positivist" to his thought. Another mid-20th-century American sociologist, Robert Nisbet, attempted to turn Durkheim into a kind of Reagan conservative before the fact in a series of books that reached a fairly wide audience (1966, 1974, 1976). Nisbet saw Durkheim as an unrelenting critic of virtually all of modernity and an advocate of a return to the social structures of medieval Europe. He was required to discount the most obvious evidence to forward such a reading, including a nearly complete dismissal of Durkheim's lifelong interest in socialism as both an intellectual topic of investigation and a personal politics.

In this book, rather than applying in advance an ideological or interpretive rubric with which to view Durkheim's thought, I try to allow Durkheim to speak as straightforwardly as possible for himself, by reading through most of his major works, both those published in his lifetime and those that emerged posthumously, while endeavoring to carefully situate his thought in the social and intellectual context of his times. My goal is to present a case for Durkheim's perspective as perhaps the most properly *sociological* to be found among the discipline's founders. The evidence is considerable that he thought through the nature of society, culture, and the complex relationship of the individual to the collective in a manner more concentrated and thorough than virtually any other thinker alive during the period (roughly 1880–1920) of the emergence of sociology.

But if he was so compelling, why is he now so incompletely understood? A good deal of the answer has to do specifically with the practices of English-speaking, and particularly American, sociologists, as noted previously. Those sociologists are, however, part of a larger social world, and some of the most basic facts of the tenor of that social world suggest that one of the main reasons we misunderstand and reject Durkheim's ideas in the contemporary West (and perhaps especially in the United States) has to do with the moral trajectories of many contemporary societies. Those trajectories are in some important ways *pathological*, to use Durkheim's language, and the social medicine required to cure the pathologies, which Durkheim explored in much of his work, is something the patient is greatly interested in avoiding, as we fail to grasp the gravity of our illness. The complexity of his ideas and their implications for politics have made it difficult for thinkers of less nuance and more simplistically defined ideological positions to grasp their descriptive and explanatory power. Those on both the traditional left and right frequently find Durkheim too catholic in his prescriptions because, although he certainly understood sociology to have a significant contribution to make to politics and policy, it was ultimately not pure ideology that drove him but rather the desire to conceive intellectual tools that could reveal the reality of society and thereby furnish reformers with accurate knowledge to apply to their task.

Durkheim lived in a social world that was faced with numerous problems (e.g., a rising individualism unhinged from moral engagement with the community and the weakening of religious ties and uncertainty that secular morality could effectively replace them), and he felt a moral imperative as an intellectual to speak to those problems, but he did so always from the perspective of a social scientist focused first and foremost on knowing the truth about the workings of the human world, even if those truths ran counter to his own *a priori* beliefs about what was to be done. This remains a tremendously powerful intellectual and moral position today, and as I describe the contours of Durkheim's thinking, I will invoke examples of social and cultural issues and problems in the contemporary world that can be fruitfully addressed from a Durkheimian framework.

There are a great many volumes on Durkheim that endeavor, as this book does, to introduce him and his thought to an audience without much previous knowledge of his work. One of the problems that limits many of these works is their way of talking about the writing and thought of Durkheim as though it simply wrote itself, divorced from the real life of a human being writing at a particular time in a particular place. This book will fully embrace the perspective of the sociology of knowledge and its central axiom: that *ideas are produced by beings who are thoroughly social and cultural— that is, who are inevitably and profoundly affected in their intellectual efforts by structures, events, and contexts of their times and locations.* Great thinkers are no different on this score than the average members of a society. What they think, and even what they *can* think, has a great deal to do with the lives they lead and the conditions in which those lives emerge.

Practically speaking, this perspective requires paying real attention to a number of sources that are almost never consulted in the writing of this kind of book—for example, the fat tome of Durkheim's letters to his nephew and intellectual colleague Marcel Mauss (Durkheim, 1998), in which we see the emergence of intellectual and political agendas in the intimate lives and interaction of these two great founders of the French social sciences. My intention is obviously not to try to unveil radically new elements of Durkheim's biography; nor will I indulge in endless and unfocused inspection of minute details of Durkheim's life. But I want to be sure to root the ideas and arguments Durkheim produced during the course of his career in the experiences and events of his life and the social and cultural structures of the France of the Third Republic in which he lived. It matters a great deal, for example, that the Dreyfus Affair took place at the height of Durkheim's academic rise, and even an introductory text should attempt to describe why this is so. A perhaps even more crucial example here has to do with the role played by the research team

Durkheim organized around his journal, *l'Année sociologique,* in his own intellectual life. Any careful discussion of his work must attempt to place it in the context of the eminently collective intellectual labor of this group, which means at the most basic level simply acknowledging that Durkheim did not produce his ideas in a vacuum but in concerted interaction with a group of close intellectual allies.

Outline of the Book

The first chapter constitutes a mini–biographical study of Durkheim, with the aims laid out previously. Chapter 2 will very briefly summarize Durkheim's views of the individual and society and sketch out his vision of sociological method; these topics will then be more fully pursued in Chapters 3 through 7.

Chapter 3 is the fattest chapter because it deals with the wide-ranging body of Durkheim's writing in which he directly addressed questions of moral solidarity. This is a topic that appeared in some form in virtually everything he wrote, but in some of the work it shows up in a more extensive manifestation. The main works considered in this chapter are *The Division of Labor in Society* and his lectures on socialism and professional ethics.

In the fourth chapter, we will closely read through two of the books Durkheim published in his lifetime that have most directly to do with his effort to lay out a sociological research method. *The Rules of Sociological Method* is a collection of essays addressing a range of methodological questions and issues, while *Suicide* was Durkheim's effort to provide a demonstration of his methodological principles by tackling a specific and compelling social fact.

Chapter 5 considers Durkheim's extensive writing on education. He lectured and wrote over the entirety of his 30-year career on this topic, and three book-length collections of these lectures are the source material examined in this chapter.

Durkheim's work on religion and the sociology of knowledge is the subject of Chapter 6. His last book, *The Elementary Forms of Religious Life,* is the focal point here, but we will also read through other important studies he produced on these topics.

In Chapter 7, we come to the conclusion of Durkheim's intellectual career. Here, we will consider the work he did in the service of the French war effort, which directly draws on his sociological ideas, and speculate on his two planned but uncompleted major studies on morality and the family.

The last chapter of the book summarizes a good deal of the most interesting work on Durkheim and in the tradition he created over the past several decades. Although the secondary literature here is far too vast to aim for exhaustiveness in this chapter, we will discuss contributions from all three of the nations (France, the United States, and the UK) whose intellectual traditions were most powerfully affected by Durkheim's thought.

1

David Émile Durkheim, Life and Times

Intellectual work is inevitably attached to a human life, and so understanding what Durkheim thought and wrote will require understanding a good deal about where and when he grew up, where he went to school, and what kinds of important experiences he had during his formative years. In this chapter, we examine some crucial and basic elements of Durkheim's biography, including descriptions of his early family life, educational trajectory, and the political and cultural events of importance that took place during his lifetime. Though these sociobiographical elements will resurface frequently throughout the text, it is in this chapter that I will lay out the broad contours of the sociology of knowledge, at both a local or micro level (his family and close networks of colleagues and interlocutors) and a broader or macro level (the broader social and political environment of the French university and social world), which is necessary for a rich understanding of Durkheim's thought.

The France That Produced Durkheim: The Second Empire, the Early Days of the Third Republic, and the Situation of French Jews

Durkheim's youth unfolded in a period marked by great political upheaval in France. The turmoil of that time sparked cultural and political debates that resonated profoundly throughout the country for the next several generations, and it marked Durkheim for the rest of his life and fundamentally informed his intellectual trajectory. The 19th century was, generally speaking, a tumultuous one in political and social terms in France. In the wake of Napoléon's fall in 1814, the French Republic had collapsed back into a monarchy that managed to survive, in varying forms, until barely a decade prior to Durkheim's birth. Then, in early 1848, amid riots and violence, King Louis Philippe abdicated before a movement that reinstated republican government. This fledgling Second Republic began quickly to sway back to the right. In June 1848, the republican military crushed a rebellion in Paris by some of the more radical elements, killing thousands and badly damaging working-class support of the new Republic. Toward the end of that year, the nephew of the former Emperor, Louis-Napoléon, was elected president, with powerful support from reactionary peasants and the urban underclass Marx had called the **lumpenproletariat**. Three years later, Louis-Napoléon enacted a coup and dissolved the Republic, and in late 1852, less than 6 years before Durkheim was born, Bonaparte declared himself the new Emperor of France.

The first 12 years of Durkheim's life were spent under the increasingly disastrous rule of the reactionary Second Empire of the newly christened Emperor Napoléon III. When the Emperor dragged the French into an ill-advised war with the Kingdom of Prussia in 1870, he sealed the fate of his Empire. The Prussians defeated and captured him at Sedan in September 1870, and a few days later the Third French Republic was proclaimed. Fighting continued under the provisional Government of National Defense until the following summer, when the defeated French negotiated for peace. But this was far from the conclusion of the fighting. The Prussians made bold assertions in the negotiations. They wanted a triumphal symbolic march into the French capital to display their victory. As had been the case in 1848, the fiesty Parisians revolted. Rejecting what they viewed as the abject surrender of Auguste Thiers, the head of the provisional national government, the workers of Paris seized control of the city in March 1871 and for the next 2 months held it as a revolutionary government that became a symbolic beacon for the socialist movement throughout Europe. In May, the regular French Army under Thiers, with the Prussians looking on, put down the **Paris Commune** in the blood of perhaps as many as 25,000 of the rebels. The horrific spectacle of Frenchmen shooting dead their fellow countrymen by the thousands would be a revolting collective memory for many decades afterward. But revolutionaries worldwide were inspired by the brief, tragic example of the Communards. Lenin, on the seizing of power of the Bolsheviks in the 1917 Russian Revolution, anxiously measured the early days of the new regime against the lifespan of the Paris uprising. Durkheim was just entering his teens when the Commune was crushed.

In the wake of the murderous defeat of the Paris Commune by France's own soldiers, the Prussians enforced significant territorial claims. They reclaimed a huge chunk of Alsace and a smaller but still substantial part of Lorraine. Almost the entirety of the Lorraine department of Moselle became part of Prussia, and even a small portion of Vosges, the department wherein lay Épinal, the town of Durkheim's birth, was annexed, as the Prussian leader Otto von Bismarck claimed the people there spoke Germanic dialects. French territory militarily occupied by the Prussians was separated from Durkheim's boyhood home by roughly the same distance that separates lower Manhattan from Greenwich, Connecticut.

One does not have to be a Freudian to believe that events of childhood can have a profound effect on an individual's adult trajectory, and all the more so as those childhood events are themselves profound and traumatic. It was a mere 12 years after Durkheim's birth, as he was undertaking the study of Hebrew in anticipation of following his father into the rabbinate, that the Prussian Army marched into Épinal.

Early Family Life and Education

This then was the broad setting in France and in Lorraine when on April 15, 1858, a son was born to an Ashkenazi Jewish French family headed by Moïse and Mélanie Durkheim in Épinal, which is situated in the Lorraine region in the far northeast of the country, on the German border. Durkheim's father was rabbi of the Vosges and Haute-Marne departments of the region, and he represented the eighth generation of rabbis in the family. Durkheim's nephew Marcel Mauss, a great founding social scientist in his own right, would later speak of their family genealogy as a kind of hagiography, full of "saints" (Fournier, 2007, p. 26). At Émile's birth, the Jewish community in Épinal was tiny, numbering only perhaps some 200 in a total population of around 12,000, but given its heritage in the rabbinical line, the Durkheim family was among the most locally important Jewish families. Three other children had preceded David Émile, as he was named, and Moïse's salary was barely sufficient to make ends meet, so Durkheim's mother began doing embroidery at home to add income to the family. Eventually this turned into a thriving family business. All three of Émile's siblings eventually went to work in it, and the husband of the oldest of the siblings, Émile's sister Rosine, eventually became its head.

Moïse was already in his 50s when little Émile was born. The other three children were born in a cluster, the youngest a full 7 years before Émile, so elementary family sociology reveals him as an outlier, the baby of the family by a good margin, the "simple fact of the order of birth" providing a strong initial clue into the "prematurely adult qualities" the "ever-somber and humorless Émile" would show throughout much of his life (Greenberg, 1976, p. 625).

Rabbi Moïse Durkheim was an Orthodox Jew, and the stringent ritual cult of Orthodox Jewish life was a central part of the early experience of David Émile Durkheim. The Judaism of the Durkheim family home was centered in an ascetic, antimystical logic in which little room was made for the expressive arts. Durkheim would later speak of having learned as a child to be incapable of experiencing pleasure without a twinge of remorse (Fournier, 2007, p. 29). Durkheim's colleague Georges Davy, speaking on the centenary of the former's birth, described him as having imbibed some important basic traits from his family environment: contempt for the merely alluring and charming; disdain of success that was unaccompanied by effort; and horror of everything not seriously anchored as the individual is by the group, facts are by their logical connections, and conduct is by moral regulation (Davy, 1960, p. 17). And yet we must not overstate things. A photograph of Moïse Durkheim reveals him without a beard and dressed in modern garb. The evidence visible in the photograph, and the fact that he permitted it to be taken in the first place, contribute to an interpretation of the familial life of the young Émile as perhaps less severely conservative than it has sometimes been portrayed (Greenberg, 1976, p. 625). The family did not speak Yiddish at home, and the father was proud of his heavily accented French. The evidence is that the family happily embraced its French identity (Fournier, 2007, p. 28).

Throughout Durkheim's adult life, a barely submerged undercurrent driving his social and political thought was the importance of the acceptance of France's Jewish community into the ranks of full-fledged French citizenry. He was almost never overt about expressing this, and he certainly did not make "the Jewish question" in French society a centerpiece of his public life, but it can be detected in myriad ways in his intellectual focus on questions of moral solidarity in contemporary French and European society. The history of Jews in France was complicated, filled with mixed episodes of optimistic acceptance and crushing, sometimes violent repression and exclusion. France had emancipated its Jewish population earlier than had any other European country, during the days of the Revolution in 1791, and French Jews therefore came frequently to replace their religious cult with a "cult of the revolution," which was especially prominent and pronounced during the Third Republic (Weber, 2004, p. 1).

This peculiar relationship of Jewish and French identities, a kind of secularized French Jewish patriotism that nonetheless had religious roots, deeply affected the thinking of many French Jews, including Durkheim. At the emancipation, there were some 40,000 French Jews, some three quarters of these Ashkenazi living in the region of Alsace-Lorraine that was Durkheim's birthplace. The remaining 10,000 or so French Jews were Sephardim living in the southern part of the country, largely in Bordeaux, Bayonne, and Provence (Weber, 2004, p. 3). By the time of the Dreyfus Affair (discussed in greater detail below) at the turn of the 20th century, the Jewish population had grown to 75,000, with more than half of these living in Paris, and they began to exercise an increasing social and cultural influence. At the same time, however, anti-Semitism, evident in only its most outward and obvious face in the case of the unfortunate Captain Alfred Dreyfus, was growing virulently. In the right-wing popular press, and in some purportedly more respectable political circles as well, French Jews were blamed for the defeat of 1870, and there was a widespread set of discourses on the cultural and political right that rejected the very idea of French citizens of Jewish ethnicity (Fournier, 2007, p. 32).

It was initially his father's wish for Émile to follow his own career path. There was an older son, Joseph-Félix, but it was recognized early on that he was something of a wastrel and clearly lacking the necessary seriousness for such a charge, while the young Émile was precocious and focused (Fournier, 2007, p. 25). His early education was thus directed toward preparing him to follow in his father's footsteps. He was enrolled in rabbinical school for a year at the age of 13, learned Biblical Hebrew in order to study the Pentateuch and the Talmud, and appeared contented with the planned trajectory of his life. At some point in his teens, however, there was a turning. He received a *baccalauréat* degree (the rough French equivalent to a high school diploma) in both Letters and Sciences at the *lycée* (high school) in Épinal, and then the decision was made in 1875 to send him off to Paris to prepare for the grueling entrance examination to the prestigious **École Normale Supérieure** (ENS), or Normal "Sup" as it is known in Paris argot. An ENS degree was a requirement for anyone seeking to join the professoriate, and this had apparently become Durkheim's new career path; it was clear by this point that the plan to succeed his father was no more.

The full details of this significant change in Durkheim's life trajectory are unfortunately not completely known. The typical narrative in this kind of case involves the trope of "losing the faith," and Durkheim certainly did cease to adhere to the religious ideas and many of the ritual practices of Judaism, but there is significant complexity here. His father had attempted in his mid-20s to undertake the study of science and philosophy in Paris himself, but he had not gotten far along this path, and it may have been the case that the young Émile was not so much rejecting his father's path in heading off to the capital as he was endeavoring to follow the career direction his father had also desired as a young man (Greenberg, 1976, p. 626). It might well also be said that Durkheim rejected not so much the values of his father but the paltry rabbi's salary, which he had seen in his father's example as insufficient to adequately provide for the family (Greenberg, 1976, p. 630).

In Paris, Durkheim enrolled in ENS preparatory classes at the *lycée* Louis-le-Grand, the vaunted institution in the heart of the Latin Quarter where many of France's leading intellectuals had studied since its founding in the mid-16th century. He was a somber youth, serious and shy, who made friends with difficulty but who was tremendously loyal to those friends he did have. Like many provincials arriving in the bustling capital, Durkheim underwent some considerable emotional stress and yearning for the cozy familial hearth he had left back in Lorraine. There is some evidence he may have begun suffering during this period from bouts of what we now call depression. Adding to the emotional pressure were failures in the ENS entrance examination the first two times he sat for it. His provincial schooling had handicapped him considerably on these national tests; in the oral interview of one of the failed efforts, he was described as "too cold and dull" (Greenberg, 1976, p. 633). However, his ascetic upbringing in the strict household of Rabbi Moïse prevented him from completely despairing at these failures, and he managed eventually to prevail through tenacious application and willpower.

Normal Sup'

The ENS occupied a status position in Third Republic France that elevated it above the normal university system, as its graduates would become the secondary and university teachers who would educate the entire country, and this pedagogical role was seen as crucially important by French republicans for the evolution of the entire society. *Normaliens,* as ENS students are called, quickly developed an identity that connected them to the institution and to one another, and the absorbing, suffocating atmosphere of the place almost inevitably shaped its graduates in certain important and long-lasting ways.

At the École Normale, Durkheim rubbed shoulders with a generation of talented scholars who would go on to occupy prestigious posts in the French academic and political worlds. Among his cohorts were the philosopher Maurice Blondel, the psychologist Pierre Janet, the linguist Ferdinand Brunot, and the historian Henri Berr. In the class one year ahead of him were two other giants of French intellectual and political life of this period, both of whom Durkheim knew well personally. The first was the philosopher Henri Bergson, who would go on to enjoy a vogue of celebrity that extended to the international intellectual community at the turn of the century and who served as something of a philosophical adversary for Durkheim in his post-ENS years. The second was a young man Durkheim first met before he had passed the ENS entrance exam, while he was enrolled at Louis-le-Grand in preparatory courses. Jean Jaurès was a year younger than Durkheim, but the polished youth achieved entry into the ENS a year earlier and graduated in the cohort just ahead of Durkheim's. The two men roomed in the same boarding house while studying for the ENS exam (Fournier, 2007, p. 36). There is some conjecture that the influence of Jaurès, who was already an atheist and a socialist by the time Durkheim met him, may have been of significant importance in further distancing Durkheim from the religious worldview of his youth. Jaurès would go on to become perhaps the most important socialist theorist and political figure in France at the turn of the century, and his assassination in July 1914 ensured France's entry into World War I. Although Durkheim never officially declared his affiliation with any political parties during his lifetime, the evidence is overwhelming that he was a reformist, non-Marxist socialist in the same vein as Jaurès.

Closely documenting Durkheim's intellectual influences while at the ENS allows us to demonstrate the inaccuracy of some common claims about the trajectory of his thought. It is widely believed that the **positivism** of Auguste Comte was the central philosophical source on which Durkheim drew, but, as we will see in later chapters, although there are undoubtedly points of commonality in the thought of the two men, Comte frequently comes under severe criticism in Durkheim's writings, and it is evident that there were other thinkers who influenced Durkheim more significantly.

He was profoundly marked in his time at the ENS by his reading of another of the dominant philosophical figures in 19th-century France, the idealist neo-Kantian Charles-Bernard Renouvier. Although he never taught in an institution of higher education, Renouvier exercised a great influence on a whole generation of French thinkers from the time of the founding of the Third Republic into the early 20th century. He agreed with Kant that our knowledge of the world cannot be a realist knowledge of things in themselves but must necessarily involve the work of our own understanding through our sensory apparatus, which inevitably distances us to a certain degree from reality. In his late work on knowledge and religion, Durkheim would take up this Kantian framework for understanding in devising his category of **collective representations**. Renouvier distinguished himself from positivism in his refusal of the necessity of a narrowly causal understanding of science. Whereas Comte posited a science of society that would, given its determinist foundation, be capable of prediction, Renouvier maintained a more interpretivist perspective, arguing that while the natural world should be seen as operating according to determinist principles, a critical scientific approach was better suited to the actual relationship of the knower to knowledge, due to the moral freedom of the human knower. Contingency and will played an important role in Renouvier's conception of the work of the scientific thinker, and this also influenced his social theory, which was based on republicanism and the moral autonomy of the individual (Jones, 2001, pp. 64–65; Lukes, 1985, p. 55). These concerns with determinism and republican individualism are present throughout Durkheim's work. Late in his career, Durkheim opined that the best way to mature one's own way of thinking was to "devote yourself to the study of a great master . . . [to] take a system apart, laying bare its innermost secrets." He went on: "This is what I did and my educator was Renouvier" (Lukes, 1985, p. 54).

Two of his professors at the ENS also proved influential on his way of thinking. The philosopher Émile Boutroux was also a neo-Kantian, and Durkheim acknowledged that it was from Boutroux that he formulated the notion that sociology, in order to develop as an independent discipline, must establish its own realm of facts and radically distinguish itself from biology and psychology (Lukes, 1985, p. 57). But arguably even more important to Durkheim's mature intellectual perspective was the historian Numa Denis Fustel de Coulanges. He had been a professor at the ENS since 1870 and became its director in 1880, the year before Durkheim arrived there as a student. He was perhaps France's most renowned historian, his fame largely dependent on his book *The Ancient City*, a penetrating and careful study of the deep roots of law and social institutions in the Roman Empire in religious ritual and belief, which deeply influenced Durkheim's own way of understanding the foundational power of religion. Fustel de Coulanges argued that ancient Indo-European religious beliefs concerning the worship of the souls of the dead, which formed the common historical heritage of Greece and Rome, had profound effects on nearly every facet of daily civil life. The organization of the family, the form of morality, and the structure of legal institutions including the most basic ones revolving around the notion of private property derived their shape from these religious roots. In his own book on religion, Durkheim would make a similar argument about the primary role of religious practices and ideas in shaping the civil life and legal and political institutions that superficially seemed distant from religion. The argumentative styles of the two books are similar, as both rely on a search for original, elementary forms of religion that are argued to give rise to all subsequent forms (Héran, 1989, pp. 369–376).

In addition to the specifics of his approach to the study of religion, Fustel de Coulanges was a source of influence to Durkheim in broader ways. His approach to scholarly life was marked by a tremendous ascetic devotion, and this quasireligious view of the intellectual life was well known to students at the École Normale, who noted his "austere radiance that imparted intellectual asceticism" (Lukes, 1985, p. 59). He also represented to his students a position on the scholar's political role that clearly demarcated political and intellectual roles and tasks. His work on the history of France necessarily involved him in intellectual and popular polemic about the contemporary political status of the country, national identity, and other such conflict-laden topics. Fustel de Coulanges clearly had positions on these and other political issues, but, as a scholar, he preferred to speak to them publicly only through the authority of his scholarly work. He recognized the inevitably political significance of intellectual work engaged with questions of morality and religion but understood the scholarly calling as forbidding overt interventions into the political arena, save in certain drastic situations. As we will see in later chapters, Durkheim adopted a similar model of the ascetic moral religion of scholarship and the importance of a line of distinction between that realm and the equally important sphere of politics.

In 1892, 3 years after Fustel de Coulanges's death, Durkheim dedicated his Latin thesis on Montesquieu to "the memory of Fustel de Coulanges." In his preface to the first volume of the sociological journal he created, *l'Année sociologique,* Durkheim invoked Fustel de Coulanges in his argument that the journal was designed not merely as a source for sociologists but also as a means to "bring sociology closer to certain special sciences ["it is above all history we are thinking of in speaking thus"] that keep themselves too distanced from it, to their own detriment and to our own" (Durkheim, 1898, p. ii).

Durkheim's reputation among peers and teachers was formidable at the ENS. A fellow student described him as "visibly older than the majority of the rest of the students, with a precocious maturity" (Davy, 1995/1919, p. 89). Fustel de Coulanges wrote of him early in his ENS years as an "[e]xcellent student, a very forceful mind both sound and original, with a remarkable maturity" (Tiryakian, 2009, p. 20). His personality could be caricatured by his enemies, one of whom described him as a "sort of automaton" whose "ice-cold" demeanor "would not have profaned the inside of a mortuary" (Lukes, 1985, p. 371). But Durkheim was, like his father, not nearly so cold as he perhaps appeared to some. This stern exterior was arguably only "a cultivated disposition" underneath which lay "an almost feminine sensitivity . . . a goodness and tenderness that blossomed only in the confines of the family and later in the presence of his intimate friends, his 'spiritual family' of *L'Année sociologique*" (Greenberg, 1976, p. 627).

He quickly became known for his penetrating intellectual skills and his love for political discussion (Fournier, 2007, p. 41). Nicknamed "the

Metaphysician" for his intimidating philosophical seriousness, Durkheim was characterized by one of his close ENS friends, Frédéric Rauh, as an "apostle, filled with his thought and the desire to disseminate it and to penetrate other minds[,] . . . who was at the same time a contemplative" (Fournier, 2007, p. 40). He was instinctively drawn to politics but rejected what he saw as the vulgarization of French political life, which made of this noble sphere something "small and mediocre," whereas he had always considered it the most serious of affairs (Davy, 1995/1919, p. 92).

Political debate in France during Durkheim's days at the ENS was between conservatives, largely Catholic, who looked back nostalgically on the monarchy and worshiped hypertraditionalist versions of the family, the Church, and the Army, and the secular supporters of the new Republic. Durkheim was clearly aligned with the secular republicans in the most general sense, but, like the religious conservatives, he recognized the damage an unrestrained individualism could do to the moral bases of French culture. One of the central topics of political debate of the time had to do with the nature of the educational system. Conservatives wanted to preserve its connection to the Church and classical pedagogical emphasis, while republicans saw the need for a revised, even revolutionized secular educational model. The educational reformer and ENS graduate Victor Duruy had spoken of the need to create a new, entirely secular French educational system led by an "aristocracy of intelligence" (Fournier, 2007, p. 43), and during the time that Durkheim was at the ENS, the statesman Jules Ferry was at work pushing such reform forward. Durkheim was one of those movingly compelled by this vision.

The German university system was seen by many of the secular republicans as a model to emulate, and Durkheim would later spend a year of government-sponsored research leave on the other side of the Rhine getting a close-up view of the German system. He came progressively to see the need for a new system of thought to adequately theorize the development of a republican society with a collapsed traditional value system that was in need of new social and cultural structures to undergird it and a secular pedagogy to bring its youth into those structures. By his second year at the ENS, he had begun to establish this new way of understanding the human world, and in short order would become the founder of a new intellectual movement, defined by the term "sociology," which tied together the dual projects of political and pedagogical action (Filloux, 1977, p. 259).

Durkheim was awarded the *agrégation,* or state teaching qualification, in 1882, and the following year he dutifully took up his first academic position as a secondary school teacher of philosophy in Sens, about 75 miles southeast of Paris. His ambition at this point was, however, already palpable, and he was aiming well beyond this backwater position toward the nation's capital, where the most prestigious academics found posts in the core institutions of the French academic system.

Early Teaching and Work: Lycées, Bordeaux, Dreyfus, a Year in Germany, and the Birth of *l'Année Sociologique*

The path to Paris proved to be long and complicated. A certain amount of paying of dues is required in the French system, and Durkheim selflessly took up this responsibility by teaching high school–age students for several years. This teaching was largely structured by the centralized French curriculum, with determined items that were to be covered by all teachers of the year-long philosophy courses that were Durkheim's charge. It was not a teaching responsibility that made much room for innovation or for direct inclusion of Durkheim's emerging ideas on sociology. He was nonetheless working furiously in this period to develop the perspective he would begin presenting in publications during these years. He was humorously referred to by his students as "Schopen," apparently short for "Arthur Schopenhauer," the German philosopher of the 19th century (Fournier, 2007, p. 63). Schopenhauer's work would certainly have been one of the elements in the syllabus to be covered in Durkheim's course, but there is little evidence that Durkheim was particularly enthusiastic about the German's ideas. Schopenhauer's extreme pessimism was incompatible with Durkheim's sense that concerted and impassioned collective work was required to solve the social problems France faced. Ever the realist, he advocated "a bit of melancholy, but not too much" (Fournier, 2007, p. 65).

In 1885, Durkheim received a scholarship to spend a year studying in Germany as part of a program organized by the Ministry of Public Instruction to strengthen the country's educational institutions by exposing France's brightest young scholars to cutting-edge German methods of research and instruction. Durkheim was highly impressed by the advances in the sociological study of morality in Germany and summarized his impressions of them in one of his first substantive publications. He became acquainted there with the work of historical economists such as Adolph Wagner (the teacher of Werner Sombart, one of the founding German sociologists) and Gustave von Schmoller, who attacked liberal political economy for treating human economic transactions outside of a social context and therefore reducing economic activity to pure egoism divorced from any moral content. In the view of Sombart and von Schmoller, society had its own nature, which had to be taken into account if economic activity were to be properly understood and regulated. Durkheim's mature work would take up a similar critical perspective on mainstream political economy. He also looked favorably on the work of the sociological jurist Rudolf von Ihering, who had just written a massive two-volume study on the purpose of the law that argued that the modern study of ethics and law would have to take place under the aegis of the social sciences. Finally, and most important, Durkheim discovered the work of Wilhelm Wundt, whom he described as a scientist of morality engaged in careful, empirical studies of *Völkerpsychologie,* or social psychology. The central unifying thread in all of this new German work on morality was its rejection of the purely deductive method and embrace of the collection of empirical facts to ground arguments about the nature of morality (Durkheim, 1975c/1887). Durkheim was tremendously excited to find others pointing in the direction he intended his own work to take, as it was only too easy in France for him to feel that he was a lone voice in the wilderness.

Durkheim's life changed in two fundamental ways in 1887. He was finally, after several years of teaching at *lycées,* where he was forced to teach a prescribed national curriculum with no possibility of integrating his own research in any real way into his pedagogical practice, awarded a university chair in "Science Sociale et Pédagogie" (in 1895, it would be renamed as simply "Science Sociale") at Bordeaux, on the southwest coast of the country. It was far from Paris, but it was nonetheless a step in the right direction. Here, over the next 15 years, he would write a good deal of the work for which he is most remembered. Three of the four books he published in his lifetime were produced during this period, in addition to lengthy and important articles for the *Année sociologique,* including those on incest, individual and collective representations, the definition of religious phenomena, and totemism, not to mention the voluminous collection of book reviews he contributed to the first several editions of the *Année.* These were tremendously productive years for him, despite the heavy teaching load with which he was burdened at Bordeaux. He managed to make the best of his numerous teaching responsibilities in the area of pedagogy by generating new, empirically based material for the lecture courses he gave. In the end, he turned his sociological perspective on the institutions of education and the topic of pedagogy to great effect. In addition to courses on education, he taught year-long courses on the family, on law and politics, on occupational ethics, on socialism, on the history of sociology, and on religion (Lukes, 1985, p. 277).

But if the Bordeaux appointment was the most outwardly visible sign of Durkheim's intellectual advance, his marriage in October 1887 was the more important change in terms of its positive effects on his ability to concentrate on his intellectual work. Louise Julie Durkheim *née* Dreyfus was from a well-off Parisian Jewish family; her father was an engineer by training who was the director of a Paris foundry (Charle, 1984, p. 46). Although Durkheim by this time no longer accepted the religious tenets of Judaism, he continued to participate in familial celebrations of Jewish holidays, and everything we know about his family environment indicates it was warm and supportive. Durkheim took up the position of familial patriarch readily and effectively, and his wife's total dedication to the familial sphere freed him from all the domestic cares that might have prevented him from dedicating himself fully to his work. His friend and colleague Georges Davy described the marriage and its relation to Durkheim's intellectual work in the following terms: "His own hearth was the image of that domestic ideal. To ground it, he had the good fortune to unite himself with an admirable companion who understood him, sustained him, aided him and totally and joyfully sacrificed her own life to the austere scholarly life of her husband" (Davy, 1919, p. 65).

His work began to emerge in a steady stream after the publication of his thesis, *The Division of Labor in Society*, in 1893. Just after finishing his second book, *The Rules of Sociological Method*, he entered a period of rich discovery, career advancement, and personal transition. In 1896, both the family patriarch, his father Moïse, *and* the second in line for the position, his brother-in-law Gerson, who had married Durkheim's eldest sister when Durkheim was yet a boy, died, in one stroke leaving Durkheim as the male head of the family. That same year, he was finally awarded a permanent chair at Bordeaux after teaching there for nearly a decade as a lecturer. *The Rules* was the subject of widespread attack and criticism, even by some ordinarily intellectually close to him, and he worked on his study of suicide with the depressing presentiment that it too would fall on deaf ears. It was in this same period, 1895 to 1896, that he taught his first course on religion, signaling a turn toward the cultural in his subsequent work. Finally, the organizational work to create the *Année* began in earnest at this same juncture. Durkheim's period of doubt and crisis was resolved by his renewed commitment to the mission of collective labor in a calling—namely, that of the establishment of sociology as a new discipline (Besnard, 2003, p. 51).

The first issue of the *Année* appeared in 1898, and 11 more fat volumes would appear in Durkheim's lifetime. Several of his most important essays were published in its pages, including the lengthy piece on primitive classification that he coauthored with Mauss and published in the first volume. One of the central reasons why he published only four books in his lifetime had to do with the *Année*, which took up much of his time over the last two decades of his life. But he saw this labor as essential to the establishment of sociology. He was absolutely devoted to the idea of collective intellectual labor and of altruistic service to the group goal of the establishment of social science as a new form of knowledge, and the idea of furthering his own career by publishing more books simply paled in comparison to that lofty goal. He even spoke of the collective work of the *Année* as a kind of quasi-religious project in language that will startle the reader expecting a doctrinaire secular approach to scientific work from him. In correspondence with one of his close collaborators, Mauss's friend Henri Hubert, Durkheim remarked: "You are quite right to say that our little group is a moral milieu as much as an intellectual one. No one senses this more acutely than I do. . . . *Our shared project assumes a shared faith* and a great mutual confidence" (Besnard, 1987a, pp. 518, 494, emphasis added).

Early in that same year of 1898, the writer Émile Zola penned his famous **"J'accuse" letter**, denouncing the French military and the government for its unjust prosecution of an Army captain, Alfred Dreyfus, for a treasonous act that there was no real evidence he had committed. In the open letter addressed to the French president, which was printed on the front page of a Paris newspaper, Zola accused the political establishment of anti-Jewish prejudice that struck at the heart of republican France. In short order, France's public figures and intellectuals divided up into opposing sides on the **Dreyfus Affair**, as it came to be known. On the one side were the conservatives, those who yearned for the monarchy or even the return of the Empire, who saw the Army and the Church as the most important social institutions in the nation and who saw Dreyfus as guilty despite the lack of evidence; on the other were the republicans of all stripes and the rest of the left, who carried the banner of the abstract principles of the French Republic and a deep reverence for the Republic's sacred entity, the individual.

Durkheim became avidly engaged in the Affair shortly after the *"J'accuse"* letter, apparently writing a letter of support to Zola, who was forced to flee the country in the face of a libel charge, and then some months later producing a powerful document that linked his sociological vision of the core principles of a just Republic to his felt need to intervene in the public realm on this issue of national debate and conscience. This was an essay, "Individualism and the Intellectuals," which we will examine in some detail in the next chapter. Generally, Durkheim's perspective on the intellectual's role in political matters centered on the need for distance and caution, although, as we will see in Chapter 3, Durkheim's intellectual project and his vision of sociology are incomprehensible without an understanding of his politics. Here, however, and in another extraordinary situation, that of France's entry into the First World War, he sidestepped this principle and became one of the most articulate and vigorous voices of intellectual activism and agitation that could be found in the country.

At Last, Paris

In July 1902, Durkheim's mother passed away after a long illness, in the same summer that he was finally accepted to a post in Paris at the Sorbonne. Again, crisis and triumph appeared in his life together, tightly entangled. The death of his mother was a trying event, with Durkheim writing a friend of the "difficult moments" while the family awaited the inevitable as their mother lay in a coma (Fournier, 2007, p. 488). A touching portrait of Durkheim's filial piety and devotion to his terminally ill mother was sketched by the rabbi of Épinal, Moïse Schuhl, who described the great scholar "matured by his studies, a leading figure of French science and letters, become once again a child at his mother's side, pushing the little wheelchair she was obliged to use to get around in her final days . . . this tableau seemed to me the illustration of the extreme, almost naïve acts of filial piety reported in the Talmud . . . which were performed by renowned rabbis for their own mothers" (Fournier, 2007, p. 487). Here, we see compelling evidence of the portrait of Durkheim as a secular, progressive republican nonetheless still deeply rooted in traditional moral community and practice.

In the spring of 1902, Ferdinand Buisson, then holder of a chair in the science of education at the Sorbonne, was elected to serve as a deputy in the French parliament. A replacement for the Sorbonne position was sought, and Durkheim was immediately seen as a frontrunner. Initially, he was lukewarm to the idea. He was worried that an even heavier load of courses in pedagogy and related matters would steal still more time from his sociological research and writing (Durkheim, 1998, p. 326; Fournier, 2007, p. 505). He was able, after some agonizing, to assure himself that the new position would not require him to alter the strongly sociological flavor of the pedagogical coursework he had been offering already at Bordeaux, and, recognizing how functionally important for the *Année* and the project of establishing sociology at the university level it would be to operate from Paris, he decided to present himself as a candidate. He was elected by a large majority to the position in July 1902. The following autumn, he began teaching at the Sorbonne as a lecturer; within 4 years, he was made a professor of the University of Paris.

His academic career was thus neatly divided into two 15-year periods, the first at Bordeaux, the second in Paris. In these Parisian years of his career and life, Durkheim took up a position as one of the most important intellectuals in the country, and his international reputation was growing as well. The crowning achievement of this Paris period was the monumental book on religion that he produced in 1912, *The Elementary Forms of Religious Life,* but he completed many other important pieces of work during this time, including a lengthy essay, cowritten with Mauss, on the sociology of knowledge (*Primitive Classification*) and several of the essays on morality that were brought together in a posthumous volume, *Sociology and Philosophy*.

The Great War and Death

The coming of World War I, or the Great War as it was known in Europe, was presaged by a signal occurrence, the assassination of Austrian Archduke Franz Ferdinand and his wife, the Duchess of Hohenberg, in late June 1914. But the French entry into the war was symbolized still more cogently by a local event. On July 31, 1914, Durkheim's close friend and former ENS schoolmate, Jean Jaurès, who had spoken out persuasively from the left on the need to avoid a European war that would potentially destroy all of the socialist left's efforts, was shot dead in a café on the Right Bank, where he was dining after leaving the offices of the socialist newspaper *l'Humanité*. On the day of his assassination, Jaurès was apparently considering an appeal to the American president, Woodrow Wilson, for intervention in the effort to maintain the peace. The next day, the French mobilized for war.

The emergency of the war brought the second major direct intervention into a political matter in Durkheim's lifetime. As he had risen to the challenge of the right-wing attack on French republican values during the Dreyfus Affair, he responded to the onset of war in Europe by applying his formidable intellectual and polemical skills to the French national cause. Durkheim was 56 at the war's beginning, too old to serve in a military capacity, but he threw himself into the propaganda effort with zeal. He authored two lengthy texts explicating the culpability of the Germans in instigating the war and edited another collection of essays intended to stiffen the French public's resolve in the grim business of the war.

If Durkheim himself was beyond the age of mobilization, this was not true for many of his intellectual associates, friends, and members of his family. His nephew Marcel Mauss, a second nephew, his brother-in-law, and his own son André shipped off for various theaters of the war, as did numerous younger collaborators on the *Année*. Of the latter, Maxime David, Antoine Bianconi, Jean Reynier, and one of Durkheim's most outstanding young students, Robert Hertz, were killed in combat within the war's first year. Durkheim's initial vigor in response to the war gradually began to change, as was doubtless true for many in France, to an anguished and fearful anticipation of horrors to come. When Hertz died near Verdun in April 1915, Durkheim wrote to Mauss, who had also been close to the deceased man, that Hertz's death greatly increased his worry for Mauss and André, as

Hertz was the first of their associates to perish with whom Durkheim had a close personal relationship (Durkheim, 1998, p. 454). Later that same year, 1915, André went missing at the Bulgarian front. Durkheim wrote to his colleague Georges Davy in January 1916 and expressed his fears: "[T]he image of this exhausted child, alone at the side of a road in the midst of night and fog . . . seizes me by the throat" (Lukes, 1985, p. 555). Then, in late February 1916, the crushing blow came: Durkheim learned that André had been killed in action in Bulgaria. He wrote to inform Mauss of the news in desperation: "This is going to hurt a great deal, but it's impossible to spare you the pain. We can no longer hang on to our illusions. André was wounded and died. He is buried in the little village of Davidovo. It hurts me to write these words, and it will hurt you to read them . . . when you respond, speak as little as possible about the irreparable. These images make me suffer" (Durkheim, 1998, pp. 501–502).

Durkheim struggled to avoid being completely shattered by this horrific event, and the work on the edited volume of war letters aided him in this regard. He wrote to Mauss that "life triumphs over death" and described how, initially fearing he would not be able to work again after André's death, he had indeed managed to return to his writing desk and told his wife: "I work, I'm saved" (Durkheim, 1998, pp. 507, 508). Yet he acknowledges in the same letter that from this point on, it is inevitable that in whatever future remains for him, "melancholy will be the mode of my life" (Durkheim, 1998, p. 508). A few months later, and only about a month before his death, he told his colleague and collaborator Georges Davy that he observed people and things in the world as one who had already departed the realm of the living (Davy, 1995/1919, p. 87). It has been suggested that Durkheim gives evidence during the war, and perhaps even before, of symptoms of what today we would call depression (Pickering & Rosati, 2008, p. 19). He was undoubtedly overworked and plagued by anguished worry during the war. Any interpreter who would make of Durkheim a bloodless positivist robot will have a great deal of work to do dealing with the voluminous evidence that the end of his life was brought on by the deep emotional wound caused by the horrific death of his beloved only son.

In early 1916, while still bitterly mourning the death of his son under the French banner, Durkheim was attacked in the press and then, stunningly, also on the floor of the French Senate as a German spy in the pay of the enemy's Ministry of War in viciously, boldly xenophobic terms. Paul Painlevé, who would briefly become prime minister in the fall of 1917 just before Durkheim's death, publicly denounced the senator who had slandered Durkheim, reminding his listeners of his efforts in propaganda for the French cause and of the recent loss of his son, and poignantly expressing his "regret that to the wound caused by a German hand to M. Durkheim's heart there has today been added an even graver injury from a French hand" (Lukes, 1985, p. 557).

Despite all the emotional distress he was enduring, Durkheim attempted to get back to his desk. According to Mauss, in March of 1917, he had started working on an introduction to the book on morality he had been contemplating for some years. His condition made it extremely difficult to concentrate, but he managed to more or less complete the introduction during the summer of 1917. In his last letter to Mauss, dated November 10, 1917, Durkheim tells him that his health has "not gotten worse" and his insomnia and nervous spasms have "disappeared." He also mentions receiving a copy of Robert Hertz's last publication, a volume of popular myths and stories told to him by other French soldiers at the front that Hertz had collected prior to his death (Durkheim, 1998, p. 585). Less than a week later, on November 15, Durkheim's daughter Marie telegrammed Mauss: "Papa passed away without suffering this morning" (Durkheim, 1998, p. 586). Mauss cryptically suggests that for approximately a year, Durkheim had known that he had a terminal illness ("a long illness the end of which he understood from its beginning, in December 1916"), but his exact cause of death is unknown (Mauss, 1925).

Conclusion

One might reasonably share Davy's view that Durkheim was a victim of the war (Davy, 1995/1919, p. 87). As was true for many in Europe in that generation, some of his deepest hopes—that is, to see a renewed French republicanism solve the problems it faced in peaceful solidarity and to watch the adult lives of his children unfold in his old age—were mercilessly annihilated in the bloodshed and turmoil. A whole generation of Frenchmen was destroyed in this grisly combat, and intellectuals took their share of the loss just as the other sectors of French life. Yet the intellectual legacy left by Durkheim was great, and we still profit significantly from a reading of his work today.

In the chapters that follow, we will explore a wide range of his thought. My effort in those chapters is to follow his writings closely, as though we were reading through them collectively. In the background of that reading, though, is the wealth of contextual information about Durkheim's life, the surface of which we have brushed in this introductory chapter. It is arguably the case that the central intellectual concern of Durkheim's adult life—the study of morality from the perspective of a new social science that would produce knowledge that could be of use in the moral regeneration of his country and modern societies more broadly—can be traced back to the details of his childhood and early adulthood.

A few questions

- In what ways might Durkheim's thought have turned out differently if he had been born a Catholic Frenchman? A French*woman*? A German Jew? A German Protestant?
- How did Durkheim think about the role of the intellectual in political matters? What factors in his own life might have contributed to the way he thought about this?
- What were the social, cultural, and political factors that made the era of Durkheim's life a unique time in European history?
- How did the social, cultural, and political contexts of Durkheim's life shape his intellectual interests?
- Does reading Durkheim's intellectual work with an eye toward his own social and historical location change our understanding of that work, and if so, in what specific ways?

2

Moral Solidarity and the New Social Science

Durkheim's Study of the Individual in Society and Society in the Individual

Durkheim wrote on a wide range of topics, from the division of labor to suicide, from treatises on method to studies of religion, from the sociology of knowledge to marriage and the family. Throughout the length and breadth of that work, two major tasks are taken up over and over again: (1) *the identification, establishing, and maintenance of moral institutions that could produce solidarity and regulate individual appetites in modernity;* and (2) *the elaboration of a unified theoretical and methodological basis for the then only-just-emerging social sciences.* In a voluminous collection of books, articles, lecture courses, and other scholarly and political interventions produced during the course of his 30-year career, he made a compelling and original case for a new science called sociology, which he believed to be uniquely capable of answering to the most profound moral dilemmas of modern human society.

Durkheim's thought developed in the context of a major moral concern linked to specific crises and problems of his era, which was undergoing rapid social and cultural change. Industrialization had brought new technology, trade, and, for some, great wealth, but it had also brought new forms of organization of human life that shocked the sensibilities of many caught up in them. The explosion in the role of machines provoked a significant alteration of the traditional world most Westerners had inhabited prior to the early 19th century. The factory system and its labor conditions changed the nature of work irrevocably. New urban living areas revolutionized family and community life and market relations. The political sweep toward democracy initiated by the French Revolution of the late 1780s and then exported around Europe and other parts of the globe swept away traditional forms and structures of government at all levels. The State rose to a position of prominence in the political landscape that it has not yet relinquished, assuming a great deal more power in the realms of the economy, politics, and education. The patriarchal family system was undone, and spousal and parental roles shifted fundamentally. The Church, which had occupied a position of cultural dominance for so long, was shaken in its supremacy, and belief itself faced the massive challenge of growing scientific knowledge spread by mass media and public education.

All of this brought advances of all sorts, and Durkheim recognized this. But he was certainly not an apologist for change of any kind at any price. Significant social change always brings significant, and frequently unanticipated, social consequences. In his scholarly work, Durkheim set about rigorously examining some of the key consequences of the political, social, and cultural changes that brought about the new kinds of societies that were emerging in the 18th and 19th centuries: highly rationalized, scientific, secularizing, industrialized, capitalist, and democratic. Durkheim, whose mission throughout his adult life has been defined as "to teach men to find in the group their own truth" (Filloux, 1977, p. 259), was interested in exploring ways to counteract the dangers created by these changes.

Within the framework of the first major theme in Durkheim's work, we see two concrete manifestations of his efforts to resolve the problem of solidarity appearing again and again in his writing, and those two ideas tell us much about his view of the individual's relationship to society, and vice versa. Durkheim was committed at once to two ideas in creative tension with each other: *The individual relies necessarily on the collectivity for all that makes him truly human, and at the same time the abstract category of the individual is in modernity the most widely shared political, moral, and religious ideal and object of veneration.*

The first solution to the problem of moral solidarity in modern society articulated by Durkheim has to do with the role he envisioned for professional corporate groups—that is, those groups made up of the members of a common profession or trade that serve to set up the moral and ethical practices of the trades, including the organization of the methods by which members of the professions are recruited and trained, and provide a collective mode of social and political action and mutual support for the individual members. The term "corporate" is derived from a Latin verb "*corporare,*" which means "to make into a body," and this is precisely what is happening in such a group: A number of otherwise separate and isolated individuals is turned into a coherent, integrated body with collective rather than merely individual interests.

Durkheim looked historically to the institution of the guilds as an example of this kind of corporate group. **Guilds** had existed in the time of the Roman Empire, then had disappeared and reemerged in a different form in medieval Europe before being dismantled with the rise of the Industrial and French Revolutions. These organizations united all the members of a particular trade or craft into a single body and pursued numerous goals in their interests, as do modern trade unions, but they were also deeply involved in the lives of their members even outside of the workplace. In his lectures on the history of the guilds (which we discuss in Chapter 3), Durkheim describes how they functioned in a certain sense as a combination of a second family and a religious group to the members. Durkheim believed that, at their best, guilds had helped to integrate individual members into a social project larger than themselves and to infuse them with a moral spirit essential for the harmonious working of the whole society. When the guilds disappeared, no new such organizational framework had emerged; while he recognized that they had some similarities, Durkheim never saw trade unions as fulfilling the same wide range of functions taken up by the guilds. Without some new social form, adapted to modern conditions, to take the place of the guilds, the glue holding the individual members of society together in a moral community was bound to weaken.

The second solution Durkheim developed in his work to respond to the problem of moral solidarity was what he called the **cult of the human person.** From at least the mid-1890s, Durkheim was convinced of the important cultural contribution that had been made to the modern Western world by religion. Beyond its undeniable role in bringing co-religionists together in a fraternal spirit of community, it had served as the earliest form of complex and collective human reasoning, groping at the reality of the world around us in ways that would ultimately lead to the rational, scientific forms of knowledge on which we depend so heavily today. Many functions fulfilled by religion were crucial to human life, and these functions would need to be performed even if religion in its historical forms passed away, which Durkheim believed it inevitably would. When religion disappeared, we would need another set of beliefs and practices that would unite society in a common cult of worship and recharge our moral batteries with periodic celebrations of its "gods" and the moral codes oriented around them.

What would take the place of religion? Durkheim believed what had emerged as a quickly universalizing sacred object that could serve as the focal point of a new secular body of beliefs and practices was *the human person*. This might sound confused, initially. How could moral solidarity and a sense of mutually invested collective identity be produced by devotion to the human individual? In clarifying, the first thing we should note is that the human person and the human individual are not the same thing, in Durkheim's view. The individual is an empirically presented entity; it is you, or me, or any other member of our society, or any other, taken as an isolated atom. The cult of the human person is not oriented toward the empirical human individual, with his or her personal interests and ideals; it points to the human person as an abstract concept that has been produced by a specific group of human societies, over a specific historical trajectory, and that is filled not with the content of individual interests and idiosyncrasies but with the interests and ideals of the society in which the individual exists. Put another way, what the members of the cult of the human person worship are the elements of the human individual that are put there by society: his ability to reason and create, her concern for her fellow human beings, his capacity to step outside of his merely biological desires and needs and to focus himself instead on transcendent ideals that involve self-sacrifice.

Durkheim alluded to this distinction between the social qualities of the human person—that is, our moral capacities—and the purely biological side of human being—the physical body itself with its material drives and desires and its requirements for basic animal survival—with his notion of *homo duplex*. The emergence of the human individual is at the core of modernity for Durkheim, and he sees our individualism as tied neatly to the social portion of our being. Our merely biological characteristics flatten us out and make us equivalent to all others of our species, but the modern rise of the differentiated self is the first moment in which true individualism emerges in human life. Nonetheless, humankind is, in modernity, becoming at once more individuated and more strictly dependent on society. As the individual has become more autonomous and free of social control of the most primitive kinds, she has nonetheless become more dependent on society and the moral bonds uniting its members. This seeming paradox was seen by Durkheim as at the root of the revolution of modernity. The central fact that emerges from Durkheim's perspective is that the individual is perhaps the central creation of modernity and that the key to directing the modern social world will involve finding an effective way to permit, and even to revel in, the movement toward individuation while at the same time seeing to it that this new individual remains morally interconnected in a functional division of labor with others. Put another way, the problem is how to reconcile two necessities, one eternal in the human world, the other a product of historical change that now asserts itself as undeniable: *integration* and *differentiation*.

Individualism and the Intellectuals: The Relation of Individual and Society Summarized

Durkheim's argument for individualism as an obligatory quasi-religion cult of the human person is present throughout his work, but a particularly focused articulation can be found in a public response he made to another figure in the French intellectual scene in a pointed exchange over the Dreyfus Affair.

In March 1898, Ferdinand Brunetière, a conservative writer, Sorbonne lecturer, and member of the prestigious Académie Française, wrote a polemically charged piece for the *Revue de deux mondes* in response to the famous Émile Zola letter that exposed the undercurrent of injustice and anti-Semitism in the charges levied against Captain Dreyfus. The article was titled "After the Trial," and in it Brunetière argued that the world of political affairs in France was in danger of absolute corruption from the emergence of a new kind of intellectual figure, the leftist "Dreyfusard." These dangerous anarchists, as Brunetière described them, were engaged in the destruction of the bonds of French society in their abstract, bloodless endorsement of universal rights and freedoms that failed to recognize the moral needs and bonds of human populations.

Brunetière's charge brought numerous public responses by advocates for Dreyfus, among them Durkheim. Writing in the pages of the *Revue bleue*, Durkheim begins by complicating the idea of individualism. Brunetière has defined it in a way, he argues, that is consistent with the "utilitarian egoism" of the philosopher and sociologist Herbert Spencer, essentially the same notion that we find in classical economics of an entirely self-interested, self-contained, self-made human actor (Durkheim, 1898/1973, p. 44). In our own time, this is the same vision of the human being adhered to on the libertarian right and left. Durkheim agrees with Brunetière that this perspective is untenable, even "anarchical," but it does not exhaust individualism (Durkheim, 1898/1973, p. 44). There is *another* variety of individualism, which descends from Kant and Rousseau, and which undergirds the French Revolution's Declaration of the Rights of Man, and this second type of individualism rejects egoism completely (Durkheim, 1898/1973, p. 45). Kant argued that morally proper action must be motivated not by specific interests and situations but rather by the common humanity that connects individuals. The famous doctrine of the general will in Rousseau is not an individual will but the sum of all such wills, and this is its claim to infallibility, not its assertive voluntarism.

At the root of both these notions, and also of Durkheim's own brand of individualism, is an essentially religious idea: *The human person is a sacred entity in precisely the same sense that gods are sacred entities in existing religions* (Durkheim, 1898/1973, p. 46). It is protected from contact by profane sources and placed in a vaunted position, outside the tawdry commerce of the mundane. Anything that intrudes upon the life, freedom, or honor of the human person horrifies us just as, for example, the Catholic is horrified when the Host is defiled in word or deed. But this new religion of individualism is distinct from existing religion in one important way: Here, the one who worships the god is himself also the god worshipped.

This form of individualism, which we might well call **moral or civic individualism** (Cladis, 2005, p. 385), is both individualistic and collectivist at once. The sacrosanct rights of the person cannot be infringed for any reason of State, yet it is a collective cult that makes this possible and calls all to its worship in a tone that is just as commanding as that we hear from the great monotheistic religions (Durkheim, 1898/1973, pp. 46, 48). This reveals the radical difference between Durkheim's individualism and that of the libertarians and classical economists. For Durkheim, the individual merits this respect precisely because of her humanity—that is, because of an attribute shared with the entire collectivity of which she is a part. Humanity itself is the sacred object, and no single individual exhausts this sacred force; it is diffused through all of them. This means that the true worship of the sacred principle of humanity requires the individual to "come out of himself and relate to others." The religion of individualism, then, is not about any specific individual but rather about the abstract category of the human person in all its myriad forms. Though it is part of us, it dominates us all the same. So here, in contradistinction to the Spencerian variety of individualism rightly criticized by Brunetière, we find not a form of egoism but a profound respect and "sympathy for all that is human," a powerful emotional response to all human suffering and a driving desire to undo the forces that cause human persons to be dominated or abused in any way (Durkheim, 1898/1973, pp. 48–49).

But how then can individualism, even if defined as Durkheim defines it, avoid ending in fracturing anarchy, as Brunetière charges? What principles can allow for harmony and order to emerge from a worldview in which all are equally meritorious of respect, all have equal rights to speak, to pose questions, to present cases? The question is a profound one, as anyone in the contemporary United States will instantly recognize. It often seems the case today in American society that anyone and everyone can pose as an authoritative speaker on nearly every topic, and debates on matters of important public policy often turn quickly from discussions of fact into mutual accusations of bias and ignorance, with no possible common ground on the qualifications of experts and sound knowledge. Durkheim argues in the strongest possible terms against such a state of affairs. The valuing of individualism of the kind he describes does not in the least commit us to a "right to incompetence," and along with his freedoms every citizen also has the responsibility to know and accept the limits of his own knowledge. On issues on which an individual is insufficiently informed or even incapable of forming any reasonable opinion at all due to a lack of required education, he is compelled to adhere to the competence of experts (Durkheim, 1898/1973, p. 49). That adherence must be based on reason—that is, it is not simply charisma, or power, or mere agreement with one's already existing ideological beliefs that should generate authority, but rather scientific or some other rational intellectual expertise and mastery. For this reason, Durkheim rejects Brunetière's insistence that abject subordination to the legal and military tribunal decisions on the affair of Captain Dreyfus are required; this is pure and blind submission to power. In a Republic, the accused must be permitted to defend himself according to a doctrine of impartial law, and reason must be the mechanism that determines the outcome (Durkheim, 1898/1973, p. 50). Nonetheless, it is inescapable that no one will be capable of the mastery required in all fields for competent judgment, so mutual deference and a collective sense of mutual reliance on one another for sound judgment will be necessary.

So moral or civic individualism is, according to Durkheim, "the only system of beliefs which can ensure the moral unity of the country" (Durkheim, 1898/1973, p. 50). Brunetière and his conservative allies argue that such work can only properly be done by religion, and Durkheim agrees, but with the qualification that religion must be more sociologically articulated. It is not fully defined by "symbols and rites . . . or temples and priests," but must be understood more broadly as "a body of collective beliefs and practices endowed with a certain authority" (Durkheim, 1898/1973, pp. 50–51). Any goal that is collectively pursued by a group of people automatically takes on the moral power that is held by religion. Religion, in other words, can change, and the question faced in Durkheim's France is not how to apply existing religion to the moral problems of French society, but what new form of religion will be capable of addressing them.

Durkheim then summarizes some of the facts of modernity that had motivated his thesis on the division of labor and social solidarity. As older, traditional forms of collective life and solidarity are undone by the new structures of modernity, "individual variations" become too strong to be limited as they previously were. The increased division of labor pushes people into differentiation and "each mind finds itself . . . reflecting a different aspect of the world, and consequently the contents of consciousness differs from one person to another" (Durkheim, 1898/1973, p. 51). Increasingly, in this state of affairs, the only commonality uniting us all is the idea of our common humanity, and it is only some set of practices and beliefs that revolve around this theme—that is, that focuses on the divine, sacred nature of the essential human character that we all share—that can hope to bind together such a diverse set of viewpoints and interests.

Brunetière offers Christian morality instead as the force to bring these disparate modern individuals together, but Durkheim cleverly shows that the development of Christian thought leads to the cult of the human person. It consists of nothing more than an increased emphasis on the individual as the source of spiritual and moral energy. In ancient Rome, pagan religions had focused almost entirely outside the individual on practical rites, and in opposition to this Christianity from its inception had emphasized the "inner faith" of the individual (Durkheim, 1898/1973, p. 52). Durkheim also notes that this focus on the interior life of the believer in Christianity, especially in its Protestant forms, had contributed to the growth of scientific inquiry, as the Christians firmly separated "the spiritual and the temporal," leaving the latter to be investigated by reason while the former was governed by faith (Durkheim, 1898/1973, p. 53). Thus, the cult of the human person is really only the logical extension of what had already been happening within Christianity.

Assaults on the rights of the individual such as that manifested by the attack on Dreyfus constitute a sacrilege to the cult, and they threaten the very existence and solidarity of a society based on such a set of beliefs. Thus, a defense of the individual Dreyfus does not undermine social order at all. It constitutes a defense of society's most basic interests and its most strongly held collective beliefs (Durkheim, 1898/1973, p. 54).

And yet, Durkheim adds, the version of individualism provided by the French revolutionary tradition, which is one of the central sources on which he is drawing, is somewhat in need of revision. This 18th-century doctrine presents only a "negative" definition of individualism insofar as it emphasizes a number of freedoms ("to think, to write, to vote") provided to the individual to allow his emergence from the "shackles" of pre-Revolutionary French social structure (Durkheim, 1898/1973, p. 55). These freedoms must be understood not as ends in themselves but only as a means to a larger collective goal. If those advances are seen as the end of the evolution of the individual, and if individualism devolves into a worship of the individual's right to reject membership in a collective that exerts effective control over her, we find ourselves in a "dangerous" situation. A similar exultation at the falling of political repression and emphasis on individual rights over against society also framed the establishment of the Third Republic of Durkheim's lifetime. In this case, an initial wave of joy was followed by a stark admission that "we did not know what to do with this hard-won freedom" (Durkheim, 1898/1973, p. 55).

The goal toward which these rights point, in Durkheim's view, is a fully harmonized socialist society. These liberties must be put to work to make "the social machine" function more effectively and smoothly, to enable each individual to climb to the heights permitted by his natural talents and abilities so that the promise "to each according to his labor!" can be made good (Durkheim, 1898/1973, p. 56). This further movement would constitute not the restraint or defeat of individualism but its completion.

The Scientific Study of Society and Its Implications in Moral Life

When Durkheim wrote, there was nothing yet that could properly be called "the sociological method." He had to invent it, and so invent it he did. In his early efforts to find inspiration for such a system of thought, Durkheim was strongly drawn to psychology, especially the work of the celebrated Théodule Ribot, because of its strong commitment to an empirical and scientific method (Fournier, 2007, pp. 73–75). The already existing French efforts at social science were, in Durkheim's view, theoretically lacking in rigor, overeager to apply tentative observations to social reform, and generally insufficiently grounded in scientific method (Fournier, 2007, p. 83).

A strong thrust of Durkheim's early methodological work thus was in the direction of establishing the scientific status of sociological method. But the true complexity of Durkheim's efforts here has been oversimplified in the textbooks and in much of sociological common knowledge. The dominant interpretation of Durkheim's methodological ideas paints him as a crude positivist who understands human action in precisely the same way the chemist understands the actions of chemical reagents. General and determinist laws, it is asserted, govern everything that can happen, and agency and consciousness, along with any notion of free will and choice, must be jettisoned. The question of the meaning of social action to actors is considered irrelevant, and the task of the sociologist is to remove herself utterly from any investment or role in moral and political matters in the interests of true scientific objectivity.

A close reading of the breadth of Durkheim's work reveals this caricature as fundamentally distorted. He was undeniably a scientific rationalist who believed the domains of the physical sciences and the human sciences were not wholly separate. He believed that humankind is part of nature, and if the elements of nature can be studied by science, then so too can human beings, individually and collectively. Yet there is much in Durkheim's writing on sociological method to suggest that he was neither a materialist nor a determinist. Even in the single work, *The Rules of Sociological Method* (Durkheim, 1982/1895), which is most often taken by readers to make a case for positivist social science, Durkheim explicitly denies the label and approaches the question of the determination of human action by social structures with a nuance seldom reflected in commentary on this book. It is clear in *The Rules* that sociology must center on **social facts** and not on individual action, and further that these social facts surpass the individual in important ways: They are external to her and they compel her in certain ways. Yet they do not completely *determine* human action. Moreover, human action cannot be studied in precisely the same ways that the natural and physical sciences proceed for reasons having to do with the impossibility of controlling the subjects studied. Only *indirect* experimentation is possible, and this limits the parameters of how and what we can know about the human world.

During the period in which he was working on his book on religion, he distances himself even more clearly from crude positivism and sounds rather like a contemporary cultural sociologist, arguing for the relative autonomy of human cultural productions from the material sources from which they spring. In his later work, the concept of collective representations becomes the central conceptual tool for Durkheim. There is still a recognition, as with the concept of social facts, that these structures provide the field in which human action can operate, but there is now a greater sense in which the *meaning* of these structures, in addition to their effects on human action, is important for the sociologist, and the contours of the beliefs involved must be studied as a factor that can in principle at least be separated from the material structures that give rise to them.

One of the central problems with much textbook summary of Durkheim's thought on sociological method has to do with an imputation of a false and even impossible consistency, when the reality is that he argued different things about this at different times. One telling example involves his sense of the sources of data relevant to sociological work. The early Durkheim was convinced that ethnographic data were extremely limited in their utility, and for this reason he advocated that sociologists confine themselves to the use of more or less official historical documents regarding social and legal structures and macro-level statistical information on practices. Later he would embrace the use of ethnographic data wholeheartedly, although he refused to limit his vision to that of the single-minded ethnographer narrowly describing one small society with no interest in broader generalizations but rather remained interested in analyses that could speak to the condition of humans in society more generally.

Another of the myths that emerge from the textbooks would have Durkheim viewing the science of sociology as radically disconnected from the realm of the moral and politics, but here again the reality is more complicated. It is powerfully telling that, as Durkheim's colleague and friend Georges Davy put it, when the outbreak of the First World War faced French society, Durkheim put aside his interest in the purely scholarly questions of the origins of totemism and exogamy and turned with a passion to the study of the sociological origins of the war (Davy, 1995/1919, p. 98). It was never the isolated task of the scientist alone, studying the abstruse ways of distant human groups such as the Arunta or the Bantu, that moved Durkheim. He was motivated by a desire to understand *contemporary* human groups and their workings, with an eye toward using knowledge of their workings to better them. From the first pages of his thesis, Durkheim rejected the idea of a purely speculative scientific project and embraced a social science that is both moral and political by nature.

The moral meaning of the scientific life is vividly apparent in an early piece of writing Durkheim produced in the form of an address to his *lycée* students at the conclusion of the 1883 school year. The main question at hand is whether men of genius are a menace to the mediocre, or whether the general health is dependent on this elect group. Durkheim cites the philosopher Ernest Renan as an example of those who side with the great in history and reject even the idea that the great should attempt to introduce high culture to the "small minds" (Durkheim, 1883/1975a, p. 412). Renan's vision is a "somber" one of serious, renunciatory thinkers on the one side, doing the work of advancing the race for all of humanity, and the frivolous, mediocre masses on the other, worshipping the great men though they do not understand them and contenting themselves with the "sweet illusions of the ignorant" (Durkheim, 1883/1975a, p. 412).

In opposition to this unapologetically aristocratic vision, there is what we might call a mass society position on the matter. Here, it is not a few great individuals who make a nation, but rather the mass of the citizenry, who can have no interest in the work produced by the poet, the artist, and the philosopher for their aristocratic patrons (Durkheim, 1883/1975a, p. 414). A society that spends energy on producing such great individuals necessarily does so at the expense of the greater majority and thereby runs the risk of creating "dangerous inequalities," so it is, in this vision, obviously preferable to prioritize the average member of the society and the "middle-class culture of the mind" that interests him (Durkheim, 1883/1975a, pp. 414, 415).

Durkheim's response is critical of both of these positions. He accepts Renan's claim that the life of the mind is superior to the common life of tradition and ignorance, but it is unconscionable in his view, if one properly understands the meaning of truth and knowledge, to deny access to it to the mass of society. "All individuals," he writes, "however humble they may be, have the right to aspire to the superior life of the mind" (Durkheim, 1883/1975a, p. 413). But Durkheim finds the argument for radical leveling and the uselessness of great men advanced by the most extreme democrats "perhaps more dangerous" than Renan's Nietzscheanism, and the third way Durkheim advocates turns out to be significantly closer to the latter than to the former (Durkheim, 1883/1975a, p. 414). It amounts to a kind of evolutionist theory of great men as moral, scientific, and spiritual points of superiority that emerge here and there to indicate to the masses, which tend toward a "satisfied mediocrity," the proper direction for the continued progress of humankind (Durkheim, 1883/1975a, p. 415).

How are they to do this? They are to provide a demonstration to the masses in their lives, but especially by their dedication to the "superior life" of the mind, that "humanity is not made to endlessly indulge in easy and vulgar pleasures," and to lead the masses to "despise that inferior life, in order to detach humanity from this mortal slumber and to persuade it to march ahead" (Durkheim, 1883/1975a, p. 416). The life of the mind, the scientific life, is the ideal to which all should aspire, even though not all will be capable of adhering to it. After explicitly naming several of the more typical categories of the "great man"—for example, the artist, the poet, and the thinker—he closes his address by calling on the young graduates not to blush in according to superior men a just deference, for "there is a certain manner of allowing oneself to be guided that does not at all take away independence," and one must know how to respect "all natural superiority" (Durkheim, 1883/1975a, p. 417).

The *Année Sociologique* Group: Collective Labor in a Calling

We might reasonably assert that Durkheim is one of the founders of the discipline of sociology based solely on his ideas, but the claim is considerably strengthened once we understand how he worked institutionally to create the discipline and preserve it from attackers. In the mid-1890s, following the publication of his *Rules of Sociological Method*, Durkheim was increasingly recognized as the central figure in the emerging French social sciences. He had perhaps won allies to his cause with the book, but he had also become a target for intellectual attacks of various orientations. Philosophers denounced what they saw as an effort to steal their thunder by rejecting their claims to speak to questions of human life and meaning without grounding them first in a social context. Psychologists and historians too saw Durkheim's new social science as an effort to trump their own disciplinary approaches.

Durkheim increasingly understood that the only effective way to push social science forward in the face of such trenchant criticism and obstinacy was to create a research center of like-minded colleagues, mostly younger men of great motivation and talent, who could, together, carve out the intellectual space needed to establish sociology in the French academic world. He was spurred on by some of his allies in the struggle, especially by Célestin Bouglé, a young philosopher who had already done much to open up one of the central French philosophical journals, the *Revue de métaphysique et de morale*, to sociological investigations. By mid-1896, Durkheim was steadily working on the project of launching a new journal that would bring together the work of a large group of associates both in France and abroad. He convinced a major Paris academic publisher, Félix Alcan, to take on the journal and set about recruiting members of the editorial team. These included Bouglé himself and a number of others who made up the organizational core of the new journal: Paul Fauconnet, Gaston Richard, Marcel Mauss, Henri Hubert, François Simiand, Maurice Halbwachs, and Hubert Bourgin. Dozens of other young scholars contributed to the journal's voluminous collection of book reviews of all the major work in fields of sociological interest, whether philosophy, ethics, law, domestic and family history and ethnography, economics, geography, criminology, linguistics, history and ethnography of religions, or aesthetics. In addition to the huge number of reviews published in each issue, there were original, often lengthy articles on topical themes, and Durkheim himself published some of his most important work here.

From 1898 to 1913, the first series of the journal carved out a space for sociology with this intensely collective form of intellectual life. There is much evidence in his correspondence with members of the editorial team that Durkheim saw the journal group as something more than a merely scholarly team; the group was a moral force as well. The collective labor of the journal and the solidarity produced by a shared project was another powerful element of its nature. As one commentator puts it, "Durkheim did not do sociology as an isolated individual, but rather as a team leader" (Tiryakian, 2009, p. 2). A good deal of the writing for the journal was done in small collective units, with close editorial supervision by Durkheim and other central figures. In the very process by which he produced his own intellectual work, Durkheim was attentive to the central rule of the doctrine he developed—that is, the eminently social nature of all human endeavor. It is evident in his correspondence that he frequently considered the *Année* a tremendous burden in terms of the time and energy he put into it, but this burden was balanced by the collective spirit and the advances made possible by individuals working together. In one startlingly clear passage in a letter to Mauss from June 1897, during the early effort to get the journal underway, Durkheim encourages his nephew to the task of working in the collective project that he sees as a central vehicle for the articulation of a radically new view of the nature of society: "I hope that from the *Année sociologique* will emerge a theory, exactly opposed to that of vulgar and simplistic historical materialism . . . , which will make religion, rather than the economy, the womb of social facts" (Durkheim, 1998, p. 71).

Prelude: The Individual and Society in the Four Great Books, and Elsewhere

Virtually the entirety of Durkheim's work offers an ongoing examination of the basic questions and themes described in this chapter. In *The Division of Labor in Society* (1984/1893), Durkheim first sketched his argument concerning the modern origins of the individual. Primitive humankind contained no individuals; human beings were simply and totally subsumed into the social collectivity and were in all essential ways interchangeable and indistinguishable. Some of his intellectual opponents, including the English philosopher and social thinker Herbert Spencer, would have had it that individualism was the rule in early human life, and that society came from this primal state after the individuals agreed to rationally bind themselves to one another. Durkheim showed clearly that it was precisely the other way round. The individual personality and the phenomenon of individualism more generally are products of the progressive growth of the division of labor in human society.

The Rules of Sociological Method presents a treatise in anti-individualist sociology. Society is a reality in and of itself, hovering above and ruling over individuals in countless ways, and the science of sociology must take collective life as its essential fact. The social fact is the central theoretical principle upon which sociology relies, and in Durkheim's formulation it reveals the dependence of the individual on the group for all of the most essential elements of her mental life and action in the world.

Suicide was a calculated effort to put the doctrines of *The Rules* into operation in an empirical study. Durkheim deliberately chose a phenomenon that seems, superficially, entirely a matter of individual psychology and pathology, and demonstrated that it is a sociological phenomenon to the core. Yet the analysis is nuanced, and Durkheim proves himself a careful and antireductionist thinker in this important study.

In his final book, *The Elementary Forms of Religious Life* (1995/1912), Durkheim once again returned to the dependence of the individual on collective life. The most basic categories by which humans have understood our world, from the earliest times to the present, have been provided to us by group life, and the individual who would escape these collective representations would become something less than human. Here, the doctrine of *homo duplex* is presented in full articulation to show how the most individual level of the human being is the body as a desiring, biological object, while the most fully human part of our being is the part that comes to us from the social and the cultural.

In his body of writing on the family, marriage, sexuality, and related topics, he argues for the marital bond and the conjugal family as among the primary contemporary institutional forces that hold the excesses of individualism at bay by tying individuals closely together into relations of interdependency and mutual responsibility. In his lectures on professional ethics and civic morals, he reveals the State and the individual as allies. The latter is a product of the growth of the former and depends utterly on the State for the production and protection of his rights and legal status. In his courses and writings on education, he produces a complex vision in which the individual is seen to naturally require the moral authority of the collectivity.

Durkheim's central concerns require considerable conceptual stretching for many contemporary readers. We are today in an age where even the social scientists produce works justifying the most antisocial forms of individualism, with scarcely a wisp of concern at the lack of moral solidarity among the atomic elements making up the human population. We see, for example, sociological bestsellers that describe the phenomenon of "families of one" in more or less celebratory terms, refusing any grander vision of social architecture and willfully refusing to see how this phenomenon of more and more people living alone, with no families and minimal connections and commitments to moral communities, is in large part the inevitable consequence of an increasingly merciless economic system that requires individuals to dedicate themselves to work (without the professional corporate groups Durkheim advocated for) in a more totalizing and dehumanizing way than has ever been the case previously. In this context, a return to Durkheim—if not to fully and uncritically embrace every aspect of his project,

then at least to endeavor to discover what can be learned from him—
promises much in the way of a more vibrantly sociological sociology.

A few questions

- What additional evidence can be seen in developments of the last century for Durkheim's notion of a cult of the human person?
- Are there other varieties of individualism beyond those described by Durkheim in his essay on individualism and the intellectuals?
- Is Durkheim's view of the scientific life compatible with contemporary conceptions of democratic culture?
- In what ways might collective intellectual work differ in substance from work produced by one individual working alone?
- How does the notion of *homo duplex* enhance the sociologist's ability to explain the social world?

3

Morality, Law, the State, and Politics

I f there is one thing that can be asserted with confidence about Durkheim, it is that he was concerned with the nature of morality for the entirety of his adult life. For Durkheim, a focus on the moral foundation of human society led inevitably to the study of the various institutions charged with the production and reproduction of moral beliefs and discipline: the family, the occupational group, and the State. According to his nephew Marcel Mauss, Durkheim was setting to work on a major book on morality at the time of his death, and the evidence of his concern for moral questions is widespread in his existing writing. All four of his major books deal with aspects of the sociology of morality, and it is not too much to say that the entirety of his investigation of the division of labor, religion, culture, and knowledge centers on moral questions. One of the central issues raised over and over again in his work has to do with the moral responsibilities of the individual to society, and vice versa. He firmly believed that morality could be studied scientifically and that a rational morality should emerge as the product of this investigation.

It is also clear that concerns of an ultimately political nature were of profound importance in Durkheim's sociology, and political issues were necessarily immersed in questions of morality for Durkheim. Though he was always careful about making explicit political allegiances and articulated an intellectual position of abstention from overt political activity, his concern that a caustic variety of egoistic individualism would undercut social solidarity and the sense of mutual responsibility for the collective pushed him toward a socialist politics. Colleagues reported that Durkheim indirectly alerted students to his political leanings by entering the lecture hall daily with a copy of the socialist paper *l'Humanité* under his arm (Clark, 1973, p. 190). In 1895 through 1896, he presented a lecture course on the history of socialism in France (Durkheim, 1962/1928), in which he endeavored to strip away the Marxist pretentions to science while at the same time underlining socialism's moral claims and arguing for Saint-Simon as the father of both socialism and social science in France. Though it was for a long time not well known in the English-speaking world, he also gave a course on the State as the chief political entity in modernity and therein produced the foundation of a theory of the State (Durkheim, 1992/1950). In that same lecture course, he discussed at length the problem of how to ensure the moral regulation of economic relations.

The first major intervention Durkheim made into this realm of moral sociology was his doctoral thesis. This study, *The Division of Labor in Society,* was published in 1893. In it, we find already, in a Durkheim barely 35 years of age, the central issues with which he would be dealing for the remainder of his scholarly life. At the core of this study is the question of the relationship between the individual personality and **social solidarity**. Durkheim found that as the individual has become more autonomous and free of social control of the more primitive kinds, s/he has nonetheless become more dependent on society and the moral bonds uniting its members. At the same time, however, certain new forces in the human world work to move us away from moral solidarity and into individualistic pursuits. This problem is at the heart of modernity, and Durkheim returned to it again and again, in various forms, throughout his career.

The Division of Labor in Society

Durkheim envisioned his thesis as an intervention into both intellectual and political debates of his day, and those debates have remained heated and ongoing affairs in our own. The early working title of the thesis was "The Relationship of Individualism and Socialism," which evolved into "The Relationship of the Individual Personality and Social Solidarity" before the definitive title emerged. The question of the nature of this relationship was posed by the emerging discipline of sociology, to be sure, but the same topic was being discussed by the politicians and the press as well. It was obvious that the cultural and legal movement of Europe at the end of the 19th century was toward greater freedom for the individual, at the same time as it seemed equally apparent that the only effective political system in modernity would have to be some kind of social democracy or democratic socialism that would acknowledge individual freedom while protecting the weak and preventing massive social inequality. How could these two cultural and political realities, individualism and socialism, be made compatible?

Political discussions in the contemporary West still revolve around this same basic tension. While classical liberalism, modern conservativism (to be distinguished from classical conservativism, which is quite a different creature), and left and right libertarianism claim that the individual should be granted the maximum of freedom from restraint possible and that individualism is entirely incompatible with any collectivist vision of society, communitarians and some (though not all) progressives argue for the need for at least some significant constraints on individual agency in order to ensure the moral and political health of the group.

This "social question" is at the root of Durkheim's career, and it is connected to the political atmosphere of the end of the French 19th century. These were years of tremendous upheaval and violence in France. In December 1893, months after Alcan had published Durkheim's thesis as a book, the anarchist Auguste Vaillant threw a bomb inside the French Chamber of Deputies; he was executed in February of the following year. His death was seen as an act of martyrdom on the anarchist left, and other attacks followed, the most severe of which was the assassination in June 1894 of the president of the Republic, Marie François Sadi Carnot, by a knife-wielding Italian assailant.

The genesis of *The Division of Labor in Society* goes back at least to 1889 and the early years of Durkheim's scholarly career. In a review in that year of the German sociologist Ferdinand Tönnies's study *Gemeinschaft und Gesellschaft* (*Community and Society*), Durkheim had criticized the latter of the two theoretical categories that undergirded the German thinker's book. *Gemeinschaft*, or community, is described by Tönnies as a form of social relations based on intimacy, tradition, and organicism (by the last term, Tönnies meant to refer simply to its holistic nature—that is, the fact that such profound social bonds could only be understood by reference to an entire social and cultural system, with all its history). Durkheim agrees with Tönnies that this was the dominant mode of social relations in premodern Europe. However, the second of the two concepts, *Gesellschaft*, which is inadequately translated into English as "society," fails in Durkheim's view to accurately describe the nature of social relations in modern, mass societies.

To grasp Tönnies's definition of *Gesellschaft*, one might think of the nature of the relationship one has with a merchant at a department store. Tönnies wants to foreground the abstract and egoistic nature of the relationship. It is, he says, not only the shopkeeper who is a merchant in a

Gesellschaft-dominated social order; the purchaser of his goods is too, and he enters the relation with the same wholly self-interested, materialist goal of getting the better of the exchange. Both parties have no more interest in or connection to one another than that dictated by their narrow pursuit of economic advantage, the seller trying to get top dollar, the buyer trying not to pay it. But, retorts Durkheim, this overlooks the deep webs of interdependency that connect the two parties. Insofar as the ever-increasing specialization of labor has meant that each of us is individually capable of less and less of the entire range of production necessary for our everyday lives, we are thrust into greater relationships of interdependence, however much exchange relationships might seem more distanced than they were in an earlier, *Gemeinschaft*-dominated social order. He set out in his first book to demonstrate what these new relations of solidarity looked like.

Durkheim divides the book into three sections. In the first and clearly the most important, which makes up roughly half of the total text, he begins methodically by defining the object of the book and discussing why a sociological perspective on it offers superior insights.

The growing division of labor in the advanced world at the turn of the 19th century was an undeniable fact. Great concentrations of labor and capital, along with massive industrial and technological innovation and the explosive growth of new bodies of technical knowledge, require a highly specialized delineation of different occupations and careers (Durkheim, 1984/1893, p. 1). Some of what Durkheim prognosticates in these opening pages will be seen by today's reader as obvious truth. For example, he predicts the eventual separation of the functions of teacher and scholar, which were still tightly intertwined in his day, and contemporary institutions of higher education, with their lower tier of masses of educators who produce no scholarship and teach hundreds if not thousands of students every term, reveal the accuracy of his prediction (Durkheim, 1984/1893, p. 2). There is, Durkheim claims, a new categorical imperative in the modern world: "Equip yourself to fulfill usefully a specific function" (Durkheim, 1984/1893, p. 4). The investigation of the meaning and the moral consequences of the growing **division of labor** must be carried out scientifically, and the abstract methods of the moralists who previously were seen as the authorities on such matters must be rejected in favor of the study of empirical reality (Durkheim, 1984/1893, pp. 5–6). Such an empirical, scientific investigation will seek to determine the "social need" or function served by the division of labor as well as its causes, and it will classify the abnormal forms the division of labor can sometimes take (Durkheim, 1984/1893, pp. 6–7). It is the question of the changes in forms of social solidarity that interests Durkheim: "[I]f pre-industrial societies were held together by common ideas and sentiments, by shared norms and values [by *Gemeinschaft* relations, in Tönnies's terms], what holds an *industrial* society [like ours] together? Or is it perhaps *not being held together at all*, but rather in the process of disintegration [as Tönnies suggests]?" (Lukes, 1985, p. 141, emphasis added).

The Method of Determining This Function

What is a **function**? It can be defined in at least two different ways, Durkheim notes, both derived from biological terminology. We can speak of the relations that exist between two or more parts of a biological system—say, the heart and the lungs, or the nervous system and the digestive system—or we can refer to relations between "movements" of the system and specific needs of the organism (Durkheim, 1984/1893, p. 11). It is the second of these definitions that Durkheim adopts.

He nuances the relationship between the sociological task of determining how the division of labor actually functions and the moral task of evaluating its contribution to civilization. It is clear that at the broadest level we cannot fall back upon merely moral terms in discussing the division of labor, as the elements of modern civilization cannot reasonably be classified as having a simple moral end. Crime and suicide rise precipitously in the contemporary world, and even the greater economic production that is one of the basic consequences of the division of labor in modern society has "nothing obligatorily moral about it" (Durkheim, 1984/1893, p. 13). Science and art too are outside the realm of the properly moral, according to Durkheim. The moral realm is limited to "rules of action" that are imposed on behavior under penalty of punishment (Durkheim, 1984/1893, p. 15). Modern society can only be considered "morally neutral," and the division of labor shares this neutrality if its sole end is to "make civilisation possible" (Durkheim, 1984/1893, p. 15). It may be that certain needs are provided for by the division of labor, but it may also be that those needs are themselves *consequences* of the division of labor (e.g., we are exhausted by our jobs and therefore need various leisure goods—vacations!—to relieve us of this exhaustion), which leaves the moral status of the division of labor unclear (Durkheim, 1984/1893, pp. 15–16).

Durkheim turns then to a discussion of social difference and identity as expressed in the division of labor. We generally think that resemblance of two individuals is more likely to lead them to recognize a bond between them than difference, yet this depends entirely on the *kind* of difference. Differences that are mutually opposed and exclusionary will likely not produce solidarity, but those that are complementary—for example, those of the abstract intellectual and the practical man—can bring us closer to one another (Durkheim, 1984/1893, p. 16). The division of labor can therefore, at least in some manifestations, have the moral effect of producing a more powerful glue to hold two or more individuals together in a social bond (Durkheim, 1984/1893, p. 17). The sexual attraction of men and women, and the division of labor that has historically sprung up along the lines of gender, provides another compelling example here. Though we might tend to think the contrary, given recent political and cultural movements in the direction of the equalization of the condition of men and women, differences between the genders were fewer in the distant past than in Durkheim's day or now. The primitive, gendered division of labor was almost certainly less developed than ours, and men and women were physically much more similar in earlier societies than they are today. How then did the sexes become more specialized and differentiated?

Durkheim's argument here has been widely attacked over the years, often unfairly by critics who have not fully understood his argument. What is generally emphasized by these critics is the fact that Durkheim invokes research, controversial today but widely cited and reported in his day, that shows systematic differences in brain sizes between the sexes and infers differences in intelligence from those physical differences. But what is generally passed over is that he does so *only in order to emphasize the point regarding the historical differentiation of men and women.* He argues that male and female brain masses were much closer to equal in size earlier in human history, so the contemporary difference in size cannot be explained by any simple allusion to natural sexual difference (Durkheim, 1984/1893, pp. 18–19).

The larger point he makes here has nothing whatever to do with biological determinism of sex differentiation, though many of his critics incorrectly assume this is his perspective. It is changes in morality and social institutions that seem responsible for the more differentiated sexual division of labor and the difference in brain sizes, not biological determinism. In many earlier societies, the institution of marriage existed only in an undeveloped state (Durkheim, 1984/1893, p. 19). It is only much later that the institution begins to tie the two individuals to monogamous and long-term fidelity, which presents a radically different field in which the differentiation of function develops. Earlier, women had performed most of the same roles men did, but once the modern marital institution was in place, they found their roles restricted to the private sphere of the family and the "affective" areas of life—for example, "art and literature," as well as nurturant care of children (Durkheim, 1984/1893, p. 20). Men, meanwhile, continued to be fully engaged in the competitive, aggressive public sphere, where they are required to test themselves constantly against others in the struggle for resources. Durkheim's intention here is not to make a case for the inferiority of women.

Rather, he shows how the evolution of the institution of marriage, along with the growing complexity of modern societies, has created two differentiated sexes that are, each of them, "incomplete" and in need of a complementary other to provide some of the functions they cannot fulfill on their own (Durkheim, 1984/1893, p. 22). He even argues that the two sexes come to construct images of self that include the complementary sexual other, as the relationship of male and female, and the solidarity it produces, comes to be understood as "natural" (Durkheim, 1984/1893, p. 22). On the issue of what causes what here, Durkheim is crystal clear: It is the functional differences that have produced the morphological ones, and not the other way round (Durkheim, 1984/1893, p. 21).

So differentiation can produce greater solidarity and mutual interdependence. It is at least a reasonable hypothesis, then, that modern societies like our own, which can maintain themselves in equilibrium only thanks to the specialization of tasks, might derive important benefits from that division of labor (Durkheim, 1984/1893, p. 23). But how can we go about demonstrating this to be so?

We must first effectively define social solidarity. There are different types of this phenomenon that must be distinguished (Durkheim, 1984/1893, p. 24). First, however, we must recognize that it cannot be found in naked form to measure in the empirical world. We must find a way to operationalize it—that is, to locate some empirical object that we can reasonably take to be an indicator of social solidarity (Durkheim, 1984/1893, p. 24). Law is a good option here, in Durkheim's view, for the greater the amount of solidarity existing among the members of a society is, the more we should see sustained and diverse social relations that will necessitate laws to govern them (Durkheim, 1984/1893, p. 25). Wherever social life is durable, it tends to become increasingly organized, and law is one of the primary forms such organization takes (Durkheim, 1984/1893, p. 25). Social solidarity is a social fact, which is a term Durkheim would make one of the core concepts of his sociological method later in *The Rules of Sociological Method*. As we will see in Chapter 4, in that later conception he would define social facts by their externality and their coercive aspect. Here, he seems merely to want to suggest that social solidarity can only be effectively understood from a sociological perspective (Durkheim, 1984/1893, p. 27). Law "reproduces the main forms of social solidarity," so the classification of the forms law takes will neatly enable us to investigate the forms of solidarity they represent (Durkheim, 1984/1893, p. 28). Broadly speaking, law takes two different forms, defined by the specific kinds of sanctions involved: Penal law consists of rules the transgression of which is punished with repressive sanction— that is, suffering imposed on the transgressor— while civil law is composed of rules that entail sanctions of a restitutory nature—that is, the guilty party is required to reestablish the state of affairs prior to his transgression of the law by some payment to the victim (Durkheim, 1984/1893, p. 29).

Mechanical Solidarity

Durkheim turns first to an examination of the kind of solidarity that is represented by penal law, which he calls **mechanical solidarity**. He begins with an investigation into the definition of criminal offense (Durkheim, 1984/1893, p. 31). A central question that should be addressed is the mechanism by which the severity of a criminal offense and the sanction that follows is determined. Some offenses are severely repressed despite the fact that they are not the most objectively harmful offenses to the life of the society, while other offenses that objectively damage society more seriously are punished less intensely. Murder, for example, is certainly understood as a great moral evil, but it may be the case that economic crimes that cause, for example, hundreds or thousands of people to lose their life savings and fall into misery cause more widespread harm to the whole society (Durkheim, 1984/1893, p. 33). Yet, as we see with great regularity in contemporary societies, economic criminals such as Jerome Kerviel, a trader at the French bank Société Générale, who lost nearly $7 billion of investors' money and received a prison sentence of a mere 3 years, or Enron's Jeffrey Skilling, who used accounting fraud to cheat employees and investors of billions of dollars while pocketing huge sums himself and was sentenced to only 24 years in prison, often receive much lighter penalties than those convicted of crimes with comparatively weak effects on the society. This shows that objective harm done to society cannot serve alone as the definition of crime (Durkheim, 1984/1893, pp. 32–33).

Penal law is, Durkheim argues, stated negatively—that is, it prescribes sanctions but says nothing of the duties to which they correspond. In civil law, on the contrary, duties, not punishments, are the content of the law (Durkheim, 1984/1893, p. 35). This is so because the duties that are punished by penal law are widely known and accepted throughout the society. No one needs to be told not to murder fellow citizens. We all know this, given our deep rooting in the moral substratum of our society, and we all feel the authority of this obligation without having to be explicitly made aware of it in the law. Civil law, on the other hand, frequently engages rights and obligations that are less well known and less firmly rooted in the deep moral roots of the society. I do not know the specifics of the law governing my ability to build a fence at the border of my property and the property of my neighbor unless I go to look it up. In penal law, the whole society participates to a significant extent in the moral sanctioning of transgressors, while in civil law, an official, the judge, is generally the arbiter of the offense and the remedy (Durkheim, 1984/1893, pp. 36–37). Because penal law is so widely and commonly agreed upon within a society, it evolves only exceedingly slowly, while civil law can and does change quickly and often (Durkheim, 1984/1893, p. 37).

At the bottom of penal law, then, there seems to be a deep and shared set of moral beliefs that envision certain acts as sufficiently offensive to morality as to merit serious punishment. This set of beliefs, which is shared by the wide swath of the members of any given society, Durkheim calls the **collective consciousness** (Durkheim, 1984/1893, p. 39). It is distinct from individual beliefs and generally is passed from one generation to the next (Durkheim, 1984/1893, p. 61). Durkheim insists that we should conceive of this collection of beliefs as transcendent of individual consciousnesses. Although individual minds are the vehicles that express the beliefs in the collective consciousness, it does not arise from the conditions of individuals but from the conditions facing the society as a whole. Penal law is fundamentally dependent on the state of the collective consciousness: What offends "strong, well-defined states" of this consciousness will be made a serious crime in the penal code (Durkheim, 1984/1893, pp. 39–40). It can reasonably be said, then, that the collective consciousness creates crime by so defining those acts that offend it, and the acts themselves are objectively morally neutral (Durkheim, 1984/1893, p. 40). This is a thoroughly **social constructionist** view of crime—that is, Durkheim argues that an act is criminal *solely* because it transgresses some deeply held conviction that is found in the collective consciousness of one or another society, not because of any inherent evil nature of the act itself.

Sanction in penal law, as noted above, is focused on punishment. Punishment is by its nature characterized by a certain emotional and moral vigor, especially in less advanced types of society (Durkheim, 1984/1893, p. 43). It can be defined effectively as "a reaction of passionate feeling" against those who transgress certain rules of conduct that is produced by the society, through the medium of some specific organized body—for example, a jury (Durkheim, 1984/1893, p. 52). This passionate, vengeful nature of punishment is motivated not merely by cruelty but more essentially by the instinct of preservation of the society, as it perceives in the transgression an imminent peril (Durkheim, 1984/1893, p. 45). While this aspect of punishment might be more readily apparent in less advanced forms of society, we can see it at work still in our own contemporary societies. A glance at the myriad television programs dealing with courtroom drama of one kind or another, where victims detail the offenses they have suffered and hosts denounce the guilty to the excitement of studio and living room audiences, reveals the truth of Durkheim's observation. The goal of punishment of offenses against the collective consciousness is to "aveng[e] . . . the outrage to morality" of the crime (Durkheim, 1984/1893, p. 47). This is eminently clear in, for example, the ferocious punishments to which serious criminals were subjected in premodern Europe, where various offenses might lead to you being broken on the wheel or publicly flogged, but the motivation of vengeance is the same in the modern world, according to Durkheim, although our forms of punishment are undoubtedly better directed than those of the past (Durkheim, 1984/1893, p. 47). However, neither the aggrieved party nor her family and close associates alone is the victim, in the broadest sense. It is *society itself* and not particular individuals that is outraged at the crime and requires expiation. Evidence for this can be found in the fact that penal law has religious origins, and religion is a fundamentally social entity that constrains individuals more or less constantly, obligating them to certain practices and beliefs that are often seemingly against their own individual interests (Durkheim, 1984/1893, p. 49). This can be most clearly seen in primitive societies, where most penal law applies to offenses against religion and other forms of tradition and custom (Durkheim, 1984/1893, p. 50). These offenses to the collective consciousness provoke a powerful response precisely because all (or nearly all) the individual consciousnesses in the society are in agreement on this belief and reinforce one another in their outrage (Durkheim, 1984/1893, p. 55).

It is important to be clear, Durkheim notes, that the link of penal law to religion is not simply historical. Contemporary penal law remains marked by religious sensibilities, for the desire we feel when this kind of crime occurs is to protect something *sacred* (Durkheim, 1984/1893, p. 56). We are avenging ourselves, in the form of the collective, and not any gods, but the illusion that it is something greater than ourselves that we avenge is important for the protection of the moral order in which we live. Punishment of crime brings the entire society, or at least all the "honest consciousnesses" (Durkheim, 1984/1893, p. 58), together in a sense of profound moral outrage against the offender. Durkheim provides an example of a moral scandal in a small town that produces widespread, seemingly spontaneous discussion of the event in the community and the expression of "[a] common indignation" (Durkheim, 1984/1893, p. 58).

Once particular acts are established as transgressions against basic beliefs in the collective consciousness, they are difficult to dislodge, whatever might be their actual objective harm to the system. But they always do harm something of significant importance: "social cohesion" (Durkheim, 1984/1893,

p. 62). This, in Durkheim's view, is enough to justify the response. Once such transgressions attain a certain place in the collective consciousness, to fail to punish them would be to allow the weakening of social bonds, and thus the punishment is a *moral* good. In this sense, decriminalization of acts still understood as powerful outrages in the moral community can only serve to weaken solidarity (Durkheim, 1984/1893, p. 62). Punishment cannot simply be justified by the philosophy of "an eye for an eye," even if that is the language in which it is frequently couched, for the reasons just given. Its ultimate function is the reaffirmation of a social bond (Durkheim, 1984/1893, pp. 62–63).

Organic Solidarity

There is another kind of social solidarity, represented in restitutory or civil law, that frames sanction not as expiation but as a simple return of the state obtaining before the infraction occurred. This Durkheim calls **organic solidarity** (Durkheim, 1984/1893, p. 68). The kind of law that serves as an indicator of this variety of solidarity is less central to the collective consciousness than criminal law, but it is nonetheless still involved to a significant degree in social solidarity (Durkheim, 1984/1893, pp. 69–70). Restitutory sanctions concern relations not between the individual and the society as a whole, as is the case with repressive sanctions, but between clearly defined and specific parties in the society whom they bind together (Durkheim, 1984/1893, p. 71). These relations can take two forms, each of which is defined by a particular kind of rule and contributes to a particular kind of solidarity. In the first, the rules and solidarity involved are purely "negative" (Durkheim, 1984/1893, p. 72). They do not help to form social bonds, but instead mark the boundaries between people and, in general, establish the relation between persons and property. This is the domain of what is known in legal discourse as **real rights** (Durkheim, 1984/1893, pp. 73, 75). It is Durkheim's contention that real rights and the **negative solidarity** they represent cannot be the basis for social relations because there must be something "beneath" them that provides moral bedrock. For people to recognize and mutually guarantee property rights, they must, first of all, have some affective bond to one another. They must, for some reason, depend upon one another and on the same society to which they belong (Durkheim, 1984/1893, p. 77). This perspective constitutes a profound criticism of the core argument of classical liberal economics.

The second kind of relation we can find expressed in restitutory law is characterized by Durkheim as "positive," and it entails "co-operation" between the involved parties. Here, we find law that defines relations of one person to another and thereby brings them together into a mutual social relationship stemming from the division of labor. Examples of bodies of law that fit under this label include a number of large bodies of contemporary law: family law, contractual law, commercial law, administrative law, and constitutional law (Durkheim, 1984/1893, p. 77). Family law defines and regulates relations among various individuals within the division of labor in the family and determines parental statuses, domestic functions, familial membership, and other such matters (Durkheim, 1984/1893, p. 78). Contractual law regulates relations between "buyer and seller . . . employers and workers . . . lender and borrower . . . innkeeper and traveler," among others (Durkheim, 1984/1893, p. 80). In yet another biological metaphor, Durkheim notes that this kind of law functions as a kind of "nervous system," ensuring that the various functions of the social body fit together properly (Durkheim, 1984/1893, p. 83).

Durkheim then sums up the two chapters he has just concluded, which are in many ways the most important in the book. **Positive solidarity**, which differs from negative solidarity in that it directly contributes to the integration of members of the society, can be understood as consisting of two types: mechanical, which integrates by binding individuals directly to the rest of the society, and organic, which creates solidarity by linking individuals to some discrete part of the larger society. In mechanical solidarity, we experience society as "a collective type" in which beliefs are widely shared; in organic solidarity, we experience it as a complex system of differentiated units and functions that form a larger whole as a result of a vast web of specific relationships (Durkheim, 1984/1893, p. 83). Individual differences in function, feelings, and personality are minimal or even nonexistent in relations of mechanical solidarity, and here what makes individuals like one another is greater and more powerful than what makes them different. Durkheim goes so far as to claim that individuals, in our contemporary sense of the term as persons with unique personalities, can only exist in societies with advanced divisions of labor and extensive organic solidarity. He attacks Herbert Spencer, who argued that the individual was severely repressed in the primitive world, by correcting a fundamental flaw in his observation: There simply *were* no individuals in the primitive world (Durkheim, 1984/1893, p. 142). Differences in function and belief are emphasized in organic solidarity, but this is in order to create a higher synthesis of discrete individuals in relations of mutual interdependence (Durkheim, 1984/1893, p. 84–85). Later in the book Durkheim will make clear he is not making a merely historical argument. While mechanical solidarity is more prevalent in the kinds of simply organized societies that seemed to be rapidly going extinct in his day (as well as in the historical societies of antiquity that gave birth to today's major world religions—for example, among the ancient Hebrews; Durkheim, 1984/1893, p. 94), we can and do still experience it today in our complex societies in which organic solidarity is the dominant form of social solidarity.

Generally speaking, however, the growing purview of organic solidarity means a significant decrease in punitive law. Domestic law, for example, has now lost most of its more repressive aspects, as Durkheim shows by turning again to comparisons with Greek and Hebrew antiquity, where, for example, filial impiety was punishable by the death penalty for many offenses (Durkheim, 1984/1893, p. 109). Societies characterized by organic solidarity have seen an almost total disappearance of religious crimes, whereas in ancient Israel and even in classical Athens, there were many such crimes. In Rome too there was a large amount of repressive religious law to vigorously punish such offenses as, for example, the profaning of holy places and exposing a corpse to sunlight (Durkheim, 1984/1893, pp. 113–114). Crimes of *lèse-majesté*—that is, offending the dignity of a sovereign, which could include a wide range of even the lightest such transgressions in previous times—are also disappearing (Durkheim, 1984/1893, p. 115). In modern society generally, we see great evidence of what Durkheim calls an "incontrovertibl[e] . . . truth": The purview of religion diminishes radically, and this means the collective consciousness, although it is not in danger of disappearing altogether, is significantly less focused and unified than it was in the past (Durkheim, 1984/1893, pp. 119, 122).

Durkheim turns again to one of his regular foils, Herbert Spencer, to register a few more blows against theories of human nature that take egoism as the primary motivating force. Spencer, a mostly neglected and forgotten figure today but seen as one of the most legitimate players in the new field of sociology in Durkheim's time, is by far the single author most cited in *The Division of Labor*, with 105 citations of nine different texts. Even Auguste Comte comes in a distant second, with less than a third as many citations (Besnard, Borlandi, & Vogt, 1993, p. 70). Durkheim unquestionably owed some debts to Spencer, but he also differed with him fundamentally on many points. Spencer and others who carried the intellectual banner of egoism and purported to base it in an understanding of evolutionary theory had not in Durkheim's view exercised the necessary "reservations and moderation" when putting Darwin's theoretical insights to work in the world of human morality. Durkheim argues that the best evolutionary analysis of the facts shows that humankind in its earliest, most primitive forms was driven fundamentally not by individualism but by a sense of altruism, which is most compellingly evident in myriad examples in the primitive world of practices involving what Durkheim would later term altruistic suicide (in his book *Suicide*, which is discussed in the next chapter), in which individuals willingly sacrifice themselves for the moral good of the group (Durkheim, 1984/1893, p. 145). Although these specific forms are seen by most of us as excessive today, there is no reason to doubt the morally healthy impulses that lie at their foundations and that continue to exist in modern society (Durkheim, 1984/1893, p. 145). There is almost no evidence, Durkheim claims, to support the theory of the social contract, which would have it that humankind came into social relations based solely on individualistic calculations of self-interest in which each individual realized his or her interests would be most efficiently obtained by giving up some freedom in order to gain the protection of the group and its rules (Durkheim, 1984/1893, p. 151). Durkheim's argument is that the individual gives up freedom for the benefits of group membership "spontaneously" because he feels the emotional satisfaction of life in the group and not because of self-interest (Durkheim, 1984/1893, p. 151).

The sustained growth of restitutory law in modernity is accompanied by a decrease in the purview of purely private contracts, and the new restitutory law that is emerging has a strongly public element—that is, it is not simply a legal formula for dealing with the claims of two agents bound by purely contractual relations. So, for example, in marriage and adoption law, there is an increasing presence of a mediating public authority, whether the Church, State (in the form of magistrates and judges), or both, standing between the two parties and representing the larger social world to which both are ultimately responsible (Durkheim, 1984/1893, pp. 155, 156). In our day, at least in the United States, much exists to counter Durkheim's claim about the trend of history, and certainly there are many who reject the very idea of an intervening public authority in, for example, marital law in order to propose fairly radical and individualist changes in that law. Durkheim would see such a development as abnormal and socially problematic, as it is unclear how law that does not aim at solidarity beyond the merely momentary and self-interested relation of the contract form could play any role in holding society together. It may be that organic solidarity as it existed at the time of his writing was not yet sufficiently developed to do the social task required, but the general form of such solidarity was as he described (Durkheim, 1984/1893, p. 174).

Durkheim's contention is that contracts of a private, individual nature always rely on a broader sense of the moral legitimacy of contracts. If there were no underlying moral sense that contracts are desirable, that we should adhere to our end of them, and that others can be counted on to do so as well, then individual contracts would not have any power whatsoever. The contract, in other words, is "of social origin" and precedes the rational calculating self-interest of the individuals involved in any given contract

(Durkheim, 1984/1893, p. 162). Later in the book, Durkheim attacks Spencer again on the latter's notion that individualist, rational cooperation is the key to understanding what holds society together. For Durkheim, such cooperation is necessarily preceded by "instinctive forces such as the affinity of blood, attachment to the same soil, the cult of their ancestors, a commonality of habits," and it can arise only once a base is established on one or another of these forces (Durkheim, 1984/1893, p. 219).

The Causes and Conditions

The second major section of the book sets out to demonstrate how the change from societies based on mechanical solidarity to societies based on organic solidarity has taken place. It begins with a discussion of the relationship of the division of labor to human happiness. How is human happiness affected, if at all, by a more or less sophisticated division of labor? Durkheim finds it first of all necessary to note something rarely seriously entertained by those blindly enthralled by a certain notion of progress, which is that it is not at all obvious that progress, as it is frequently defined as a more rationalized world with more sophisticated technology and greater individualism, increases human happiness (Durkheim, 1984/1893, p. 186). Happiness has a certain relative quality; the primitive can be just as happy in his condition as any modern is in hers (Durkheim, 1984/1893, p. 189). There are some key indicators that suggest that happiness is *decreasing* in modernity. Rising levels of suicide, which seem to have been a rare phenomenon in early human society, point in this direction, and the fact that suicides seem most prevalent in precisely the parts of modern society most touched by the primary characteristics of modernity (e.g., in large cities) is still more evidence of this hypothesis (Durkheim, 1984/1893, pp. 191–192). The social scientist, therefore, would do well to give up facile ideas about the relationship of the social changes Durkheim is investigating in this book (from one type of solidarity to another) and happiness and to endeavor more rigorously to find the *causes* of those changes (Durkheim, 1984/1893, p. 194).

The concentration of population in towns, which became cities, which became metropolises, was in itself one of the primary causal factors involved here (Durkheim, 1984/1893, p. 201). Rapidly developing means of communication (e.g., print media, mail, telegraph) decreased the distance between elements of society still more dramatically (Durkheim, 1984/1893, p. 203). These changes in demographics and communicative media produced greater **dynamic or moral density**, by which Durkheim means simply that people were drawn into more frequent interaction (Durkheim, 1984/1893, p. 201). To be sure, the moral bonds that are involved here are not those prevalent in feudal villages, but Durkheim is taking a strong stand against social theories that would see in the condition of town and urban life a necessary cause of greater isolation. He is here again challenging the position of Tönnies, who had argued that modernity brought the purely individualist, anticommunal ethic of *Gesellschaft*.

This greater social density required a greater division of labor; Durkheim states this as a sociological law (Durkheim, 1984/1893, pp. 205, 206). This extended, invigorated division of labor, then, as an essentially automatic product of its operation, produced a host of new human desires and needs, but we must be careful, in keeping with Durkheim's warning, not to equate the existence of those new needs and the means to satisfy them with greater happiness (Durkheim, 1984/1893, pp. 212, 214, 216).

There are a number of substantial social and cultural consequences of the development of the modern division of labor. As the division of labor increases, the collective consciousness grows less concrete and more abstract, and this is most evident in the changes that take place in "the most vital of all its elements . . . the notion of deity" (Durkheim, 1984/1893, p. 230). The conception of gods grows increasingly more transcendent and becomes more highly rationalized and universalized (Durkheim, 1984/1893, p. 231–232). There is also a progressive weakening of tradition and the power of elders, as the aged increasingly no longer occupy positions of respect and become instead objects of pity (Durkheim, 1984/1893, p. 236). In the cities especially, the young take on positions of power and the old are swept away (Durkheim, 1984/1893, p. 237). The collective consciousness in the form it takes in all premodern societies relies heavily on the past as its basis, but this shifts dramatically in modernity. Finally, and even though dynamic or moral density increases with greater social density in a form consistent with organic solidarity, at the same time "society spreads out"—that is, although there are many people living in close proximity to one another, they are no longer as tightly located near the moral centers of authority, and individuals cannot be as effectively enveloped by the collective's moral judgment as was true in societies characterized by mechanical solidarity (Durkheim, 1984/1893, p. 238). Heredity becomes a less important factor in the determination of the trajectory of individuals, not because its organic and psychological bases have weakened but because individuals are driven to acquire ideas and skills heredity cannot pass on to them in order to survive (Durkheim, 1984/1893, p. 261).

The Abnormal Forms

In the book's final section, which makes up only about one seventh of the total page count in the English translation, Durkheim turns to an advance response to critics who might see the foregoing analysis as too utopian—that is to say, as too convinced that social evolution in modernity is inevitably in the direction of more and better solidarity through the intricacies of the workings of the division of labor. Here, he not only describes some of the ways in which what he sees as the normal evolution of the division of labor can be disturbed and derailed, he also advocates for a politics capable of responding to these abnormalities.

The **anomic division of labor** is the result of a failure of the division of labor to produce solidarity because of a lack of norms—that is, because there is insufficient regulation of the relationships between the various elements of the division of labor (Durkheim, 1984/1893, p. 304). If the division of labor is pushed too far, it can become a disintegrative, anomic force (Durkheim, 1984/1893, p. 294). Durkheim suggests we see examples of this kind of development in situations of "industrial or commercial crises" and of pronounced antagonism and conflict of labor and capital (Durkheim, 1984/1893, p. 292). Such problems of anomie in the division of labor can only be effectively regulated by some party external to the division of labor itself—that is, the State (Durkheim, 1984/1893, p. 295).

Some critics of the modern division of labor (we might well think of Marx here) insinuate that it necessarily pushes the division of labor to the point that the worker feels himself reduced to the level of a machine (Durkheim, 1984/1893, p. 306). Against the idea that the worker needs a greatly expanded hand in the overall productive process in order not to feel his labor power abused and restricted, Durkheim believes that it is sufficient for the individual worker to know that he contributes to a process larger than his part in it, for he will thereby see that what he produces in his labors is a part of a larger project (Durkheim, 1984/1893, p. 306). Marx famously suggested that the workers be converted into philosophers and artists for at least part of their day in addition to performing manual labor. Durkheim is much more firmly realist, even while he shares Marx's sense that injustice in the division of labor is a problem that will have to be resolved. It is not necessary, or likely, for the worker to be able to take on a wide variety of tasks or come to a deep understanding of the entire chain of production of which he is a part, as in Marx's speculative dream of life after the revolution. It is enough to stave off anomie in the division of labor, Durkheim writes, if the worker vaguely sees the end goal to which he contributes through his labor and therefore has a sense of the usefulness of his own contribution to that larger process (Durkheim, 1984/1893, p. 308).

Another abnormal form is what Durkheim calls the **forced division of labor,** where there is pronounced inequality of opportunity and some workers feel trapped in positions below what they feel they deserve. It is not regulation *per se* of access to positions that creates this abnormality, since even the most highly regulated division of labor—for example, in caste societies—can be seen as acceptable to those involved (Durkheim, 1984/1893, p. 312). The division of labor must emerge spontaneously to create solidarity, but this does not mean that all workers have the same objective possibility of being in all positions. Durkheim assumes nothing about what is "natural" for members of any given society to desire in terms of hierarchy and social differentiation. It is something of a byword in some intellectual circles today that the innate desire and need of all human creatures is a social order without hierarchy of any kind, with a concomitant recognition of the absolute equality of abilities of all people. Durkheim did not adhere to this utopian fantasy. He believed that functions of disparate kinds will exist in all societies, and individuals will be differently suited to fill them, and it is perfectly possible for even fairly rigid systems of class or even caste distinction to be seen as acceptable by the members of a given society (Durkheim, 1984/1893, p. 312). Solidarity in the division of labor does not require total equality of outcomes, nor even of opportunity. Social inequalities will exist, and that is perfectly acceptable so long as they roughly map natural inequalities (Durkheim, 1984/1893, p. 313). Durkheim accepts basic differences in aptitude and talent in the human population, but he also recognizes that real injustice can exist in the outcomes of the division of labor, and the concern for justice will have to be paramount if this abnormal form is to be avoided (Durkheim, 1984/1893, p. 321).

The final abnormal form of the division of labor consists in a situation wherein individual effort is not given appropriate scope and the various elements of the division of labor are not effectively coordinated (Durkheim, 1984/1893, p. 323). This variation has been called the **bureaucratic division of labor** (Besnard, Borlandi, & Vogt, 1993, p. 198). In stifling individual activity, this abnormal form cuts at the heart of organic solidarity, which brings the members of the society together not only in regulating them but also in increasing the vibrancy of the activity of the entire social body (Durkheim, 1984/1893, p. 328).

In the book's brief conclusion, Durkheim returns to the moral function of the division of labor. It is essential in the creation of lasting solidarity, through the "system of rights and duties" it produces (Durkheim, 1984/1893, pp. 337–338). He points directly to the moral crisis of the France of his day, in which the progress of organic solidarity has not been rapid and thorough enough to stave off decay and individualization (Durkheim, 1984/1893, p. 339), and closes with a call for action based on the results of his study:

> We need to put a stop to this anomie, and to find ways of harmonious co-operation between those organs that still clash discordantly together. We need

to introduce into their relationships a greater justice by diminishing those external inequalities that are the source of our ills. . . . [O]ur first duty at the present time is to fashion a morality for ourselves. (Durkheim, 1984/1893, p. 340)

On Socialism

For some time, much interpretive work has been done, especially in American sociology, to get Durkheim away from socialism and to characterize his political sensibilities as oriented more toward the political right. But this may be one of the rare occasions on which we would do well to heed the reactionary critics of Durkheim in his own day, for whom there was no question but that he was a socialist. According to Marcel Mauss, the issue of socialism was of importance to Durkheim from his days at the École Normale. We have already seen that his first idea for a thesis title placed the question right up front: "The Relationship of Individualism and Socialism." Durkheim turned his attention to an academic study of socialism in 1895, when he gave the first course in what was intended at the time as an ongoing project on the topic.

It is quite likely that the disaster of the Paris Commune (which occurred, let us recall, when he was only 13 years old) had a role to play in Durkheim's thinking about socialism. Any kind of socialism that presented itself as militant and based in Marxian ideas of violent class conflict, as was the case in the Commune, rubbed against Durkheim's experiences and his fundamental conviction that society had to find the means of solidarity if it were to advance. But this did not mean a turn against socialism. On the contrary, during the First World War, he wrote to his friend the philosopher Xavier Léon, describing his hopes for the future: "Our salvation lies in socialism discarding its out of date slogans or in the formation of a new Socialism which goes back to the French tradition. I see so clearly what this might be!" (Lukes, 1985, p. 321). A close examination of his thinking on this topic, especially when it is melded into a consideration of his work on religion (which is described in Chapter 6), will suggest that Durkheim saw in the solidarity of a non-Marxist socialism the way beyond religion, which would harness religion's powerful ability to create moral solidarity but firmly ground it in empirical matters of social well-being and justice rather than supernatural falsehoods and myth.

The Socialism Course: Socialism and Saint-Simon

There is a problem to be addressed right out of the gate, in Durkheim's view, that stems from the inaccurate claims some socialists make for the scientific status of their political ideology. Socialism is not simply another way of saying "sociology"—that is to say, it is not a scientific analysis of society. Though there were certainly in Durkheim's day European Marxists who were already claiming the theoretical doctrines of historical materialism as the human science equivalent of the laws of physics, Durkheim maintains that socialism is "a cry of grief, sometimes of anger" in response to the moral and political "malaise" of the time (Durkheim, 1962/1928, p. 41). But if it is not a science, it should certainly be the object of scientific investigation. It is "a social fact of the highest importance" (Durkheim, 1962/1928, p. 42), and we cannot well understand social conditions of modernity unless we are familiar with the origins and nature of one of the most influential ideological systems produced by those conditions and aiming to reform them. Socialism as a social fact will be studied by sociology, just as sociology studies other such facts, for example, "suicide, the family, marriage, crime, punishment, responsibility, and religion" (Durkheim, 1962/1928, p. 44).

The question of definition must be broached before any further analysis can be made. What *is* **socialism**? There are many differing doctrines that claim the term. At the time Durkheim was delivering his course on socialism, French socialist theories and parties ranged from the Marxist and revolutionary Parti ouvrier français (French Workers' Party), led by Marx's son-in-law Paul Lafargue, to the reformist Fédération des travailleurs socialistes de France (Federation of Socialist Workers of France). Radical syndicalist theorist Georges Sorel had considerable political influence in workers' politics, and Durkheim's schoolmate and friend, Jean Jaurès, had become by century's end one of the most influential and unifying forces in socialist circles. While Durkheim was in Bordeaux, his nephew Marcel Mauss was in Paris, working closely with Lucien Herr, the librarian at the École Normale and a figurehead of the socialist movement. There were massive differences in the political programs and theoretical principles of each of these varieties of socialism.

Recognizing this plurality of competing parties and theorists, Durkheim cast the definitional net widely: "We denote as socialist every doctrine which demands the connection of all economic functions, or of certain among them, which are at the present time diffuse, to the directing and conscious centers of society" (Durkheim, 1962/1928, p. 54). By the end of this lecture, though, he has gone still further. Socialism, he writes, is not simply a doctrine about the economic organization of society; it is the hope for "a rearrangement of the social structure" (Durkheim, 1962/1928, p. 61). Here, we see a perspective quite familiar from his earliest work on the division of labor. Economics, and for that matter any other single aspect of social life, cannot be properly considered in isolation from the whole of social life. A proper analysis of the functioning of any particular slice of human endeavor must place it in its structural field, recognize its interconnections with the other elements surrounding it, and account for their mutual influences. This far at least, the traditional Parsonian interpretation of Durkheim as a systems theorist is correct. Durkheim saw it as the height of intellectual obscurity and muddle-headedness to believe parts of a necessarily integrated whole could be understood alone. Socialism is a perspective on the organization of social life in the broadest sense.

Clear definition requires avoiding false equivalencies. We must be clear that, as philosophies of economic and political policy and practical programs, socialism and **communism** are quite distinct. Socialism dates only from the early 19th century, as it required modern economic conditions and industry to emerge, while communist doctrines go back to antiquity (Durkheim, 1962/1928, pp. 78, 80). Plato's utopian society, where property was to be shared and an ascetic denial of material indulgence was the normative rule, was organized on neatly communist principles (Durkheim, 1962/1928, p. 67). But socialism is not utopian; it is eminently practical. Unlike communism, it links the State and industrial activity instead of placing industrial life outside the State and thereby insulating it from interference from the State. Durkheim's criticism of communism is harsh. He sees it as simply unrealistic in endeavoring to separate political elites from those who actually do the work in the society and to elevate them above the laborers. In communism, he argues, not only production but consumption too is regulated, whereas socialism aims to direct only the former. In socialism, production is communal and consumption is private, while the reverse is true in communism (Durkheim, 1962/1928, p. 71). He provides a telling analogy: Communism is to socialism as "the organization of certain colonies of polyps [to] that of superior animals" (Durkheim, 1962/1928, p. 71). Communism aims to be a universal moral doctrine speaking to all social systems throughout history, whereas socialism is formulated specifically as a response to modern social systems and their specific dilemmas (Durkheim, 1962/1928, p. 73).

There are, of course, a few broad common points that connect the two doctrines. Both fear "economic particularism," or the threat to society posed by individuals pursuing purely private interests, and both reject the classical liberal idea that the "free play of egoism" can alone produce social order (Durkheim, 1962/1928, p. 75). For both, the needs of the group trump the desires of particular individuals, and "radical and intransigent individualism" is to be opposed and countered in social policy under both systems (Durkheim, 1962/1928, pp. 75, 76). But communism considers all private property dangerous to the collective interest, whereas socialism rejects only private ownership of the largest, most essential parts of the economy. Communism wants to suppress individual interests, while socialism wants to "socialize" them (Durkheim, 1962/1928, pp. 75, 88). For communism, the State and the economy become manifestations of, respectively, sacred and profane, whereas for socialism the State is desacralized so that it can play a role in the everyday life of the economy (Durkheim, 1962/1928, p. 77). Communism has been attractive precisely because it promises everything. But reality is hard edged; even were a socialist state to emerge overnight, impoverishment and suffering would still exist (Durkheim, 1962/1928, p. 90). Durkheim is, here as elsewhere, a resolutely anti-utopian thinker.

After this introductory task of distinguishing socialism from communism, Durkheim turns to the thinker he sees as the key figure in French socialist thought: Claude Henri de Rouvroy, Count of Saint-Simon, or simply Saint-Simon as he is commonly known. Born in 1760 into an aristocratic family, Saint-Simon had by the end of his life created a social theory that established French positivism and greatly influenced generations of radical social thinkers to come. Despite his privileged position of birth, Saint-Simon lived an unstable life, marked by periods of extreme poverty, thanks to his dedication to his intellectual work (Durkheim, 1962/1928, p. 122). Durkheim classifies him as a "man of a single idea . . . [to] reorganize European societies by giving them science and industry as bases" (Durkheim, 1962/1928, p. 123). Such a reorganization of the European social order would require a new system of ideas, and Saint-Simon firmly believed that the human sciences needed to model themselves after the natural sciences insofar as humankind is merely one more part of the natural world (Durkheim, 1962/1928, p. 135). Positivist philosophy, Durkheim argues, while frequently credited as Auguste Comte's innovation, was actually created by Comte's teacher, Saint-Simon, and positivism led to "positive sociology"—that is, a vision of the social sciences that would integrate them into the already existing natural sciences (Durkheim, 1962/1928, p. 142). His refutation of Comte's originality here could scarcely be more vigorous:

> We can see here all that Auguste Comte, and consequently all that the thinkers of the 19th century, owe him. In [Saint-Simon] we encounter the seeds already developed of all the ideas which have fed the thinking of our time. We have just found in it positive philosophy, positivist sociology. We will see that we will also find socialism in it. . . . [T]he Comtists . . . have even gone so far as saying it was to Comte that Saint-Simon owed everything that was accurate and original in his doctrine. But the facts refute such an interpretation. (Durkheim, 1962/1928, p. 143)

The actual distinction between Comte and Saint-Simon had to do with the fact that the latter moved quickly from scholarly theory building and scientific analysis to application in the political and moral realms, while

Comte kept science and policy more clearly separated. Saint-Simon lacked the "scientific patience" of Comte, eager as he was to implement his political philosophy as policy (Durkheim, 1962/1928, p. 146). The core of Comte's positivist system, however, originates in Saint-Simon. As was noted in the first chapter, Comte is frequently claimed, in the face of considerable evidence, as Durkheim's central intellectual source of inspiration, but if we follow the reading Durkheim makes of Comte's relationship to his mentor Saint-Simon here, we would perhaps do well to talk instead of Durkheim's influence by Saint-Simon. In a footnote in his introduction to the English translation of Durkheim's lectures on socialism, Alvin Gouldner demonstrates how the charged nature of this relationship has contributed to fundamental misunderstandings about the relationship. Textbooks on sociology still today (more than a half century after Gouldner wrote) claim Comte as the founder of sociology despite the evidence Durkheim presents that Saint-Simon can be seen as at least as central a figure in the development of French positivism, which for Durkheim is the crucial philosophical movement presaging the birth of sociology. Saint-Simon and not Comte was, according to Durkheim, "the first who resolutely freed himself from the . . . prejudices" of prepositivist philosophy, which separated the study of humankind from the natural sciences (Durkheim, 1962/1928, p. 143). Why, then, Gouldner asks, do we not find Saint-Simon in our sociology textbooks? Durkheim points to the answer: It is because Saint-Simon is not only the founder of French positivism but also one of the fathers of French socialism.

Saint-Simon gave a painstaking account, which Durkheim summarizes, of the origins of the modern industrial system in the massive historical and social transition from the Europe of the Middle Ages to the coming of the French Revolution. Europe in the 11th century was dominated by two institutions, the Army and the Clergy, and their leaders; economic activity was as dependent on the lords as intellectual activity was on the priests (Durkheim, 1962/1928, p. 148). Saint-Simon calls this a military and theological system (Durkheim, 1962/1928, p. 148). In the following century, however, two new social forces emerged: "the free commune and exact science"—that is, the newly emancipated communities of merchants and craftsmen and the emergent experimental secular scholars, which challenged the existing rulers of the two realms of economy and knowledge (Durkheim, 1962/1928, p. 149). These two new forces signaled the progressive diminution of the power of the Army and the Clergy. These "two seeds of destruction" began to grow here, and eventually they would come to fundamentally challenge clericalism and feudalism (Durkheim, 1962/1928, p. 150). While the Middle Ages are incorrectly characterized as the Dark Ages, when all thought was in danger of extinction, the truth is that they prepared the way forward to modernity and even "contained [it] in embryo" (Durkheim, 1962/1928, p. 150).

By the 16th century, aided and pushed along by further innovations in knowledge and productive capacity, including the invention of printing and the Copernican discovery of the heliocentric reality of our planet's place, these forces in opposition to the old system began an offensive that would culminate in the French Revolution (Durkheim, 1962/1928, p. 151). The power at the top of the military system was considerably weakened with Louis XIV's move to weaken the nobility's power and the severe limits placed on royal power in England by the Glorious Revolution of 1688 (Durkheim, 1962/1928, p. 152). By the 18th century, the attack on the feudal order had become generalized (Durkheim, 1962/1928, p. 153). In a concise sociological history of this period of several centuries, Saint-Simon shows that the old society bore within itself the seeds of a new society, one fundamentally antagonistic to and incompatible with the old system. Whereas the medieval system was predicated on social aggression and war, the new rising industrial system was, according to Saint-Simon, oriented fundamentally to peace and prosperity (Durkheim, 1962/1928, p. 157). Saint-Simon was himself firmly opposed to violent revolution, as he believed violence could only destroy (Durkheim, 1962/1928, p. 171).

Then came the French Revolution and the final, total overturning of the old military and theological system. Yet the Revolution merely cleared the ground and failed to construct anything lasting in the way of a "new body of rational beliefs that all minds could accept" to take the place of what had been demolished (Durkheim, 1962/1928, p. 159). Because of this failure to replace the old institutions, some of the demolished structures simply reemerged from the ruins of the Revolution, and royal authority rose from the grave to reclaim power in the wake of the failure of Napoléon (Durkheim, 1962/1928, p. 160). Saint-Simon, like Durkheim, thus recognized the potential danger of revolutions that destroyed old ways of life but failed to create new institutions to replace those that had been rent asunder. At the same time, Saint-Simon vigorously opposed the reactionary intellectuals who attempted from time to time to reestablish the old system, and Durkheim is sympathetic to him here as well, for "[a] system which the centuries have built and destroyed cannot be re-established . . . [and] it is neither possible nor useful to restore the old system in its entirety" (Durkheim, 1962/1928, p. 168, 170). In Saint-Simon's view, it was the task of socialist organization of the economy to fulfill the promise of the Revolution and put in place the new institutions that would take the place of the old.

Saint-Simon provides a sociological explanation for the failure of the Revolution to complete in one leap the move from the old theological and military order to a new industrial one. He believed intermediary stages generally intervene between large-scale revolutions of the entire social structure, and what sprang up in the years preceding the Revolution in the gap left by the weakening priestly and feudal powers were two new and autonomous groups: on the one hand, lawyers; on the other, "metaphysicians," or spiritualist philosophers (Durkheim, 1962/1928, pp. 161, 162). These lawyers and metaphysicians challenged the feudal lords and priests, but they could offer no way forward to the industrial socialist order Saint-Simon championed. They became the dominant groups in the revolutionary assemblies and pushed over the teetering old system, but all their action was consonant with "their nature and their past," which meant they were incapable of positive action. They merely articulated radical restrictions on the old powers that eventually reduced them to a husk of their formerly robust state (Durkheim, 1962/1928, p. 163). In this move, Saint-Simon presents a theory of history in three stages (feudal/theological, juridical/metaphysical, socialist/positivist), the precursor of the better-known **Law of Three Stages** that is the centerpiece of the work of Auguste Comte. Durkheim argues that Comte's framework is directly taken from that of Saint-Simon (Durkheim, 1962/1928, p. 165).

Durkheim then moves on to the particulars of Saint-Simon's vision of the post-Revolutionary establishment of the industrial system. The core goal of industrialization, Saint-Simon believed, is to increase humankind's mastery of the material world, and thus "[s]ociety will be fully in harmony with itself only when it is totally industrialized" (Durkheim, 1962/1928, p. 173). Saint-Simon's view of industrialization and its various and serious discontents is startlingly uncritical; Durkheim cites his belief that "the most favorable state of affairs for industry is . . . the most favorable to society" (Durkheim, 1962/1928, p. 174), an assertion with which Marxists would certainly have a field day. Durkheim notes that Saint-Simon is clearly distinguished from the classical liberal economists who neatly separate economic life and the realm of politics, for Saint-Simon believes economics is "the whole substance of politics"; indeed, politics is nothing more than and nothing less than "the science of production" (Durkheim, 1962/1928, p. 179). While the classical economists see economic action as purely private action, Saint-Simon insisted it was part of a systemic unity, and the collective therefore had an interest in controlling it (Durkheim, 1962/1928, p. 180).

Saint-Simon's vision of the socialist society is in some regards fairly radical. He believed that only the "producers of useful things" should be permitted to play a role in setting the direction of society, while the owner, on the other hand, insofar as he is not a producer, cannot even be considered a fully participating member of an industrial society (Durkheim, 1962/1928,

p. 174). Saint-Simon distinguishes between those he calls "bourgeois"—that is, those who live on unearned income—and those he labels "industrials"—that is, those who "make their wealth productive" (Durkheim, 1962/1928, p. 175). These latter would be permitted to play a role in the political administration of the industrial society. But those who do not work, in Saint-Simon's definition of the term, are "useless" and cannot be permitted any participation in the political decision making. They will be seen as "aliens," tolerated but stripped of any real political power (Durkheim, 1962/1928, p. 175).

As for scholars, they constitute the "indispensable auxiliaries of industry" (Durkheim, 1962/1928, p. 176). In Saint-Simon's vision, the core of society is made up of "two great families": the "secondary class" of intellectuals ("industrials of theory") and the "fundamental class" of producers ("scholars of application"). Intellectuals should be given substantial autonomy in their theoretical realm, but the industrials will ultimately decide what is to be done in practice (Durkheim, 1962/1928, p. 176).

Though the specifics changed as his thought matured, Saint-Simon consistently insisted that the political organization of fully industrialized and rationalized societies would be guided by three principles: The regulation of social life should be in the hands of the industrials; as science is necessary for industrial organization, the scholars must assist the industrials in their work; and, thus, there must be a close relationship and synergy between the functions of "science and art, theory and practice, the spiritual and the temporal," which must be separate but constantly in contact with one another (Durkheim, 1962/1928, p. 184). Early on, he theorized a structure of three chambers that together would be responsible for directing political life: a chamber of invention (consisting of 300 engineers and artists who would draw up plans for public works), a chamber of study (300 scholars, one third mathematicians, one third physicists, and one third physiologists) that would examine those public work projects and direct public education, and a chamber of execution (consisting of the heads of all branches of commercial farming and manufacturing industries) that would implement the public work projects (Durkheim, 1962/1928, p. 181). Later, he specified only three ministries (finance, interior, and marine), with a body of scholars, the Institute. The Institute would be responsible for the creation of a "national catechism" that would be used to teach the basic principles around which the society is organized. It would also exercise oversight over all instruction to ensure that nothing contrary to the national catechism was purveyed in schools (Durkheim, 1962/1928, p. 182). The Institute was to consist of an Academy of Sciences (scholars of political economy) and an Academy of Morals made up of "moralists" ranging in occupation among lawyers, theologians, poets, painters, sculptors, and musicians (Durkheim, 1962/1928,

p. 183). This Academy of Morals would be charged with establishing a "system of moral rules in harmony with the conditions of existence of an industrial society." Above these two Academies, there would be a "supreme scientific College," which would be given the task of coordinating the work of the Academies (Durkheim, 1962/1928, p. 183).

Saint-Simon was suspicious of all existing government, including parliamentary democracy, as too driven by the narrow, self-interested agendas of the rulers, but in his view the government of fully industrialized socialist societies such as he envisioned would be guided not by the will of the strongest but by capability in science and industry (Durkheim, 1962/1928, p. 191). In such a society, "truth alone . . . speaks" as the scholars reveal the "laws of social hygiene" and the industrials then decide how to put them into practice (Durkheim, 1962/1928, p. 196). Science is the sole legitimate authority in Saint-Simon's vision. In such a society, there would be no privilege of birth or station, and a principle of total equality would reign. The administration would be superior to the rest of the population in no way other than in knowledge: "[T]hey are simply better informed than those who execute what they have decided" (Durkheim, 1962/1928, p. 193). The role of government for Saint-Simon had essentially to do with a police function, and this would progressively be reduced under the rule of the industrials and the scholars. Socialism is not in this vision authoritarian, as it will shrink the police power of government, in the name not of power but of reason (Durkheim, 1962/1928, p. 194). Durkheim notes a curious convergence here with the classical economists, though Saint-Simon arrives at this point not through individualism and privatization but through collectivism and socialism.

Liberty is defined by Saint-Simon not as the freedom to obstruct as an isolated individual but as the ability to "develop . . . without hindrance and with every possible extension, a temporal or spiritual capacity advantageous to society" (Durkheim, 1962/1928, p. 198). Property rights are indispensable in any society, but they may take many forms, and they will evolve in the Saint-Simonian vision such that those who will not or cannot be productive will not be permitted to exercise over their possessions "excessive rights which hinder production" (Durkheim, 1962/1928, pp. 199, 202). Whereas communism would seek to alleviate social conflict by impoverishing everyone and attacking the very idea of material prosperity, Saint-Simon envisions a kind of socialism with the power to eliminate poverty by raising the standard of living for the poor and expropriating idle owners (Durkheim, 1962/1928, p. 210).

Durkheim next turns to a discussion of Saint-Simon's thought on religion and internationalism. He saw purely national motivations and interests as a form of egoism (Durkheim, 1962/1928, p. 217). The Greeks and Romans were morally inferior because they felt only national sentiments (Durkheim, 1962/1928, p. 218). But the contemporary Europe of Saint-Simon's day is no better. The Europe of the Middle Ages was superior to 19th-century Europe precisely because the Roman Church made much of Europe a *de facto* common project, a positive aspect of the medieval world that is usually overlooked (Durkheim, 1962/1928, p. 222). Fully rationalized industrial socialist societies would necessarily be pointed outward to an international cosmopolitanism (Durkheim, 1962/1928, p. 219). Although the Church cannot be looked to as the engine of such a renewed, industrial internationalism, principles of moral solidarity that originated in religion will be required for the future, as abstract reason alone cannot fully ground the new social model required. In his late book *Nouveau christianisme,* or *The New Christianity,* the champion of a secular positivist philosophy calls for a new international religion modeled in some important ways on Christianity (Durkheim, 1962/1928, p. 223). Durkheim argues that Saint-Simon had never understood positivism and science as excluding religion entirely, and that he believed that "one must naturally lead to the other" (Durkheim, 1962/1928, p. 224). Science and religion have the same objective for Saint-Simon: to attack intellectual pluralism and seek to find a universal law. Religion and philosophy discover the same laws. The law of gravity, for example, does not oppose God, as it is quite simply "the idea of the immutable law by which God governs the Universe" (Durkheim, 1962/1928, p. 226).

Much of what Durkheim cites from Saint-Simon on religion presages his own discussion of the topic in later writings, especially *The Elementary Forms of Religious Life* (which is discussed in Chapter 6). The mission of religion is not to teach the faithful to disregard material reality and concentrate instead on the supernatural but to "emphasize the unity of reality" (Durkheim, 1962/1928, p. 225). Christianity moved humanity in the direction of international unity, but it was now necessary to go beyond it by taking up the same project and pushing it still farther (Durkheim, 1962/1928, p. 226). Saint-Simon understands history to have a tripartite structure here, again presaging the Law of Three Stages of his student Comte: Early religious thinking obscures the individual and emphasizes the group; then, with monotheism, the individual comes to the fore for a time and is progressive in his limited historical sphere; but now the individual must be exceeded by a return to moral unity and collectivism (Durkheim, 1962/1928, p. 227). This is remarkably similar to Comte's vision of a theological epoch followed by a metaphysical period, culminating in a move into positive science.

Saint-Simon was unable to finish *The New Christianity* before his death, but what he did finish suggests that the new religion he proposed would be based on morality, with theology having a much reduced role (Durkheim, 1962/1928, p. 229). This is in keeping with original historical Christianity, which was based on fundamental moral principles (e.g., that all men act like brothers), though these principles were later warped by the later Church into obscure rites and mysticism (Durkheim, 1962/1928, p. 230). *The New Christianity* begins with the credo "I believe in God," but how precisely will God be defined in this new system? Saint-Simon's God is not anthropomorphic—that is, it is not a living, personal God, but a God present in all nature, and both physical and moral laws are part of the divine (Durkheim, 1962/1928, p. 232). The goal of this religion is the utilitarian end of the greatest happiness of humankind (Durkheim, 1962/1928, p. 233). This is a pantheistic God, both religious and scientific at once (Durkheim, 1962/1928, p. 234).

Durkheim closes his lecture course on socialism and Saint-Simon with some critical remarks. Saint-Simon believed that individuals in the future would and should pursue only economic interests, which would, however, be harmonized by the collective (Durkheim, 1962/1928, p. 235). Economic appetites would be freed of restraints, and at the same time they would be fulfilled by the newly capable socialist economy (Durkheim, 1962/1928, p. 241). For Durkheim, however, this vision misunderstands human nature in an important way. Economic needs and desires cannot have the final word because man is incapable of limiting his desires without external, moral constraints (Durkheim, 1962/1928, pp. 241–242). There is a need for a moral force superior to the individual that "cries out 'You must go no further'" and informs her instead to be content with what she has (Durkheim, 1962/1928, p. 243). Though Saint-Simon pointed to a moral, secular religion at the end of his life, his premise that economic interests alone could drive the new society indicates he had not fully understood just how foundational moral constraint and discipline are to human life.

Durkheim was working on his book-length study of suicide (which we discuss in Chapter 4) at the same time he was giving these lectures, and we see here the same social theory he developed in that book in which a society that would endeavor to meet ever-increasing human desire must necessarily founder, for such desires are unlimited unless limits are externally imposed. This was the role that had been played by religion, which Saint-Simon wishes to completely dethrone and secularize. Durkheim, as we will see in discussing *The Elementary Forms of Religious Life,* was not so certain that such an effort could succeed. In any event, Saint-Simon's "industrialist solution" remains unsatisfactory, notwithstanding the many points on which Durkheim's thought is clearly consonant with that of Saint-Simon (Durkheim, 1962/1928, p. 245). Durkheim here alludes, yet again, to the possibility that "professional groupings, or corporations" will be able to step in for religion as the new force of moral restraint (Durkheim, 1962/1928, p. 245). Saint-Simon does not recognize this need.

This course is tremendously important in understanding the legacy of Durkheim's thought. The question of socialism and its role in organizing an industrial society that had shaken off the traditional forms of solidarity had been present in Durkheim's thinking from at least his days at the École Normale. That Durkheim believed some kind of socialist organization of the economy was a necessity is without question. Mauss, in his introduction to the first edition of this incomplete text, emphasizes the "regret" Durkheim felt at never having returned to the study to complete it (Durkheim, 1962/1928, p. 35).

Additional Writing by Durkheim on Socialism

Durkheim's view of socialism comes into still clearer focus when we examine a few key reviews he wrote of books on the topic. Antonio Labriola was an Italian Marxist philosopher who greatly influenced the most important Italian Marxist thinker, Antonio Gramsci. Durkheim reviewed his book, *Essays on the Materialist Conception of History,* in the *Revue philosophique* in 1897. Insofar as Labriola's perspective is seen only as a theoretical recognition that the explanation of social life has to come not from the ideas of those in the society in question but from deeper causes of which they are not aware and that can be found in the manner in which individuals are arranged in groups, Durkheim was in agreement (Durkheim 1978a/1897, p. 127). The collective consciousness must be connected to something real, and this something is simply the members of the society in the specific way in which they are arranged and grouped together. However, Labriola and Marx go astray when they attempt to reduce *everything* to economics. Durkheim responds that if we were to choose only one institution as the primary site for the study of society, it would be not economics but religion. "Everything," he wrote, "is religious in principle," and all other institutions and forms of social life ("law, ethics, science, political forms") come from religion, which is the most primitive institution (Durkheim 1978a/1897, p. 129).

But this does not condemn us, as the Marxists and other materialists might charge, to idealism. Durkheim has no wish simply to turn over the Marxian relationship of economics and all ideology (including religion) in which the former is understood as the causal and material principle, while the latter is a mere caused and immaterial epiphenomenon, and put religion in the place the Marxists reserve for economics. Economics is not to be reduced in all its manifestations to an effect of the causal powers of religion, and once economics exists, it can attain a certain autonomy and even in limited ways change that from which it originally sprang (Durkheim 1978a/1897, p. 130). But we must recognize that the historical and ethnological facts indicate that it is derived from a more primitive institution—namely, religion. Given this sense of the relative importance of economics in the social order, Durkheim sees no reason to believe that the significant changes in European economy in his time indicate any necessary revolutionary overturning of the existing order (Durkheim 1978a/1897, p. 130).

In another review for the *Revue philosophique*—this of a book, *Socialism and Social Science,* by an *Année* contributor, Gaston Richard, and written in this same year (1897)—Durkheim reiterates several of the basic arguments of his socialism course. Socialism, the essence of which is neatly summarized in the work of Saint-Simon, must be kept distinct from sociology (Durkheim, 1978b/1897, p. 132). Despite its occasional claims to the contrary (especially from some disciples of Marx), socialism is not a scientific undertaking (Durkheim, 1978b/1897, p. 136). This is not, however, to say there is nothing of use in Marx. On the contrary, *Capital* certainly contains "suggestive" and "fertile intuitions," even if it cannot merit the term "science" precisely because of its speculative and undemonstrated arguments (Durkheim, 1978b/1897, p. 137). But sociology is called to be intimately interested in socialism, minimally as a topic of research, for the same reason he gives in the lecture course on socialism: Socialism is an important indicator of a broader "social malaise," and if sociology would understand that malaise and hope to offer scientific knowledge about it to those in political positions, it cannot dispense with a study of socialism (Durkheim, 1978b/1897, p. 137).

Professional Ethics and Civic Morals

Professional Ethics and Civic Morals is another set of course lectures that were unpublished in Durkheim's lifetime. We know that Durkheim gave a course on this topic during his last decade in Bordeaux and then twice (in 1904–1905 and again in 1912) at the Sorbonne. His lectures were generally thoroughly written out, the prose scarcely distinguishable from that of his published work, and this posthumously published course provides a clear exposition of his thinking on the role of occupational groups and the State in producing and sustaining systems of moral rules and conduct.

The Guild and Professional Ethics

In the first major section of the course (on professional ethics), Durkheim sets out a definition for the sociological study of morals and rights. Unlike philosophers, who are frequently content to abstractly discuss morality in the absence of empirical facts, sociologists must consult "moral and juridical facts," which are defined as "rules of conduct that have sanction" (Durkheim, 1992/1950, pp. 1, 2). All moral systems are collective affairs, as the power of the group is the only power that can maintain morality (Durkheim, 1992/1950, p. 7). There are, he argues, two kinds of moral rules: those that are equally applicable to all and those that apply only to some select subset of individuals. Rules of universal moral application are themselves of two kinds: universal rules concerning the obligations each of us has to his or her own self and universal rules governing our relations with others (Durkheim, 1992/1950, p. 3). Moral rules that are not universal include those that are specific to gender, age, and citizenship status, but the most diverse of these are those that accrue to us as a result of our particular place in the division of labor. This is the realm of **professional ethics** (Durkheim, 1992/1950, p. 4). Systems of professional ethics can be in conflict among themselves; for example, the code of the scientist is not that of the soldier (Durkheim, 1992/1950, p. 5).

Such professional ethics are matters with which the society as a whole is generally unconcerned, so the work to make and maintain them is the task of special groups of the involved parties. Durkheim notes a general rule on moral systems: The more a group's contact is "frequent and intimate," the denser its moral life will be—that is, it will have a more intricate body of moral rules surrounding the life of the group (Durkheim, 1992/1950, pp. 7–8).

He turns next to the realm of ethics that is perhaps of the most obvious relevance for today's reader. The economic functions, he notes, are in the Europe of his day generally not morally regulated (Durkheim, 1992/1950, p. 9). Is this a normal, desirable state of affairs? Interestingly, both the classical economists *and* most socialist theorists respond affirmatively (Durkheim, 1992/1950, p. 10). Durkheim, however, argues that any social function that lacks a moral code to guide and limit its activity will break down into the disaster of unregulated and bottomless individual desires. Not only will this distort economic matters, but inevitably it will affect the rest of social life as well, given the disproportionate amount of time people spend in the work world today. This is a principle we will find argued at length in his book on suicide in the next chapter. There is no miraculous "free hand of the market" to mysteriously and automatically bring order to economic affairs; only a moral system can do that (Durkheim, 1992/1950, p. 12). Even if the market could regulate itself, he goes on, production itself is not a legitimate social end. Human society cannot be justified if it fails to "bring a little peace to men . . . in their mutual intercourse," and if production is achieved by removing the possibility for that peace, its cost is greater than its benefit (Durkheim, 1992/1950, p. 16).

The professional group that is called to create this moral framework to guide economic affairs is the corporate body, or "craft union" (Durkheim, 1992/1950, p. 13). It is now in an enervated state, Durkheim acknowledges, but must be reinvigorated. At the beginning of any inquiry into what new forms they will have to take, though, there must be a historical investigation of what forms they took in the past. Thus, Durkheim embarks on a mini-history of the medieval guilds of the *Ancien Régime* (Durkheim, 1992/1950, p. 17).

He directly confronts the argument, championed by many advocates of progress in his day, that the guild is a retrograde institution of a social order that is now antiquated. In fact, the guilds are far more ancient than even the Middle Ages. They date to the emergence in Europe of the first towns and the end of purely agricultural economies. In ancient Rome, the guilds became over time one of the key elements in the administration of the Roman State. But the destruction of the Roman Empire brought about the collapse of the guilds, and they did not reemerge in Europe until the 11th and 12th centuries. By the 13th century, they were again flourishing (Durkheim, 1992/1950, pp. 18–19).

Durkheim sees the guild's longevity, as well as the fact that it could disappear with the fall of Rome and then reappear later, as evidence that it must respond to some fundamental and lasting social requirements (Durkheim, 1992/1950, p. 19). Yet he acknowledges a slide by the guilds in the last years of the Old Regime toward what he calls "corporate egotism" (Durkheim, 1992/1950, p. 20). He sounds here almost as if he were responding to contemporary voices on the right in their accusations of the excesses of some labor unions. Yes, he argues, the guilds did, in the last days before the French Revolution, turn away from their task of making labor ethical and morally regulated and instead concentrated corruptly on advancing as much as possible the narrow interests of the guild members over those of the rest of the society. But recognizing the excesses of that particular moment in their history, when corruption was widespread through the *entirety* of French society, does not require a thoroughgoing rejection of the entire corporative institution (Durkheim, 1992/1950, p. 20).

In ancient Rome, the guilds had none of the "labor bargaining" functions they took on in the Old Regime (the same function by which contemporary labor unions are often centrally defined, at least by nonsociologists). They did not regulate work methods in their industries, or set rules on apprenticeship processes, or work toward the establishment of exclusive rights to certain labor by their members. The guild in Rome was instead "a religious *collegium*":

> Each had its own particular deity, its own ritual which, when the means were available, was celebrated in a specially dedicated temple. In the same way as each family had their *lar familiaris,* each city its *genius publicus,* each *collegium* had its tutelary god or *genius collegii.* This cult practiced by the crafts always had its festivals and these festivals were celebrated with sacrifices. (Durkheim, 1992/1950, p. 20)

The guild was, in other words, a thoroughly religious institution in its origins, and this is the source of its moral authority and historical function. At guild festivals, gifts were distributed from the common fund to all the members, just as presents are given in familial holiday celebrations. Guilds with sufficient common wealth had their own burial vaults where members could be interred, as in a family plot. The guild in Rome, in short, was a moral and religious community that modeled and in some ways substituted for the familial bonds of blood. Guild members referred to one another as "*sodales,*" a term that "expresses a spiritual kinship implying close brotherhood," and the patron and patroness of guild collegiums behaved in the style of parents with respect to the other guild members (Durkheim, 1992/1950, p. 21).

While the guilds of the medieval period moved away from some of this familial and religious structure, they did not fail to produce a warm moral environment for members. Medieval guild members would attend Sunday Mass together and then hold collective feasts afterward. They also used common funds to support members in states of hardship; for example, the cooks of Paris used a significant portion of their guild dues to support poor elders of their profession (Durkheim, 1992/1950, p. 22). Monitoring of guild business with an eye to proper ethics became an important function during this period. Merchants and craftsmen were prevented by their fellows from deceiving customers about the quality of merchandise. Butchers were prohibited by their guild from selling poor-quality meat. Knife makers, or cutlers, could not sell cheaply made knives whose poor-quality handles were disguised with gaudy covers (Durkheim, 1992/1950, p. 23).

Membership in such groups of mutual activity and interest is bound to draw those involved into close relationships. The root of moral solidarity, Durkheim argues, is our desire for peace and order, and, as in the family, where moral solidarity produces and encourages an altruistic spirit and great loyalty to the group, so too was it in the medieval guilds (Durkheim, 1992/1950, pp. 24–25). It is not just consanguinity that produces powerful moral bonds; a "close community of ideas, sentiments, and interests" is arguably just as important (Durkheim, 1992/1950, p. 25).

The family and the guild are connected, in Durkheim's argument, in an evolutionary fashion. Craft work began in the familial setting, but eventually making a living through a craft trade meant finding and competing with other craftsmen for customers to purchase the goods, and the guilds emerged organically from this labor process that had begun in the setting of the family and therefore retained some of the features of the family (Durkheim, 1992/1950, p. 26). This is all the historical view of the matter, though Durkheim makes clear that he recognizes that future manifestations of the guild may or may not retain these familial characteristics (Durkheim, 1992/1950, p. 27). Though the future will certainly be unable to escape the influence of the past, the specific manner in which it works itself out is not wholly predictable.

It is clear, however, that *some* kind of guild-like institution is a functional necessity, and Durkheim emphasizes that the issue does not have to do with what he considers the superficial framing of the question by those in the political debates of the time (and in our own): that is, whether the economy itself is fundamentally directed by private citizens and companies or by the collective, that is, the State. Even if, by a stroke of luck, it were possible to realize the socialists' dream and establish collective ownership, without the moral regulation of the new guilds, nothing would be solved (Durkheim, 1992/1950, p. 30). It is the "raising of moral standards," and not mere changes in who owns what, that will reinvigorate the economic world (Durkheim, 1992/1950, p. 31).

Durkheim provides a bit more guild history, this time in order to tease out the institution's relation historically to the State. In Rome, the guild *collegia* were initially removed from the administrative structures of the State, and when they were finally integrated into the State apparatus it was only at the cost of being made a powerless cog and "reduced to a kind of servitude" (Durkheim, 1992/1950, p. 32). In the Middle Ages, the situation was quite different. From the 11th century, the guilds were dominated by the Third Estate—that is, the bourgeoisie or craftsmen, whose role in the State was becoming more and more important. The guilds were also "the basic element of the commune" (Durkheim, 1992/1950, p. 34).

From this brief historical interlude, Durkheim concludes that the guilds of the future will need to integrate themselves effectively into the State without being fully dominated by it as had been the case in Rome (Durkheim, 1992/1950, p. 36). He provides a tantalizingly brief practical sketch of what this might look like: national guilds for all the important industries, each with an elected administrative council heading it and holding the power to regulate the business of that guild; and the simultaneous existence of "subsidiary and regional organs" at local levels for each national guild to increase democratic involvement in the institution (Durkheim, 1992/1950, p. 37). In this future setting, he imagines a question that was evidently of concern to some critics in his day, as it is to some of those on the right today who worry greatly about purportedly coerced union membership: the compulsory nature of guild membership. Ultimately, in his view, once the new guilds are established, it will be such a "handicap" for individuals to remain outside them that they will join freely and with no coercion. In any event, he goes on, it was in his day compulsory for all French citizens to be members of a communal parish, and the same principle should certainly apply to professions, especially given the role as a political unit the guilds will play in Durkheim's anticipation (Durkheim, 1992/1950, p. 39).

Civic Morals: The State, Property Right, and Contract

In the book's second section, Durkheim undertakes a lengthy discussion of the form, nature, and history of the **State** and its role in producing moral solidarity. He begins by presenting the theory of the emergence of the State of his teacher at the ENS, Fustel de Coulanges. This theory postulated that the most primitive form of society was the patriarchal family, and this organizational form descended to the State in a historical process that Fustel de Coulanges traced in his work. Durkheim argues, on the contrary, that the State is not derived in this simplified way from the patriarchal family but represents a new form of authority, "original and specific" in its nature (Durkheim, 1992/1950, p. 45).

The State is, in Durkheim's definition, "a group of officials *sui generis,* within which representations and acts of volition involving the collectivity are worked out, although they are not the product of collectivity" (Durkheim, 1992/1950, pp. 49–50). Though the State is clearly involved in the expression of the collective consciousness, the two entities cannot be equated. The State is a much more delimited thing and the collective consciousness diffuse in the extreme. The State constitutes only one element of the collective consciousness, the part that is most self-aware, limited, and clear in its conceptions. The more obscure and irrational manifestations of the collective consciousness—for example, "myths, religious or moral legends, and so on"—exist outside the boundaries of the State (Durkheim, 1992/1950, p. 50). The State has the responsibility of elaborating a limited number of collective representations that are more "conscious and specific" than most such representations (Durkheim, 1992/1950, p. 50).

What is the purpose of the State? Durkheim presents two opposing responses to this question, from the individualists (Herbert Spencer) and classical economists (Immanuel Kant and Jean-Jacques Rousseau) on the one hand and the spiritualists (G. W. F. Hegel) on the other (Durkheim, 1992/1950, p. 51). The first group argues that the State exists only to look after and protect the rights of individuals, a position Durkheim rejects peremptorily as inconsistent with empirical facts (Durkheim, 1992/1950, pp. 52, 53). The spiritualist theory presents a vision of the State in which it has goals that wholly transcend and are completely unrelated to individual goals (Durkheim, 1992/1950, p. 54). Here, the individual, far from being served by the State, is the mere servant of these larger aims of the State.

Durkheim is not satisfied with either of these approaches. The individualists and the classical economists misunderstand the source of the individual's importance. Both Kant and Spencer argue for a theory of individual right that stems from the inherent nature of the human individual, but Durkheim responds vigorously that it is not the individual's particular constitution that determines his rights. Rather, rights accrue according to the value society attaches to the individual (Durkheim, 1992/1950, pp. 66, 67). This is a fully sociological theory of rights. Kant declares the individual wholly autonomous, but such radical autonomy is in Durkheim's view inconsistent with the nature of human existence, which is social through and through. The autonomy of the individual can only be relative to the "state of public opinion" in a given social milieu (Durkheim, 1992/1950, p. 68). The rights of individuals evolve and change, precisely because they are not derived from nature but from society.

Hegel's view is problematic as well. It is clear that the individual is far more than just a servant of the goals of the State. Kant's vision of the individual as endowed with an essentially sacred status is, in Durkheim's view, correct, even if Kant is mistaken as to the origins of that status. So is it a contradiction that we find in modernity the singular importance of the individual and the unquestionably growing power of the State? Not at all. It is the State itself that is responsible for the emergence of the autonomous individual (Durkheim, 1992/1950, p. 57). The individual emerges only because the State produces him through legislation and then sustains him through police protection. If we examine the historical record, we find that in the period of human history before the State existed or when it was less expansive and powerful than in Durkheim's day, the individual was nothing in comparison to her status today. Individuals are without question freer in mass societies with large, powerful States than in small-scale societies, in large part because members can be more carefully, effectively, and constantly scrutinized and policed in the latter (Durkheim, 1992/1950, p. 61). The view, which we in the United States hear echoed to us daily in the news by various political figures on the libertarian right and left, that the State is the enemy of the individual and seeks constantly to repress him, does not stand up to serious scrutiny. It is, after all, the State that freed family members from the tyranny of patriarchal domination and broke the fetters placed on citizens and workers by the local political and economic groups that controlled them under feudalism (Durkheim, 1992/1950, p. 64).

The State's function, then, has been to bring the individual into the position he currently holds, and its duty is to sustain the "cult of the human person" it established (Durkheim, 1992/1950, p. 69). Both capitalist and socialist theories of the State go astray in seeing its fundamental duty as a mere economic machine or a power that must be restrained in order to allow individuals to pursue merely material individual interests. Durkheim asserts that the State must be primarily an "organ of moral discipline" that undergirds this new cult that is, in his view, destined to take the place of religious cults of the past (Durkheim, 1992/1950, pp. 69, 72).

But the State ultimately also points beyond itself to a global moral community, based in the cult of the human person, wherein national aims are subordinated to fully universal, human ones (Durkheim, 1992/1950, p. 73). Durkheim recognizes that a global moral community is not a practical possibility in the absence of a global society. Without it, internationalism can seem just an "egoistic individualism" to which individuals resort in order to claim freedom from all national morals and laws (Durkheim, 1992/1950, p. 74). We begin, though, to move toward the creation of that global society when we move from understanding patriotism in the limited sense of the past—that is, as something produced in national groups only during times of conflict with other national groups. The moral bravery and selflessness inspired by war is not simply disdained by Durkheim, who concedes that such conflicts produce "brilliantly devoted service" (Durkheim, 1992/1950, p. 75). Yet he believes another kind of patriotism is imaginable, wherein the moral selflessless of the citizen is directed not outwardly but inwardly. In this new internationalist style of patriotic moral spirit, individual States will cultivate a morality consisting of the pursuit not of military might or wealth but of the status of "being the most just, the best organized and in possessing the best moral constitution" (Durkheim, 1992/1950, p. 75).

Durkheim next moves to a consideration of democratic States specifically. Historically, he notes, democracies have only differed from monarchies in degree, as both are governments of minorities (in Durkheim's day, women did not vote in France, and in most contemporary democracies, only a minority actually cast votes). The difference is that the specific minority that governs changes in a democracy. If we define **democracy** as a society "where everyone has a share in directing communal life," only very primitive forms of society qualify (Durkheim, 1992/1950, p. 78). In this sense, democracy is an "archaic . . . form of society" (Durkheim, 1992/1950, p. 78).

Democracies are likewise not government by the people, since the governing power in modern democracies (as against the primitive democracies just mentioned) is always a small group of elites within the State (Durkheim, 1992/1950, p. 82). Just as democracies are not actually forms in which everyone governs, so no form of elite rule can ever be absolute (Durkheim, 1992/1950, p. 87). Such elites may have great power over individuals, but they are much less able to resist or undo "the structure of society." Durkheim gives the example of the French King Louis XIV, who was able to issue *lettres de cachet* (arbitrary orders without any possibility of appeal) against anyone but was far less free to do as he pleased in the face of opposition from the Church (Durkheim, 1992/1950, p. 87).

After this effort to weaken the distinction between democracy and seemingly more highly centralized and hierarchized forms of government, Durkheim argues that modern democratic States are tending toward a more hierarchically organized form (Durkheim, 1992/1950, p. 88). In a democratic State thus envisioned, the role of the State is not simply to uncritically and directly express the will of the mass but to take this "unreflective" form of thought and "superimpose" on it the superior understanding of governing elites (Durkheim, 1992/1950, p. 92). He is unapologetic in his elitism here, as he asserts that the representatives of the State understand more fully than the average citizen does what can and cannot be done and what must and must not be done. It is Durkheim's position that a major problem is created in contemporary democracies by the fact that, in the sweeping away of tradition that took place in establishing democratic government in the great bourgeois revolutions, there has been no subsequent putting into place of any "deep-rooted ideas and sentiments" that could prevent the society from being shaken to its core by "the first gusts of doubt or debate" (Durkheim, 1992/1950, p. 93). Democratic States, that is, must be stronger, not weaker, if they are to survive, and the "constant flux and instability" of changing governing parties and coalitions is generally a force of "disorder" (Durkheim, 1992/1950, p. 94). One might imagine him speaking these lines to those we hear today speaking in smug satisfaction that "checks and balances" essentially prevent a governing party from being able to implement any agenda, however limited, or even from passing a federal budget.

This needed additional strength of the State will come, however, not simply from the top down, by giving more power to the State itself, but by creating and invigorating new intermediary groups and institutions, and especially the kind of corporate, guild-like groups with which he began these lectures, that stand between the individual and the State (Durkheim, 1992/1950, pp. 96, 106). The State must derive its powers from both individuals and such groups. Rejecting the view of Rousseau, who sees only the individual and the State, Durkheim argues that invigorated "secondary cadres" will increase the solidity of the State in numerous ways, not the least of which have to do with taking up responsibilities currently left to individuals for which the latter are not well suited (Durkheim, 1992/1950, p. 96). In this section, he even hints that, in a future, more organized form of democratic State with vibrant professional guilds, the individual might be unburdened at least partially of a responsibility she has in our current forms of democracy for which she is largely unsuited and that she frequently exercises in ways that merely reflect her own self-interest rather than an enlightened view of the needs of the society: He is talking here about voting (Durkheim, 1992/1950, pp. 96–97).

The next lecture marks another transition in the text. After focusing in the foregoing on the ethical responsibilities specific to given professional groups and civic morality as defined by membership in a State, Durkheim takes up the topic of general moral duties humans have, independent of their membership in specific groups or nations. The duty not to kill one's fellows is paramount here. He argues that homicide is seen as the most grievous offense today precisely because the individual has become an "object of a sacred respect" (Durkheim, 1992/1950, p. 113). In modernity, we see homicide decreasing for this reason, and the lowering of the homicide rate is proof that we are moving away from the state of the public consciousness driven fundamentally by the passions that prevailed in past epochs (Durkheim, 1992/1950, p. 119). When homicide does occur in the modern world, strong passions and moral commitments to groups that reduce the sacredness of the individual are often behind it—for example, war or the *vendetta* (Durkheim, 1992/1950, pp. 116, 117).

The remaining chapters in the book take up questions concerning the rights of property and contracts. Attacks on property are prohibited in modern society because of a historical process by which certain things came to be understood as so closely related to a person that they could share the inviolability that accrued to him as a sacred human person (Durkheim, 1992/1950, p. 121). It might seem, especially if we adhere to a view of society centered on individuals, such as that of John Stuart Mill (whom Durkheim cites here), that property rights naturally emerge from the inherent freedom individuals have to dispose as they will of the fruits of their labor. Here, we find a theory of **property right** based in the labor of the individual. Durkheim argues, on the contrary, that it might just as well seem self-evident, once we understand the deeply social nature of humankind, that we are from our birth indebted to the society in which we live and that this debt might reasonably include the requirement to dedicate some portion of the fruits of our labors to the social group without which we could not exist

(Durkheim, 1992/1950, p. 122). Understanding the emergence of property rights will require a more penetrating examination of the situation than is suggested by Mill's axiom.

Property is obtained through labor, to be sure, but not only thus. It may also come through exchange, and by legacy or inheritance (Durkheim, 1992/1950, p. 123). Moreover, factors beyond my labor determine the value of my property—for example, I have more fertile land than another, and a given amount of labor on that fertile land therefore produces more crops for me than the same amount of labor does for another person. In Durkheim's argument, "a mere whim of fashion" can increase or decrease the value of property, which is always dependent on public opinion (Durkheim, 1992/1950, p. 126).

A historical investigation into the matter reveals that individual property is always historically rooted in a notion of collective property. Individuals may come to exercise property rights over something only after the collectivity to which they belong has possessed those rights (Durkheim, 1992/1950, p. 129). The first entity to exercise a claim to possess property was the whole of humankind, since the soil is everywhere connected (Durkheim, 1992/1950, p. 129). The individual right to property is determined then by antecedence, or, more crudely put, by who gets there first (Durkheim, 1992/1950, pp. 130–131). Here, Durkheim is following Kant, who argued that the earth is the property of the human race, and we then may parcel it out individually (Durkheim, 1992/1950, p. 133).

Some things, however, cannot be objects of property. In Rome, the *res sacrae,* or sacred things, were outside of all economic transaction and could not be owned by any party (Durkheim, 1992/1950, p. 137). Such sacred things are prohibited from ownership by *taboo*—that is, recognizing something as consecrated and therefore to be set apart from other, mundane things (Durkheim, 1992/1950, p. 143). Durkheim invokes the Polynesian religious concept as an equivalent of the Roman *sacer,* from which we derive our term "sacred." From these notions, we get the power of the notion of ownership, for the thing that is taken as the property of a given person is understood to be surrounded by a vacuum that prevents approach by all others (Durkheim, 1992/1950, p. 143). The *taboo* of property rights can be seen in the reluctance individuals in modern societies often have to touch even things that are not yet actually legally the property of someone else but only symbolically so. Think of the disapprobation that would be directed at someone who took fruit from the cart of another supermarket shopper, reasoning (technically accurately) that the latter had not yet purchased it and it was therefore still in the stock of the store to sell!

So the origins of property can be seen in the structure of "certain religious beliefs" (Durkheim, 1992/1950, pp. 143–144). Kings in Tahiti were understood to be sacred beings, and their sacredness is contagious, so whatever they touch becomes marked with that sacred power and thereby becomes the king's property. For this reason, kings there must be borne aloft by others when they travel so as not to make contact with the ground and thereby make the whole Earth their possession (Durkheim, 1992/1950, p. 144).

The right to property is a distinct kind of right because it invalidates by definition concurrent rights (Durkheim, 1992/1950, p. 146). Once a thing is owned by someone, any possibility of the right of property being exerted over that thing by another person is excluded. There is also a kind of moral bond established between the owner and the thing, and this causes the property to change in status as the owner does. Hence, if the owner dies, his heirs get the property (Durkheim, 1992/1950, p. 146). As sacred things are contagious, so too is property. Hence, the young of a domestic animal or, in earlier times, the child of a slave are also the property of the owner (Durkheim, 1992/1950, p. 148).

The most ancient form of property is landed property, and it is in this form that we can most clearly see the notion of the sacredness of property emerging (Durkheim, 1992/1950, p. 149). In the great agricultural kingdoms of the past, where landed property emerged, all individual land holdings were surrounded by a strip of unowned land that separated it from other, nearby, owned parcels. This band of a few feet had to remain completely uncultivated, and tilling it opened you to the risk of being slain as sacrilegious (Durkheim, 1992/1950, p. 151). It was, Durkheim asserts in citing Fustel de Coulanges, *res sancta* (Durkheim, 1992/1950, p. 151). As is the case with sacred things, property must be protected. The tradition of lifting the betrothed over the threshold of the house is based in the recognition that she is not yet of the ownership of the house, and so she cannot pass over the limit on her own. Often an expiation must be made to protect her transgression of the sacred property boundary, which is a kind of "magic circle" (Durkheim, 1992/1950, p. 152). Fustel de Coulanges had argued that this idea originates in a cult of the dead, who are buried on the family property and become almost god-like ancestral figures, thus making the land sacred (Durkheim, 1992/1950, p. 153). Durkheim counters that the reality is somewhat more complex and that the family religious cult in such societies was not limited to a cult of the dead ancestors. Harvesting too played an important role in such cults, and he describes the practice of the sacrifice of the first fruits of the harvest, which are given to the gods and cannot be touched by others (Durkheim, 1992/1950, pp. 154, 155).

There is historical evidence that entry into a newly constructed home required a kind of sacrifice in many societies, and only those who have performed such may enter the house. The logic was that building the home disturbed the "guardian spirits of the soil" who therefore had to be appropriately propitiated (Durkheim, 1992/1950, p. 157). This is an indication of a larger fact of the religious root of property right: Human property right is only a subsidiary version of the original property rights of the gods, and our property rights are made possible only by the gods' original ownership of the land, which has consecrated it and therefore protected it against challenge from other potential human owners once an owner has made his morally correct claim (Durkheim, 1992/1950, p. 157). Thus, property rights are not rooted in any notion of the sacred respect for the person of the owner but in the respect of the guardian spirits who were the primary owners.

In this section, Durkheim anticipates some of the most fundamental arguments on which he would elaborate in much greater detail in *The Elementary Forms of Religious Life*. While obviously the idea that there are guardian spirits who have consecrated the land is a difficult idea to square with reality, these religious principles are a symbolic translation of real social needs and collective interests (Durkheim, 1992/1950, p. 160). Religion, he argues, is the primordial form in which societies first become self-conscious and reflect on their reality, and so much that comes later in the way of more sophisticated reasoning and categorization has its roots in religion. But how did we come to believe that the soil is sacred and inhabited by gods in the first place? The gods are nothing more or less than the symbolic and personified understanding of the collective forces operating on the groups in question (Durkheim, 1992/1950, p. 161). He describes clan totemism, the form of primitive religion that would centrally occupy his attention in *The Elementary Forms*, as the religious origin of this idea. The soil is considered already appropriated by the clan/group/god, and all sacredness is the issue of this entity (Durkheim, 1992/1950, p. 162). In this vision, the sacrifice of the first fruits is the most primitive incarnation of a tax—that is, taxes originate in the sacred offering we owe to the clan/group/god (Durkheim, 1992/1950, p. 163).

Given this original position in which only extrahuman entities can own the land, how does the individual ever come to have his own property? Initially, it is a leader of the group who is awarded such sacred rights, as he is the very representative of the group (Durkheim, 1992/1950, p. 165). Then, over time, others in the group are permitted to exercise such rights as patriarchal power decreases (Durkheim, 1992/1950, p. 166). Personal property, as opposed to individual rights to landed property, was initially considered profane. However, in time, and as industry and trade advanced, this moveable property began to be seen as more significant, though it is evident that it is still of a lesser sacred power than landed property (Durkheim, 1992/1950, p. 167).

Durkheim now moves to the **right of contract.** The two fundamental ways to become an owner of something, he reiterates, are through an exchange that is governed by a contract and inheritance (Durkheim, 1992/1950, p. 173). He sees the latter as an essentially antiquated and dying form connected to family right, and so it is his sense that property right can be expected to be founded going forward fundamentally in the contract (Durkheim, 1992/1950, pp. 174, 175).

It may seem that the phenomenon of contract is primitive, but it emerges at a relatively late date (Durkheim, 1992/1950, p. 176). A contract is the mechanism by which ownership is transferred from one party to another, and as such it relies on the existence of other legal and moral frameworks for its efficacy. The two parties must already be recognized as legally vetted agents capable of executing contracts, and there must be a legal and moral framework establishing the legitimacy of the contract itself (Durkheim, 1992/1950, p. 177). In this way, marriage, which is a contractual relationship, nonetheless requires the existing structure of the family, which is not contractual, for its foundation (Durkheim, 1992/1950, p. 177). The idea of a contract would make no sense unless the parties to it were already protected by a body of law and informed by a moral community of the trustworthiness of the contract and the other party.

The two members of the contractual exchange must have something of sacredness about them, which comes ultimately from the group, in order for a contract to exist (Durkheim, 1992/1950, p. 178). In clan exchange, the members were all of the same blood, so the sacred bond was understood. When a contract was made between members of different groups, originally, a **blood covenant** was often necessary, where the blood is explicitly invoked into the contract as a way of solidifying it (Durkheim, 1992/1950, p. 180). Breaking bread together is also a kind of communion that roots a contract in blood, since "[f]ood makes blood and blood makes life" (Durkheim, 1992/1950, p. 180).

Like the blood covenant, the **real contract,** a form of exchange in which the obligation to complete the agreed-upon exchange is contained in the actual handing over of the first thing in the exchange, is a primitive ancestor of the modern contract, but neither are actually contracts in our contemporary usage since, in both, it is not the wills of the two parties involved that are important (Durkheim, 1992/1950, p. 181). Rather, in both blood covenant and real contract, it is "a state or condition of persons or of things," and not merely two individual wills, that seals these exchanges (Durkheim, 1992/1950, p. 181).

Early contracts could be sealed by oaths or the invocation of gods. The formulaic nature of the oath was the binding force, and in this we see a clear residue of magical power. In this sense, "[t]he juridical formula is only a substitute for sacred formalities and rites" (Durkheim, 1992/1950, p. 182). Generally speaking, in early contracts, ritual was a required element to make the contract binding (Durkheim, 1992/1950, p. 183). These rituals formally bound one both to the other party and to the deities (Durkheim, 1992/1950, p. 193). The early contract sealed by ritual means is the root of the contemporary contract by mutual consent, although we no longer actually engage in the ritual, owing to the lack of time and other exigencies of the modern world (Durkheim, 1992/1950, p. 194). The weak force of the wills involved or the actual words uttered themselves, shorn of religious and ritual meanings, could not hope to give the contract the required power. The force that binds the parties is "supplied from without" (Durkheim, 1992/1950, p. 194).

Durkheim closes these lectures with a few notes as to the current trajectory of contract. The idea of the **just contract**—that is, a contractual form that takes into account the status of knowledge and coercion of the two parties and declares a contract null and void if one or the other party has been misled or forced to act—is the future of contract law, consistent with the enshrinement of the human person as a sacred entity (Durkheim, 1992/1950, p. 208). Although he has clearly argued that much of the deeply collectivist nature of the history of contract remains present in contemporary contract, it is certainly the case that the role played by the wills of the two parties to the contract is greatly increased in the contemporary world. As the notion of justice becomes more central to the contract, so too will it and the concomitant idea of equity become the driving force in property right generally (Durkheim, 1992/1950, p. 215). Justice and equity as basic elements of the contemporary consciousness regarding property and contract will demand the imminent dismantling of inheritance, which is fundamentally contrary to equity (Durkheim, 1992/1950, pp. 216–218).

Conclusion

The Division of Labor in Society is a book that every student of society should read and then periodically reread. Like great texts generally, it rewards the careful student who will come back to it again and again with fresh insights each time. When Durkheim delivered the thesis, its radically innovative approach was patently obvious. During the thesis defense, one of the members of the jury, Paul Janet, banged loudly on the table and invoked the name of God in response to Durkheim's unabashedly secular and scientific approach (Fournier, 2007, p. 186). Others, however, moved by the brilliance of the work, applauded vigorously at Durkheim's answers to the jury

(Fournier, 2007, p. 188). It is unquestionable that the book's influence, especially on American sociology, has been massive. A study of the two major sociological journals in the United States (the *American Journal of Sociology* and the *American Sociological Review*) revealed *The Division of Labor* as by far the most cited of all of Durkheim's four major books (Besnard, Borlandi, & Vogt, 1993, p. 218).

The studies of socialism and professional ethics are much less well known in the English-speaking world, and for this and other reasons Durkheim's thought about politics and the State is widely misunderstood and mischaracterized. Even otherwise thoughtful commentators on Durkheim get this muddled. In a well-known introduction to Durkheim's thought, Robert Nisbet (1974, p. 151) brings up the lectures on socialism, only to claim peremptorily and without evidence that the subject was not one of any significant importance in either his own life or his intellectual work. Robert Alun Jones (1986, p. 18), in a short book that admirably summarizes the four major published studies of Durkheim's lifetime, nonetheless offhandedly writes of "Durkheim's antipathy for politics."

The truth is that Durkheim's whole oeuvre is marked by the struggle to theorize a moral prescription for the ills of modern individualist society, and a fundamentally socialist vision, with a central role for renewed, reinvigorated, and augmented guild-like trade associations, was at the base of this prescription.

A few questions

- What is the evidence, if any, of the continued existence of mechanical solidarity in the modern world?
- How does Durkheim's analysis of economic morality stand up in the contemporary world?
- How are unions as they exist in the contemporary United States and Western Europe like and unlike the new corporative, guild-like bodies Durkheim was calling for in his work?
- What are the risks to sociology of acknowledging a figure like Saint-Simon as a founder of sociological thought?
- Who gets the better of the debate about the state of solidarity in the contemporary Western world, Durkheim or Tönnies?

4

Establishing a Social Science

The last half decade prior to the turning of the 19th century into the 20th was a tremendously productive time for Durkheim. In addition to starting the sociological journal *l'Année sociologique* during this period, he published two of the four major books produced during his lifetime, *The Rules of Sociological Method* and *Suicide.* In these books, issues surrounding the establishment of a properly sociological method of inquiry and investigation are paramount. Durkheim argued at length in both for a definition of sociology that carved out an entirely new epistemological space for the discipline, an approach that involved taking what he called social facts as data that could not be reduced to the individual level, despite the fact that they appear to us most obviously in real consequences in the lives of individuals. In *Suicide,* Durkheim also took on a specific social problem of Europe of the late 19th century—namely, the rising suicide rate—and investigated its broader social and cultural causes, making a powerful argument that some of the fundamental social glue of Western society was being weakened by contemporary cultural change.

In addition to his principal thesis on the division of labor, Durkheim was required, as were all students endeavoring to receive the title that enabled them to teach at university, to complete a secondary thesis in Latin. He chose to write on the work of the Baron de Montesquieu, one of the most important social theorists of the French Enlightenment and the author of a work, *The Spirit of the Laws,* considered a classic study in comparative political and social theory. Here, we see Durkheim already working toward the establishing of a method for this new social science.

Durkheim presents Montesquieu as a forerunner of his own approach to sociological method. Montesquieu had marked a break from previous study of law, which was mired in the simplicities of **contract theory** (in which law is understood as outside nature altogether and residing solely in willed agreements of individuals, as in Hobbes) or saw only a few basic principles of law as stemming from human nature and almost all the rest of empirical law as a purely human creation. By contrast, according to Durkheim, Montesquieu saw all law as emerging from man's nature as a social being (Durkheim, 1960, p. 21). His three types of legal regime (despotisms, monarchies, and republics) were based not on *a priori* principles but on historical and personal accounts and what existed in the way of ethnographic material in his time. He looked for the causes of these types of regime in factors such as climate, geography, and the volume of the population. Whereas earlier studies of law relied on deductive reasoning, moving from general ideas about humankind to particular cases, Montesquieu marked the move into inductive reasoning starting from case studies and, through the comparative method, a movement toward general theory (Durkheim, 1960, p. 52). Montesquieu also recognized the need to see the interconnections between parts of the social order—for example, law, morality, and trade—that were previously considered to be unrelated; this methodological move is critical in Durkheim's view for the emergence of the modern social sciences (Durkheim, 1960, p. 57). He also doubtless appreciated Montesquieu's vigorous concern for the public interest and his sense that individual citizens of the French Republic owed to it a debt they could never fully repay. Although Durkheim also criticizes his predecessor on a number of important points—for example, his failure to conceptualize change in social structure within a basically evolutionary framework of increasing complexity and variation—he sees Montesquieu as an important predecessor of his own efforts. But the real work was yet to be done, and Durkheim saw himself as the one to do it.

The Rules of Sociological Method

The book's title is likely inspired by Descartes, whose *Discourse on Method* was an inspiration for all French thinkers of this period. It is, however, not a book on sociological method, in the contemporary usage of that term—that is, Durkheim is not describing the practical specifics of sociological research. This is an exercise of a more fundamental kind, with the goal of establishing the basic conceptual language of the new discipline. The chapters were initially published as four separate pieces in the *Revue philosophique* in the summer of 1894 (Borlandi & Mucchielli, 1995, p. 8). The book itself was published by the end of that same year, and Durkheim likely wrote these pieces during 1893 and the first part of 1894, just after having completed his two theses.

This book is frequently referred to by those who want to see Durkheim as a positivist and a disciple of Auguste Comte, yet he explicitly denies the term and the heritage in the pages of *The Rules,* plainly rejecting what he labels "the positivist metaphysics of Comte and Spencer" (Durkheim, 1982/1895, p. 33). The positivist view that all knowledge must be demonstrable through empirical evidence available to sensory experience and that therefore all deductive reasoning is flawed and theory *per se* cannot exist if it cannot be empirically verified is a particular reduction of the broader view Durkheim claims as his own in this book. In the first preface to *The Rules,* Durkheim proclaims his method to be neither purely materialist nor idealist, and he avoids the term "positivism" completely in his self-description. He is, he tells us, a *rationalist* (Durkheim, 1982/1895, p. xxxiv), one who seeks to extend scientific reasoning of cause and effect and the generation of abstract laws that govern all empirical instances.

What Is a Social Fact?

In this brief first chapter of the book, Durkheim defines the central concept of *The Rules,* the foundational concept of sociology that sets it apart from existing disciplines and methods of inquiry into the human condition: This is the social fact. A social fact is a "way of acting, thinking and feeling" defined by two characteristics of its action on humans: It is external to the individual consciousness and it works through coercion, imposing itself on us regardless of our individual will (Durkheim, 1982/1895, p. 52). Language is perhaps the example Durkheim gives that is most easily illustrated. Each of us has a language, or perhaps we should better say that a language has each of *us.* It pre-existed us, and we were not consulted and asked to vote on whether to be immersed in it. Once we are in it, however, it inexorably imposes a vocabulary on us. In nearly every case, our language will outlive us and will externally and coercively be passed along in turn to our children, and to their children, and so on. Durkheim gives money as another example. The American dollar is not my invention, but I am forced to use it if I wish to engage in economic transactions with my fellows in this country, whatever my own thoughts that, for example, those pre-euro French francs I remember that bore the faces of some of my favorite artists and musicians, such as Claude Debussy, Eugène Delacroix, and Paul Cezanne, are more aesthetically attractive bills (Durkheim, 1982/1895, p. 51).

Social facts impose themselves in varying ways. We may be directly punished or ostracized for failing to adhere to them (others will eventually shun me if I insist on avoiding English and instead speak my own invented language), or the effects may be somewhat less direct but still powerful (my old French francs will not be accepted at the supermarket when I attempt to use them to purchase my bread and peanut butter; Durkheim, 1982/1895, p. 52).

To this point, the examples Durkheim has given are **institutions**—that is, well-established social facts that endure for some time. Another kind of social fact, more ephemeral but still quite consequential in its effects on human action beyond these institutions, can be seen in what Durkheim calls **social currents** (Durkheim, 1982/1895, p. 52). These are "the great movements of enthusiasm, indignation, and pity in a crowd [which] do not originate in any one of the particular individual consciousnesses"—that is, the powerful forces that move individuals acting collectively in ways that are beyond their individual control (Durkheim, 1982/1895, p. 52). Durkheim's contemporary, the psychologist Gustave Le Bon, spoke of the crowd psychology that could move a group of individuals to act spontaneously and in concert, and Durkheim's language here is comparable. He describes how a social current can drive a group of individuals who seem quite normal and harmless to action we would not anticipate from them individually, even heinous acts (Durkheim, 1982/1895, p. 53). On a more subdued scale, we might think of the normally mild-mannered college professor who, surrounded by 10,000 of his fellow fans at a raucous college basketball game, may shriek insults at referees in chorus with the rest of the crowd. Such currents need not be so ephemeral in their effects, though, as in the case of the action of a crowd acting collectively at some particular occasion or other. They are present too as "state[s] of the collective mind" that are empirically evident in some statistical regularities of human populations such as rates of marriage, childbirth, or suicide in particular social strata (Durkheim, 1982/1895, p. 55). The existence of such facts is only to be had in the macro-level statistical data on whole populations.

The dual defining characteristics of the social fact can be neatly observed in the entire process by which children are socialized. How does it happen that a child is made a member of a social group? By the external action of others who force the child to keep to a specific daily schedule, to observe rules of self-presentation and interaction, and to act on moral principles that over time will become habitual and seem "natural" (Durkheim, 1982/1895, pp. 53–54).

It is not universality—that is, presence in the mind of all individuals of a collectivity—that defines a social fact (Durkheim, 1982/1895, p. 54). Some ideas or practices may be universally shared at the individual level without rising to the level of social facts. Durkheim insists that the defining element here has to do with the notion that social facts exist as states of the *collective mind*, not merely of all the individual minds, and states of the collective mind can be observed independently of a mere addition of individual states of mind. "[L]egal and moral rules, aphorisms and popular sayings, articles of faith in which religious or political sects epitomize their beliefs, and standards of taste drawn up by literary schools" are all examples of such states of the collective mind (Durkheim, 1982/1895, p. 55).

Toward the end of the chapter, in a footnote, Durkheim makes the first of many criticisms of the thought of the philosopher and sociologist Gabriel Tarde that can be found in the book. Though largely forgotten today, Tarde was an important figure in the development of sociology in France during Durkheim's day—indeed, one of the strongest competitors to Durkheim for supremacy in this emerging field. His own view of sociology was, in strong distinction to Durkheim's, firmly rooted in psychology. He argued from a position of **methodological individualism**—that is, that society could be nothing more than the sum of individual dispositions and actions, and everything in the human world could be explained in his view by recourse to two central, simple concepts. Most human action is **imitation**, large-scale mimicry of established patterns of behavior that spread over wide expanses of the human world. Change is brought about through **innovation**, explosive and unpredictable spontaneous divergence from the established patterns of doing things. Tarde had been a strenuous opponent of Durkheim's thought since *The Division of Labor in Society,* which he critically reviewed. In this first assault on Tarde in *The Rules,* Durkheim attacks the concept of imitation as a possible competitor to social fact as the foundational category for sociology. Imitation does not adequately point to the central elements of the social fact. On the contrary, Tarde's concept privileges the mere repetition of some act as the foundational theoretical moment, whereas Durkheim sees its externality and its coercive imposition as the real causal power behind the repetition. But not only does Tarde's concept fail to get to the real core of the social fact, it is also simply too vague and confused, describing numerous varied events at individual and collective levels, to serve as the central tool in the sociologist's theoretical kit (Durkheim, 1982/1895, p. 59).

In the book's second preface, written in 1901, Durkheim revisits the argument in the first chapter, clarifying a number of points and responding to criticisms. The externality of social facts, he argues here, does not mean they can necessarily be reduced to the material world, though they are entities with an existence independent of the human mind that have the same kind of objective influence over individuals that objects in the physical environment do (Durkheim, 1982/1895, p. 35). The sociologist's task, given the social fact as a theoretical tool, is to put herself in the same state of mind as the physicist, the chemist, or the physiologist and put aside the potentially distorting expectations of common sense as she probes the hidden laws of human action (Durkheim, 1982/1895, p. 37). The social fact leads us to a rejection of methodological individualism. Here, Durkheim revisits an analogy he had already used at least twice in the chapters of the book. The biologist knows that a living entity is composed of a vast collection of inorganic "mineral substances" in interaction, yet he also understands that life is not simply a result of the sum total of all those inorganic substances. It is a new and original phenomenon in and of itself. So too, then, the sociologist must not presume that the entity society can be reduced to the addition of all the individual elements that make it up (Durkheim, 1982/1895, pp. 39–40).

Some critics had overemphasized the coercive aspect of social facts, and Durkheim addressed this misreading of the book in this preface. While social facts do impose themselves on subjects, they are also, at the same time, and without contradiction, empowering and readily embraced by those they coerce: "[T]hey impose obligations on us and we love them; they place constraints upon us and yet we find satisfaction in the way they function, and in that very constraint" (Durkheim, 1982/1895, p. 47). Their constraint is, moreover, powerful but not fully determining of human action (Durkheim, 1982/1895, p. 47).

Durkheim also turns in this second preface to an elaboration of perhaps the central conceptual category of much of his later work—that is, collective representations. These, he says, "express . . . the way in which the group thinks of itself in its relationships with the objects which affect it"—for example, a representation of a clan totem in a totemic society tells us how the group understands its origins and its place in the universe, and a prohibition indicates a collective need to preserve some aspect of the group's self-definition by indicating the kinds of things "people like us do not do" (Durkheim, 1982/1895, pp. 40–41). Collective representations, examples of which are to be found in "[m]yths, popular legends, religious conceptions of every kind, moral beliefs," are completely distinct from the individual representations that are an affair of single human minds (Durkheim, 1982/1895, p. 41). The concept remains mostly implicit in the chapters of *The Rules,* but Durkheim would develop it with more rigor in later work, especially the book on suicide (discussed below) and an 1898 essay on individual and collective representations (discussed in Chapter 6).

The Observation of Social Facts

Once we have a definition of the social fact as a thing, to be studied as such, where do we look for them and how do we know when we have found one? Common sense—that is, our preconceptions about the way things "must" work based on our everyday experiential framework—again comes under attack here. We must be sure to avoid taking our preconceived ideas about social facts for the facts themselves. We form myriad representations of the world that are oriented to our practical goals and raw experience, and these can be useful even when they are patently false. Since Copernicus, we have known that what seems to the senses to be the sun's daily journey across the sky is something else entirely, and yet in many ways we continue to operate in our everyday lives as though the commonsense view were true. When the goal is scientific knowledge, however, such commonsense representations are dangerous (Durkheim, 1982/1895, p. 61). In the social sciences, this problem is even more difficult than in the physical sciences, since our ideas about society and its various aspects, which are of indispensable value in our everyday lives, greatly predate the rise of the social scientific way of seeing society and therefore have deep roots (Durkheim, 1982/1895, p. 62).

In this second chapter of *The Rules,* Durkheim carefully separates himself from some of his predecessors in the social sciences on this matter. He sees Auguste Comte as fundamentally guilty of building up as reality just this kind of abstraction unconnected to things in the world. The idea for which Comte is most remembered is his **Law of Three Stages** of evolution, which is seen as governing human knowledge and the social organization within which it is produced. In this conception, knowledge and social structure evolve inevitably through theological, metaphysical, and positive stages, each one superior to its predecessor, and Comte thus hypostatizes a notion of progress. He builds an entire intellectual edifice around this notion, never troubling himself to verify that the real world actually conforms to the representation (Durkheim, 1982/1895, pp. 63–64). Unfortunately for Comte, Durkheim notes, it does not; what exists are merely "particular societies which are born, develop and die independently of one another" (Durkheim, 1982/1895, p. 64).

Herbert Spencer is also subjected to criticism here. Spencer begins with two conceptual categories, industrial societies and military societies, and then fills up a whole history of human society based on these conceptual categories that are insufficiently verified against reality (Durkheim, 1982/1895, pp. 64–65). Durkheim is not entirely dismissing the idea of ideal types like these Spencerian categories, but he is asserting that we cannot legitimately arrive at them before we examine empirical reality without the aid of such *a priori* categories that will carve it up before we have even understood what is there.

Social facts must be treated in the same way the physical sciences treat physical objects, and Durkheim is quite given in this and the other chapters of the book to direct comparisons of physics and sociology:

> [J]ust as our representations of things perceived by the senses spring from those things themselves and express them more or less accurately, our representation of morality springs from observing the rules that function before our very eyes and perceives them systematically. Consequently it is these rules and not the cursory view we have of them which constitute the subject matter of science, just as the subject matter of physics consists of actual physical bodies and not the idea that ordinary people have of it. (Durkheim, 1982/1895, p. 66)

He argues that too much in one of sociology's fellow social sciences, economics, is driven by just the kind of error he finds in Comte and Spencer. The vaunted law of supply and demand, which grounds so much in the discourse of modern economics, has never been inductively demonstrated to be true. Economists have instead, he argues, contented themselves with "dialectical argument[s]" to the effect that individuals ought to behave in this way if they properly understand their interests (Durkheim, 1982/1895, pp. 68–69). The proper procedure for a scientifically grounded understanding of value must avoid taking perceptions of value as the object of study instead of "the values actually exchanged in economic transactions," and a properly scientific sociological study of morality must begin not with conceptions of moral ideals but with "the sum total of rules that in effect determine behavior" (Durkheim, 1982/1895, p. 69). It must be noted that this text provides grist for the mill of those who would present Durkheim as a positivist. He seems here to be arguing for a narrowly, empirically rooted construction of sociological research. Moreover, when he writes of the necessity to study social phenomena "detached from the conscious beings who form their own mental representations of them," he provides evidence for those who would accuse him, in his early work at least, of a naïve position on the question of the objectivity of the social sciences. How, precisely, is the sociologist, who we must assume is herself one of the "conscious beings" who inevitably "form . . . mental representations [of] social phenomena," to so completely liberate herself of all her pre-existing categories and representations in approaching a field of research (Durkheim, 1982/1895, p. 70)?

A social fact cannot simply be modified or overthrown by an act of will (Durkheim, 1982/1895, p. 70). Durkheim argues that social facts are perhaps more complex but also easier to separate from their representations than psychological facts, which by their natures are representations of the individual, seemingly inseparable from those individuals (Durkheim,

1982/1895, p. 71). Social things are, on the contrary, clearly separate from individual representations of them; for example, we find law objectively present in legal statutes, fashion concretely and collectively represented in actual clothing, and artistic taste externally revealed in the works of art themselves (Durkheim, 1982/1895, pp. 71–72).

The essence of this chapter is contained in three corollaries Durkheim presents to the general law on social facts as things presented earlier in the chapter. The first states that the sociologist "must systematically discard all preconceptions" (Durkheim, 1982/1895, p. 72). The method of Descartes, famously ticking off the list of aspects of his knowledge he cannot adequately ground until he reaches bedrock, is invoked as the model. The "ordinary person" is here opposed to the sociologist, and the latter is charged with the difficult task of moving above his own, potentially deep investment in moral and political beliefs in order to get to hard, objective analysis (Durkheim, 1982/1895, p. 73). This is much more difficult than in the physical sciences, as no physicists are as deeply invested in any moral vision of the action of electrons as social scientists are in matters of politics and morality. Additionally, the sociologist risks appearing to others as a "vivisectionist" when he insists on a dispassionate analysis of the nature of some intimately held social belief (Durkheim, 1982/1895, p. 73). Durkheim quotes at length a historian of religion who argues that the scientific study of religion cannot do without religious sensibility in order to annihilate this perspective: "Feeling is an object for scientific study, not the criterion of scientific truth" (Durkheim, 1982/1895, p. 74).

The second corollary reads thus: "The subject matter of research must only include a group of phenomena defined beforehand by certain common external characteristics and all phenomena which correspond to this definition must be so included" (Durkheim, 1982/1895, p. 75). Herbert Spencer is trotted out again here as an example of the failure to adhere to this rule of sociological inquiry. In his historical discussion of the marital institution, Spencer had failed to make the distinction between two kinds of monogamy— that enforced by law and that arising merely as a matter of practice—and as a result he failed to distinguish the significant differences between the *de facto* monogamy produced by necessities of the environment (such as poverty) and modern legal monogamy, thereby arriving at a strange history in which the earliest and latest forms of marriage are the same, with a detour in between away from monogamy (Durkheim, 1982/1895, p. 77).

We come finally to the third corollary: "[W]hen the sociologist undertakes to investigate any order of social facts he must strive to consider them from a viewpoint where they present themselves in isolation from their individual manifestations" (Durkheim, 1982/1895, pp. 82–83). Here, Durkheim is reiterating the often-repeated trope in the book that social facts must not be reduced to the individual level. They exist as such apart from their individual manifestations, as a kind of law of social order and its consequences. The social fact is "a fixed object . . . which leaves no room for subjective impressions or personal observations" (Durkheim, 1982/1895, p. 82). The application of a legal rule, he goes on, may have myriad individual manifestations, each of which will have its unique characteristics and idiosyncrasies, but the rule itself exists distinct from those individual manifestations and "there are no two ways of perceiving it" (Durkheim, 1982/1895, p. 82).

The Normal and the Pathological

This third chapter is perhaps the best known in the book, presenting a distinction that has over time become one of the snippets by which Durkheim's thought is presented in textbooks. That it is a biological analogy should not surprise us, as he uses such analogies throughout the book.

He begins with an interesting argument about the relationship of scientific knowledge to practical matters of ethics and morality. There are those who argue that science cannot tell us anything about what we ought or ought not to desire (Durkheim, 1982/1895, p. 85). Durkheim, perhaps surprisingly to some readers, given some of what he had claimed in the previous chapter concerning the necessarily dispassionate relationship of the sociologist to the object studied, disagrees strongly. What good can it do, he argues, to pursue scientific knowledge of reality if it does not serve us in our practical lives (Durkheim, 1982/1895, p. 85)? Then, a directly biological analogy is asserted in axiomatic fashion: "For societies, as for individuals, health is good and desirable; sickness . . . is bad and must be avoided" (Durkheim, 1982/1895, p. 86). Given this axiom, if sociological science can find a way to distinguish between **the normal and the pathological**, then we can certainly apply this principle practically and work to privilege normal forms and mitigate pathological ones.

How can we define the normal? We might think pain is a reliable indicator of abnormality, but the absence of pain, and even the presence of pleasure, can be signs of pathology (Durkheim, 1982/1895, p. 87). In the biological realm, we know that many cancers cause no pain in initial stages, although we would surely say the body is in a state of ill health when a tumor that has the potential eventually to kill the individual is growing in his body. Not all conditions that cause pain and weaken the body are morbid. In some species, for example, reproduction brings on death for the mother, and it sometimes does for our species as well, yet we rightly do not see this as a rationale for classifying birth as a morbid event (Durkheim,

1982/1895, p. 88). Even disease can in some cases have beneficial effects: For example, vaccinations give us weakened quantities of a disease in order to inoculate us against it (Durkheim, 1982/1895, p. 89).

The normal is finally defined by Durkheim as "those facts which appear in the most common forms" (Durkheim, 1982/1895, p. 91). We get to the normal, he argues, by thinking about a hypothetical being who would have "the most frequently occurring characteristics for the species in their most frequent forms" (Durkheim, 1982/1895, p. 91). It is, in other words, the typical, average nature of a phenomenon that makes it normal, and the pathological, it follows, is found in atypical, abnormal, deviant forms: "[T]he normal type merges into the average type . . . and any deviation from the standard of healthiness is a morbid phenomenon" (Durkheim, 1982/1895, pp. 91–92). There are no universal rules here, as what is pathological can only be defined in relation to a given species and only at a given stage of the development of that species (Durkheim, 1982/1895, p. 92). So something that is normal in one society may be pathological in another, and the same phenomenon may change status within the developmental trajectory of a single society.

Durkheim examines an example in the Europe of his day: Is the economic order dominant at the *fin-de-siècle,* with its emphasis on *laissez-faire* and a lack of state regulation of the economy, normal or pathological? He clearly sees it as pathological in the broadest sense, but it is the dominant form, the average type, in most of Western Europe, so how can such a classification be justified? Sometimes, he argues, social elements that once were productive of positive consequences can live on in later stages, even as regular and widespread (and, therefore, seemingly normal), despite the fact that the conditions that gave rise to them in the past have disappeared or radically changed. So we have to look carefully to determine whether the historical conditions that gave rise to the need for a *laissez-faire,* noninterventionist economy are still in place in the present day to make a scientific call on whether it is now normal or pathological (Durkheim, 1982/1895, p. 95).

There is doubtless a Darwinian angle to this argument. The organism that has the most typical characteristics is most likely to survive, while deviants are more likely not to survive, and the same is true, Durkheim argues, of societies (Durkheim, 1982/1895, p. 93). But this is an area where Durkheim's case is particularly vulnerable. In the biological realm, deviance can sometimes advantage the deviants; for example, the mutations of a given animal species with coloration patterns that provided better camouflage may be better able to elude predators. It seems apparent here that Durkheim's knowledge of evolutionary biology was limited, certainly in historical comparison with our own time, but perhaps even by reference to the state of biological knowledge of his day. It is not clear that we can talk about competition for resources in the relations between human groups or societies in the same way as in the standard evolutionary model that focuses on competition between individual organisms, and this is a significant potential problem for Durkheim's argument. He does note a bit later in this chapter that we cannot know, given a normal state, that it is also the maximally useful, functional state, but only that it is more useful than the pathological forms that have opposed it, which leaves the door slightly open to the possibility of deviant change that would become normal later (Durkheim, 1982/1895, p. 96).

At the end of this first section of the chapter, we find three rules for defining the process by which we determine whether a social fact is normal or pathological. The first stipulates that a social fact is normal for a given kind of society (**social type**) at a given stage in its development if it can be found in the "average society of that species . . . at the corresponding phase of its evolution." The second rule provides a way of verifying the first: Check to determine that the character of the fact in question "is related to the general conditions of collective life in the social type under consideration." This verification, he goes on in the third rule, is required when we are examining a fact in a society that has not "yet gone through its complete evolution" (Durkheim, 1982/1895, p. 97). The complicated question of determining the precise point in its given evolution a particular society is at in the moment we are studying it is passed over by Durkheim in silence.

In the following section of the chapter, Durkheim gives an example to demonstrate the utility of his method and to stress again the much greater difficulty of the determination of normal and pathological in sociological analysis as opposed to in the biological sciences. Crime, he suggests, is apparently unarguably pathological; even the criminologists accept this seeming fact. Yet it is present in all societies, and it had in Durkheim's time been rising in all of Europe since the start of the 19th century. France, in particular, had seen a 300% increase in crime over the course of that century (Durkheim does not tell us the source of this statistic). It may well be that high levels of crime are an obvious indication of pathology, but the omnipresence of the phenomenon would seem to point in the direction of normalcy. This is, however, not enough to merit the classification; for this, it would also have to be demonstrated that crime is a "factor in public health" (Durkheim, 1982/1895, p. 98). How could such a thing be shown?

What is crime, first of all? It is an act that "offends certain collective feelings" (Durkheim, 1982/1895, p. 99). A bit of historical and anthropological research shows that what is seen as the most offensive crime in one society, at one time in history, can be viewed quite differently elsewhere, but all societies define some actions as criminal insofar as they offend those collective sentiments. No society without crime, then, is imaginable, as even a society of saints would produce crime. The bar in such a saintly society would simply be raised, and if no murders occurred, impertinent words or snoring in the monastic cells would perhaps become serious criminal offenses (Durkheim, 1982/1895, p. 100). Crime is necessary in any society, Durkheim argues, because it is intimately connected to "the basic conditions of social life" (Durkheim, 1982/1895, p. 101). It can in fact be the site at which we discover the need for legal change. The criminal example of Socrates, punished by execution, revealed the limits of freedom of thought and expression in the Athens of his day (Durkheim, 1982/1895, p. 102). In *The Division of Labor*, Durkheim had argued that crime serves a valuable function in uniting the rest of the community in moral outrage against the criminal and his act. The criminal provides us an opportunity to reaffirm to ourselves the boundaries of our moral universe. The criminal is thus not a mere parasite on the normal society but a contributor to normalcy, again so long as he is not present in excessive quantities. Durkheim concludes the chapter, however, without a word on how to begin to determine the normal levels of crime in given social types.

If crime is not in and of itself pathological, we must turn away from objectives in dealing with it that are based on the utopian ideal of eliminating it altogether. Punishment cannot be driven by the desire to cure crime or the criminal (Durkheim, 1982/1895, p. 103). Durkheim here provides a striking analogy for the task of the political leader. He must think of his role as like "that of the doctor," working to cure the patient of pathology when it truly and actually exists, but generally limiting himself to maintaining the normal functioning of the organism, which includes a good deal of necessary deviance (Durkheim, 1982/1895, p. 104).

Rules for Classification of Social Types

In this brief chapter, Durkheim attempts to present the first steps toward a method for establishing what he calls **social species**, by which he means to indicate discrete social groups that are united by their immersion in the same social facts and collective representations. Sociology, he argues, occupies a middle ground in the classification of human groups between the extreme **nominalism** of history, which finds each society an incomparable, unique entity, and the extreme **realism** of philosophy, which sees humanity as a whole as the only real group (Durkheim, 1982/1895, p. 108). The social species is a category designed to occupy an intermediary position that permits empirical and comparative study of human groups (Durkheim, 1982/1895, pp. 108, 109).

The more historically oriented researcher would perhaps suggest that any effort at constructing social species would have to wait for a full empirical study of all existing societies, after which by inductive reasoning one might make a go at social species. Durkheim rejects this, noting simply that such exhaustive empirical work cannot prevent us from the more urgent task of comparative knowledge of social entities. When we study any given society, it is not possible even at that level to exhaustively catalog all the facts concerning it, so we will quickly be defeated by a problem with no solution (Durkheim, 1982/1895, p. 110). Rather than bog down in this quagmire, Durkheim turns quickly to an effort to sketch the most elementary social species, which he assumed, given his axiomatic evolutionism, would produce as progeny all subsequent species through variation and selection. This most elementary form is the primitive "horde" of a single segment—that is, societies that trace their origins to one ancestor and cannot be subdivided into subgroups distinguished along characteristics such as totem identity or exogamous marriage (Durkheim, 1982/1895, p. 113). This makes the horde a more elementary, primitive group than the clan, which also claims a common ancestor, because the latter is frequently broken up into tribal subgroups with different totems and various rules of interrelation and intermarriage. After hordes and clans, social species differentiate by adding degrees of polysegmental complexity, each new social species distinguished by the species preceding it in that it is simply two or more of the previous species united. Thus, he presents "simple polysegments . . . polysegmentary societies of simple composition . . . [and] polysegmentary societies of double composition," the first exemplified by Australian and indigenous American tribes, the second by unions of those tribes, and the third by the Germanic tribe of the late European Iron Age (Durkheim, 1982/1895, p. 114).

Rules for the Explanation of Social Facts

Durkheim now turns to the task of explaining social facts. Explanation requires locating two separate entities: the cause of the social fact and the function it fulfills (Durkheim, 1982/1895, p. 123). Spencer is here criticized yet again for conflating these two tasks. He and Comte alike, according to Durkheim, have attempted to explain social facts by the faulty method of recourse to a ground in purportedly more general laws of psychology (Durkheim, 1982/1895, p. 125). Spencer, in the fashion of contemporary rational choice theorists, wants to reduce the ends of society to individual ends. Durkheim here recalls the biological analogy he had used earlier of the new reality produced by inorganic chemicals individually coming together to create life (Durkheim, 1982/1895, p. 128). Society cannot be understood as a mere summing up of all the individuals in it, and social facts cannot be understood by simply adding up all the individual motivations of the members of a society.

Durkheim gives us a helpful footnote on the distinction of individual consciousness and the collective consciousness. Some critics of the latter notion argued that there simply is nothing to posit as its source of origin beyond the origin of individual consciousness—that is, the human mind or brain. Durkheim argues that we do not need such a source, for we do not need to hypostatize the collective consciousness in order to recognize its importance and its difference from the consciousness of individuals. The mind is the source of both, but in the one case, we are dealing with a collection of objects bounded by a single organic being, while in the other we take combinations of organic beings as the source and the combined objects they produce in common as the relevant products (Durkheim, 1982/1895, p. 145). Collective representations are ultimately not caused by individual states of consciousness but by "the conditions under which the body social as a whole exists"—that is, by states of affairs that affect groups of people together (Durkheim, 1982/1895, p. 131). The cause of a social fact is thus always to be sought in preceding social facts, and its function must always be found in its relationship to some social end (Durkheim, 1982/1895, p. 134). He is here making an argument for social morphology or social structure as the causal agent in the collective consciousness and collective representations; the size and density of the group, for example, are among the common causal factors of social facts (Durkheim, 1982/1895, p. 136). In the end, Durkheim's position on psychological reductionism is quite clear: If we explain a social fact by means of a psychological phenomenon, we can be certain such an explanation is incorrect (Durkheim, 1982/1895, p. 129).

Durkheim then describes two approaches to the relation of the individual and society that are in opposition to his own in order to demonstrate the deficiencies of both. On the one hand, thinkers such as Thomas Hobbes and Jean-Jacques Rousseau see a break in continuity between the individual and society. In this view, humans instinctively dislike and avoid communal life and must be forced to it for their own good; this is the social contract theory (Durkheim, 1982/1895, p. 142). On the other hand, there are those such as Spencer, natural law philosophers, and the liberal economists who see social life as something that emerges naturally and spontaneously but who find its basis and its cause in the individual (Durkheim, 1982/1895, p. 143). Against both, Durkheim argues for a primal social order that exercises constraint over the individual, but it is a constraint to which the individual willingly submits, recognizing in it and its source something grander and greater than himself (Durkheim, 1982/1895, pp. 143–144). In a footnote, he responds in advance to those who might take him as a defender of constraint *per se*. It is not the constraint exercised by mere physical force or wealth to which he is referring but that of intellectual or moral superiority—that is, the constraint exercised by scientific reason and the authority of moral institutions and experts (Durkheim, 1982/1895, p. 146). The sociology Durkheim is defending in this chapter "would see in the spirit of discipline the essential condition for all common life, while at the same time founding it on reason and truth" (Durkheim, 1982/1895, p. 144).

Rules for Establishing Sociological Proofs

The last chapter in the book deals with the complex issue of causality in the social sciences, a difficult topic treated here all too briefly and insufficiently. Most of the chapter is a commentary on and critique of John Stuart Mill's 1843 book *A System of Logic,* wherein the English philosopher had put forth the five types of inductive reasoning in scientific research that became known as **Mill's Methods**, a number of ways by which Mill argued relations of causality could be established between two or more phenomena.

Sociology's only proper method, Durkheim begins, is "indirect experimentation, or the comparative method" (Durkheim, 1982/1895, p. 147). Experimentation in the physical and natural sciences requires the manipulation of phenomena in a controlled way that is not possible in the social sciences. Human groups cannot be, for example, subjected differentially to massive poverty to see if all respond in the same ways or if different responses emerge, for moral as well as methodological reasons. But **indirect experimentation** offers the hope of getting to the same intellectual goal we seek in experimentation, which is the establishment of relations of causality. How should we think about cause in the social sciences? Durkheim here brings Mill into the discussion. Mill, Durkheim claims, rejects the idea that the social sciences can even perform indirect experiments. Worse still from Durkheim's perspective, he denies that a given effect always and only has one cause, arguing instead that "the same consequence . . . can be due now to one cause, now to another" (Durkheim, 1982/1895, p. 148). But it is, Durkheim asserts, only the philosophers who question causality in this way, as the scientist assumes it as the basis for the scientific method (Durkheim, 1982/1895, p. 149). Those who would argue, for example, that suicide may have various causes are simply confusing different kinds of suicide, which may have different causes because they are not the same phenomenon (Durkheim, 1982/1895, p. 150). Durkheim is pointing ahead to his effort in the book on suicide to establish at least four different types of what might seem to the uncritical observer to be one and the same phenomenon.

Durkheim then goes through Mill's five methods of induction in succession, rejecting the applicability of four of the five in the social sciences. The first three Mill calls the methods of, respectively, agreement, difference, and the joint method of agreement and difference. These three show cause by looking for characteristics present or absent in a number of compared cases. All three, Durkheim argues, require an overly exhaustive cataloging of the various facts present in different societies in order to compare them for agreement or difference. We can ultimately "never be assured . . . that two peoples match each other or differ from each other in every respect save one," and so such reasoning simply will not work in the social sciences (Durkheim, 1982/1895, p. 151). In the physical and life sciences, this is also unattainable in principle, yet we can get close enough in physics and chemistry, and sometimes even in biology, to make for a "proof" that appears "adequate" (Durkheim, 1982/1895, p. 151).

The fourth method, that of residues, is rejected in sociology because it requires knowledge of a sufficient number of causal laws to make it possible to reason by eliminating given causal options from a range, and thus it is appropriate only for sciences that are comparatively advanced, not those which, like sociology in Durkheim's day, are only just emerging (Durkheim, 1982/1895, p. 150). This leaves only Mill's final method, that of **concomitant variation**. Here, Mill describes the reasoning thus: Any phenomenon that varies whenever another phenomenon varies is either a cause or an effect of the first, or it is connected to it through some fact of causation. This can be applied in sociology, Durkheim argues rather slyly, because "[a]s soon as we have proved that in a certain number of cases two phenomena vary with each other, we may be certain that we are confronted with a law" (Durkheim, 1982/1895, p. 153). Concomitant variation can be examined in three ways: by looking at facts from various parts of one society, from several societies of the same species, or several societies from different species (Durkheim, 1982/1895, p. 155). He turns again to suicide to illustrate his argument. In the first kind of concomitant variation, we can look at suicide in different regions, classes, genders, or age groups for the same society (Durkheim, 1982/1895, p. 155). We can also study suicide comparatively among societies of the same species (e.g., modern France and modern Germany) or across social species (e.g., modern France and Australian aboriginal tribes). Whenever we seek to study an institution or some legal or moral rule or practice that extends equally over a given society, we cannot use the first type but are required to study more than one society (Durkheim, 1982/1895, p. 156). Ultimately, Durkheim asserts rather ambitiously, a complex social fact can only be well understood by "follow[ing] its entire development throughout all social species" (Durkheim, 1982/1895, p. 157).

In the book's conclusion, Durkheim reminds the reader that sociology requires no positivism, no evolutionism, no idealism, and no stance on free will and determinism. Its one fundamental philosophical and scientific principle is that of causality (Durkheim, 1982/1895, p. 159). It seeks to adapt theoretical terms from biology such as "species," "organ," "function," "health," and "morbidity," borrowing parts of their definitions from the biological sciences but also recognizing the need to transform them in applying them to the study of human groups rather than the human organism (Durkheim, 1982/1895, p. 160). Sociology must avoid commitment to political positions of individualism, communism, or socialism. It must see no scientific value at all in such ideas, but it must approach them as aspects of society to be studied in the scientific manner described throughout the book. This, however, does not mean sociology must completely forgo any interest in practical matters of policy (Durkheim, 1982/1895, p. 160). Its objectivity will treat institutions "with respect but without idolatry" (Durkheim, 1982/1895, p. 161). It must be objective, and it must disdain the generalist methods of mere philosophers, such as Comte and Spencer, who remain disconnected from true scientific method. This will necessarily mean it will be able to attract only the intellectually rigorous few to its study, but it should be prepared to give up merely worldly success (Durkheim, 1982/1895, p. 163). If it does not remove itself from the political battles and refuses to renounce the popular ideas and ways of expressing arguments and therefore presents itself as possessor of "no special competence," it cannot hope for the authority necessary "to quell passions and dispel prejudices" (Durkheim, 1982/1895, p. 163).

Suicide: A Study in Sociology

As is evident in the frequent use Durkheim makes in *The Rules* of facts related to suicide, he was working on his study of the latter topic at the same time as he compiled the essays that make up the chapters of the earlier book. But why did Durkheim want to write a book on suicide in the first place, and why has that book arguably become, for American sociologists at least, the core Durkheim text?

A number of factors should be mentioned in an explanation of Durkheim's interest in suicide. Much of Europe was concerned with the phenomenon, along with other trends in population demography, during the mid to late 19th century. During this period, population statistics were being analyzed with acuity and something approaching modern statistical tools for the first time, and some of the facts seemed worrisome to many observers. Suicide rates seemed to be rising in parts of Europe, and it was surmised by some observers that this presented a profound social problem likely related to the broad social and cultural changes related to secularization and industrialization that were sweeping Europe in the 19th century. Less than two decades before Durkheim published his study, another book on the subject, by the Italian statistician Enrico Morselli, thoroughly described the same statistical landscape presented by Durkheim and came to the conclusion that modern civilization intensified the struggle for existence by increasing the psychological pressures and strains on those people in the places most saturated with mental stimulation, who tended to be the middle classes in the large metropolitan areas (Johnson, 1994, p. 138).

There was also a personal context for Durkheim. A close friend from his student days at the École Normale, Victor Hommay, had committed suicide in 1886, and Durkheim struggled to make sense of his friend's demise. In the obituary he wrote for Hommay, Durkheim wrote with great fondness of their relationship:

> During our three years at the École, we truly lived the same life; we studied in the same room, we had the same courses, we even spent together nearly all our free time. During our long conversations, how many projects we planned for one another, which I cannot recall now without sadness and bitterness! (Durkheim, 1887, pp. 14–15)

He also quoted from a letter Hommay wrote him while he was teaching in a *lycée* in the provinces after his *agrégation*, in which his friend reflects nostalgically on "those good years at the École . . . where we so lived the true life" and bitterly reflects on how in comparison to that effervescent time "my current life seems pale, discolored, monotonous, insipid" (Durkheim, 1887, p. 17).

The discussion of his friend's temperament shows affinities with the argument he would make in *Suicide* concerning one of the four types of suicide, egoistic suicide. Hommay's family, and later, and still more intensely, his ENS comrades and the intense collective atmosphere of the school, provided him with profound social integration that he felt lacking when he was separated from those integrating communities and as a result suffered from what we would today probably call depression.

Finally, there was an intellectual angle of great interest to Durkheim. The establishment of a social science with its own set of unique analytic lenses and methodologies required empirical illustration, and Durkheim was interested in finding a topic that could be used to effectively illustrate the new contributions of sociology to knowledge of the human condition. In 1888 to 1889, he had given a lecture course on the topic. Suicide, he recognized, was an excellent candidate for a study designed to prove the unique explanatory ability of sociology to speak to social problems that traditionally had been relegated to purely individualist arguments. Statistics were readily available, and Durkheim, with the help of his nephew Mauss, eagerly mobilized them.

The 1897 book was not Durkheim's first confrontation with the topic of suicide. He had published an article titled "Suicide and the Birth Rate: A Study in Moral Statistics" in 1888, almost a decade before *Suicide*. In this piece, Durkheim had argued that rising suicide rates and falling birth rates, which tended to appear together (and on both France had among the worst rates on the continent), are indicators of societal ill health. Both are effects of a more general social malaise, and societies of sounder moral glue will show lower suicide rates than those where the social fabric is weaker (Durkheim, 1994/1888, p. 116). Though the terms are somewhat more vague in this early study, some of the elements of the conceptual framework of *Suicide,* as well as of *The Rules,* are present here in germinal form. We find an argument in the article for health and disease as sociological concepts. We also find a rejection of the idea that all suicides can be considered in the same analytic category and an effort to distinguish among different kinds of suicide with different causes. Durkheim presents only two types here: suicides that result from defects of the individual himself and suicides that are caused by social malaise rather than psychological or biological illness (Durkheim, 1994/1888, p. 130). He suggests, as he will with more theoretical specificity in *Suicide,* that there is an inverse relationship between marital and familial solidarity and suicide, and therefore that the sickness of rising suicide rates can be combated by reinforcing marital and familial structures and institutions.

As in *The Division of Labor,* and also as would be the case later in *The Elementary Forms, Suicide* is divided into three subsections. Here, the three *livres* within the book take up, respectively, the nonsocial causes that are generally invoked to explain suicide, which Durkheim intends to show are inadequate for a full treatment of the topic; then the description of the four sociological types of suicide Durkheim believes he has found and the two conceptual categories (**social integration** and **moral regulation**) that produce them (see Table 4.1); and finally an examination of the entire structure of society as it contributes to suicide.

The Extra-Social Influences

Durkheim begins with a careful effort to define the terms of the study. How is suicide to be distinguished from other kinds of death? What counts

Table 4.1

Conceptual Category	*Excessive*	*Insufficient*
Social integration	Altruistic suicide	Egoistic suicide
Moral regulation	Fatalistic suicide	Anomic suicide

as a suicide? Suicides are certainly a species of death, Durkheim argues, but clearly not all deaths are suicides. Suicides have the special quality of being the deed of the victim himself (Durkheim, 2006/1897, p. 19). Suicide is "any death resulting directly or indirectly from a positive or negative act by the victim him or herself" (Durkheim, 2006/1897, p. 17), he writes. But this still leaves problems. What of such deaths in which the victim is not aware that what he is doing will lead to death (e.g., a man under the influence of hallucination who leaps to his death from a tall building; Durkheim, 2006/1897, p. 17)? It is not precisely the intent of the actor to kill himself we are trying to ascertain, says Durkheim, as there are phenomena we should class as suicides that do not involve the desire to die on the part of the victim. But we can know more or less certainly whether the act is likely to produce death, and the actor generally knows this information too. There are serious questions we might raise concerning this definition. Durkheim claims that a soldier who marches off to sure death to preserve the lives of others in his regiment should be considered to know the effects of his action (Durkheim, 2006/1897, p. 18). Is this really so? Are there not at least some such situations in which the actor acts believing, for example, that death is possible but less than certain? Are these suicides by the definition Durkheim gives? How can we distinguish cases here without recourse to intent, which Durkheim is eager to avoid?

These questions notwithstanding, Durkheim completes his definition of suicide by adding "which he was aware would produce this result" to the first proposed definition above (Durkheim, 2006/1897, p. 19). He then moves on to consider suicide as a social fact. Looking at suicide rates in different European countries across a span of a few decades reveals a great deal of regularity in the figures, in addition to changes that seem to be more regular than mere chance would allow (Durkheim, 2006/1897, p. 23). Moreover, the suicide rates across time seem to demonstrate less variation even than mortality rates. This is startling because it reveals that the phenomena that cause suicides are at least as stable as the phenomena that cause mortality more generally (Durkheim, 2006/1897, p. 24). Another fact of interest is that mortality rates seem more or less constant across Europe when one controls for the "degree of civilization" (by which Durkheim merely means the level of economic and social development), while suicide rates vary considerably from one country to another (Durkheim, 2006/1897, p. 27). This indicates that the suicide rate is "specific to every social group and can be considered as a characteristic index" (Durkheim, 2006/1897, p. 27).

After this introduction, the first book turns to a treatment of extra-social factors in suicide. He considers in separate chapters four different such factors: psychopathology, heredity, climatological effects, and the effect of imitation. In all four cases, the conclusion is that, individually and collectively, these nonsocial factors cannot explain the regularity of suicide rates demonstrated in the introduction. It was still occasionally advanced in Durkheim's day that suicide itself constituted evidence of a psychopathic state, absent any other evidence, but Durkheim demolishes this argument. Monomania, or the pathological obsession with a single subject or idea, is almost universally rejected clinically, he argues, because the current understanding of mental illness is that it cannot affect an individual in such a limited way, leaving him to remain perfectly reasonable in every other aspect of life (Durkheim, 2006/1897, p. 38). Certainly some suicides are psychopaths and can be shown to be so by evidence from their behavior, but many others are not and thus this factor cannot explain "the collective tendency to suicide in general" (Durkheim, 2006/1897, pp. 45, 46). Durkheim also compares national rates of suicide and madness and finds no clear relation of the two (Durkheim, 2006/1897, p. 56). The chapter on hereditary effects on suicide begins with a nuanced discussion of race, as the framing of heredity in Durkheim's day tended to be oriented not on family but on racial and ethnic type. Durkheim here makes, in just a few pages, a radically constructionist argument about **race** that would be the envy of just about any contemporary race theorist. It may well be, he argues, that "the word 'race' does not nowadays correspond to anything definite at all" (Durkheim, 2006/1897, p. 69). Paleontologists alone are interested in "the original races of mankind," and those groups that are in Durkheim's day carelessly called "races" "appear to be no more than nations or societies of peoples, sharing a kinship of civilization rather than of blood" (Durkheim, 2006/1897, p. 69). This sounds as though he is reducing the category "race" to our contemporary one of "ethnicity," a radical enough move, but he is indicating something still more striking: "Seen in this way, race eventually becomes almost the same thing as nationality" (Durkheim, 2006/1897, p. 69).

After this critical beginning, Durkheim agrees to accept the "broad human types" in Europe as races in order to determine whether any systematic differences in suicide rates can be traced along these lines. He takes the different European races from Morselli: the Germanic, the Celto-Roman, the Slavic, and the Uralo-Altaic, the last of which is too numerically limited to test for suicide rates (Durkheim, 2006/1897, p. 70). The suggested order of these groups given by Morselli is, from greatest to least, Germanic, Celto-Roman, and Slavic. But the effort to sustain this instantly falls apart when data are more carefully examined. The diversity of suicide rates within these racial groups is great, and there are some Germanic groups (e.g., the Flemings and the Anglo-Saxons) with suicide rates lower than those of the other two "racial" groups (Durkheim, 2006/1897, p. 71). The complications that foil racial theories here are most evident when we look at specific societies containing several racial stocks. Switzerland contains peoples of both Germanic and Celto-Roman stock, and the Valais canton, with the highest proportion of Germanic-origin inhabitants, has the lowest suicide rate, while cantons with nearly entirely Celto-Roman populations have much higher suicide rates. This and other evidence shows, Durkheim tells us, that what appear to be effects of "blood" when we see Germanic peoples with generally higher suicide rates are in fact effects of "the civilization in which they were brought up" (Durkheim, 2006/1897, p. 74).

Variations in climate and the changes of season are considered next. The data show that the suicide rate is highest in Europe in the middle latitudes, and for all countries suicide rates are higher in the mild part of the annual weather cycle, and particularly in the summer, than in the harsher period (Durkheim, 2006/1897, pp. 93, 95). This would seem to make a *de facto* case for the causal effect on suicide of higher temperatures. But again, the purportedly self-evident fact is exposed as too simple. Suicides are more frequent in the spring than in the autumn, although temperatures are generally higher in the latter period (Durkheim, 2006/1897, p. 100). The statistics show that suicide rates across Europe begin to climb in January and continue to do so until June, when they begin to recede, although the temperatures do not reach their hottest until July and August (Durkheim, 2006/1897, p. 101). So if it is not temperature that is the causal element here, what is it? Durkheim argues that it is the increase in daylight that is most directly related to increased suicide rates; the latter rise rapidly as does the former from January to April, then the increase in both slows from April to June (Durkheim, 2006/1897, p. 106). In all seasons, he shows, the majority of suicides take place during daylight hours (Durkheim, 2006/1897, p. 107). But it is not daylight itself that is the causal element here, according to Durkheim. It is the increased intensity of social life that takes place during the daylight hours (Durkheim, 2006/1897, p. 110). He ends the chapter without explaining how this intensification of social life could contribute to heightened suicide rates, merely pointing to the analysis to come in the second book.

Prior to moving to that consideration, though, he takes on the last extra-social factor, which is that of imitation. The argument here goes that suicides are in many cases the result of **mimicry**—that is, of individuals learning of the actions of previous suicides and copying their act. Durkheim has a specific target in mind in this chapter, though the target is named only in the footnotes: This is Gabriel Tarde, who we saw so frequently at the receiving end of heavy argumentative artillery in *The Rules*. In placing imitation in his sights in the study of suicide, Durkheim certainly meant to subject his foe's central theoretical concept to a thorough thrashing. It is not too much to classify *Suicide* as a fundamentally "anti-Tarde book," as he is the most cited author in the book who is not a specialist on the topic of suicide (Besnard, 2003, p. 74).

Durkheim begins by noting that the concept of imitation is insufficiently stable in its usage. At least three different definitions of the term can be found in Tarde's work, two of which are not imitation at all. In the first case, it is claimed that numerous individuals can be affected together by some cause to come to have the same emotional or mental state, as when mobs gather and are driven to mutual action. But there is no imitation here; instead, there is a new act spontaneously and collectively undertaken by several individuals at once (Durkheim, 2006/1897, p. 117). The second type is illustrated by the example of fashion, where people will copy existing styles and modes of dress because of a desire to fit into the society in which they live (Durkheim, 2006/1897, p. 117). Here too there is no imitation *per se,* but merely the result of social pressure to conform, and therefore a rational act producing the reproduction (Durkheim, 2006/1897, p. 120). Only in the third definition of the term, wherein we reproduce some action that has happened before us or of which we have heard "solely because it has happened in front of us or because we have heard it spoken about" (Durkheim, 2006/1897, p. 117), can we legitimately speak of imitation. The repetition must take place without any "explicit or implicit intellectual process" intervening between the act imitated and the imitation (Durkheim, 2006/1897, p. 123); in other words, we are dealing with pure contagion without any intermediary. By cleansing the definition of a will to imitate, Durkheim is presenting a definition with which Tarde would likely not have agreed. Moreover, it is not evident why he thinks the definition needs to be limited in this way. He gives as examples, in addition to a literary allusion to Rabelais, laughing, yawning, and crying in imitation of another performing these acts, as well as "the idea of homicide . . . transferred from one consciousness to another" (Durkheim, 2006/1897, p. 117).

Durkheim then goes on to refute the weight of contagion on suicide rates by arguing that we should be able to see patterns of emanation starting in large cities and capitals, which, as the centers of attention and innovation in any society, would be the places where such purported waves of contagious suicide would begin. Yet the statistics do not show the pattern we would expect in such a case, which would be higher suicide rates in the central cities, such as Paris, and then progressively decreasing rates as one moves out farther from the site of original contagion (Durkheim, 2006/1897, pp. 129–130). Durkheim closes the chapter with another stern rebuke to the unnamed Tarde: The idea that imitation is "the prime source of all collective life," which was Tarde's thesis, is "ill-founded" and a "sort of dogma" (Durkheim, 2006/1897, pp. 142, 143). He will later in the book subject Tarde's ideas to still more critical decimation.

Social Types and Causes

In book two, Durkheim starts with a description of the methodology of the study. Determining cause is a difficult, if not impossible, business, and Durkheim notes that his method is to start not from the specific characteristics of the suicides but from their causes (Durkheim, 2006/1897, p. 147). Then, from those causes, the suicides can be grouped into different types. So Durkheim will start not with an account of the particular suicides but with an account of the particular social situations that cause or provoke them. He concludes this short chapter by noting that the search for causes cannot depend ultimately on the sense subjects have of motives, for social subjects themselves are most often ignorant of the real causes of their actions (Durkheim, 2006/1897, p. 151).

Durkheim turns first to the effects religious faith has on suicide. A glance at European national suicide rates shows that countries with a dominant Catholic population have lower rates than those countries with dominant Protestant populations (Durkheim, 2006/1897, p. 156). But this could be a result of national rather than religious differences, so Durkheim consults comparative data within the same society and finds the same fact. Switzerland is a prime case: Cantons in which Catholicism dominates have suicide rates four to five times lower than the Protestant cantons (Durkheim, 2006/1897, p. 159). Suicide rates for Jewish populations have tended to be the lowest of all three religious faiths, though Durkheim notes that in recent times the Jewish rate seemed to be increasing. He suggests the reason may have to do with something other than religion—namely, that Jews are disproportionately represented in large cities and the "intellectual professions," two characteristics that tend to produce higher suicide rates (Durkheim, 2006/1897, p. 161). This seems clear, Durkheim claims, even when we control for other possible causal factors—for example, national characteristics, level of economic prosperity, and minority or majority status of the religion in a particular society.

What religious differences could be behind these distinct suicide rates? For Jews, Durkheim suggests, it may be the minoritarian and embattled cultural position they occupy in Europe, which pushes them to solidarity and a "particularly rigorous discipline" (Durkheim, 2006/1897, p. 161). But Catholics make up majorities in many parts of the continent, so this logic is not universal. The fundamental causal element in the differences is located in the cohesion and vitality of a religion's "collective credo" (Durkheim, 2006/1897, p. 165). In Protestantism, broadly speaking, we find less strongly integrated churches wherein the individual is "the author of his own belief" (Durkheim, 2006/1897, p. 163). This might seem a positive factor, especially in the cultural language of contemporary radically individualist societies like the United States, but Durkheim suggests that such an approach to the serious questions of religion (sin and expiation, eternal life or damnation) leaves individuals in many cases who are intellectually and spiritually unequipped for the labor vulnerable to confusion and despair. In Catholicism and Judaism generally, on the other hand, the body of collective doctrine propounded by tradition is quite extensive and strong. Members of these two faiths find ready-made structures for solving religious problems: formulaic prayers that relieve the difficulty of personal invention, an authoritative hierarchy to be consulted in times of question, and a large historical body of material that examines virtually every conceivable existential human problem from the authoritative perspective of the faith. Seeming exceptions to the rule of religious suicide rates are explainable once we understand the real cause. For example, suicide rates in England, a Protestant country, are comparable to those in Catholic countries because the particular variety of Protestantism found there (Anglicanism) is structurally very much like Catholicism, with a large body of collectively accepted doctrine and significant internal hierarchy and structure (Durkheim, 2006/1897, pp. 166–167). Another fact of English society that points out the similarity to Catholic societies is the large number of clergy, for "the more intense religious life, the more men are needed to direct it" and "the more numerous [religious] authorities, the more closely they surround the individual and contain him" (Durkheim, 2006/1897, pp. 167, 168). In general, the greater the desire for individual study of religious matters, the greater the propensity to this type of suicide, which he labels **egoistic suicide**.

This general cause, however, seems weakened by the fact that the pursuit of religious education is general in Judaism, while Jews experience lessened propensity to suicide (Durkheim, 2006/1897, p. 174). Durkheim attempts to explain this by the specific factors contributing to the Jewish desire for knowledge. Because of their minority status in all societies (Durkheim is writing before the creation of the state of Israel), Jews "seek an education not in order to replace their collective prejudices by rational ideas, but simply to be better armed for the struggle" (Durkheim, 2006/1897, p. 175).

Durkheim concludes this chapter with a clarification that he is not arguing that knowledge is the cause of the suicides. On the contrary, knowledge itself cannot be blamed for the suicidal impulse (Durkheim, 2006/1897, p. 176). It is the response (and the only one possible, per Durkheim) to the already existing fact of the loss of collective, traditional forms of dogma. In other words, he believes it is inevitable that the growth of individual knowledge will continue but that it will have mixed (both positive and negative) consequences.

In the subsequent chapter, Durkheim examines another dimension of this same type of suicide. Religion protects believers, he argues, because of its power as a community that infuses members with the strength of numbers, tradition, and security. Could other such communities show similar effects on suicide? In a word, yes. The integrative capacities of both familial and national political communities are shown to provide protection against suicide. In every age category save the youngest he examined, those aged 16 to 25, the married had lower suicide rates than the unmarried. Durkheim surmises from this fact that premature marriage has a negative effect on the suicide rate, and this is especially so for men (Durkheim, 2006/1897, p. 186). The general immunity that marriage provides to both men and women must be due to one of two causes: Either it is about "matrimonial selection," wherein those who cannot marry are defective in various ways (disabled, extremely poor) and therefore more likely to kill themselves, or the "influence of the domestic environment" is providing the same kind of integration provided by well-oiled churches (Durkheim, 2006/1897, p. 190). The matrimonial selection option fails to account for the heightened suicide rates of the young married (Durkheim, 2006/1897, p. 192).

The data show that the presence of children in a marriage provides still further protection over and above the presence of a spouse for both men and women. Durkheim finds that when the numbers are closely examined and taken apart appropriately, it is solely the factor of children in a marriage that provides protection for women, and marriages that are childless actually aggravate suicide rates for women, though not for men. The reason why the effect does not appear when overall rates for married and unmarried women are compared is that the number of women in childless marriages is quite small compared to those in marriages with children (Durkheim, 2006/1897, pp. 199–200). So the conjugal bond affects men and women quite differently. With children, it provides protection for both, and the protection grows as the number of children does, because, as Durkheim argues, the moral intensity of an integrative group is greater as it is denser in numbers (Durkheim, 2006/1897, pp. 211, 216), but childless marriages harm women and protect men.

Major political upheavals on the order of popular wars and national crises (e.g., think today of 9/11 and, at least in its early days, the subsequent war in Afghanistan with respect to the population in the United States) reduce the number of suicides (Durkheim, 2006/1897, p. 218). The reason is that they increase feelings of national unity and, in focusing the group on a clear and given goal, are able, at least briefly, to provide more intense social integration (Durkheim, 2006/1897, p. 223).

As too little integration can aggravate suicide rates, so too can too much. When individuals feel themselves so tightly integrated into a group that they lose the grasp on the importance of their individual selves, they can sacrifice themselves more readily to the perceived good of the group. In many forms of societies at earlier developmental stages, the elderly felt a strong compulsion to act to terminate their own lives once they could no longer play an active role in the group. Durkheim gives the example of the Rock of Ancestors, from which elder male Goths would throw themselves to their doom (Durkheim, 2006/1897, p. 235). In such primitive societies, it is also common to find suicides of women on the deaths of their husbands and of servants on the deaths of their masters (Durkheim, 2006/1897, p. 236). Moral pressure is exerted on the individual, who feels such suicides as a duty. Japanese *seppuku,* or *hara kiri,* is another example, wherein the perceived sense of loss of social prestige or honor is enough to drive the individual to annihilate himself (Durkheim, 2006/1897, p. 240). Traditional, caste-based India, he argues, is one of the primary locations to look for this kind of suicide (Durkheim, 2006/1897, p. 241).

There are three subvarieties of this second type of suicide: obligatory, voluntary, and acute **altruistic suicide** (Durkheim, 2006/1897, p. 245). Durkheim suggests that this variety of suicide is most typical of "inferior societies," though he does discuss some contemporary examples (Durkheim, 2006/1897, p. 246). He describes Christian martyrs, who do not actually kill themselves yet actively embrace their preventable deaths. Soldiers in military situations are the chief example he gives from the contemporary world. Their training and the exigencies of combat can facilitate the weakening of the notion of individuality in favor of a group identity. A powerful example is provided by one of Durkheim's own students and colleagues, the young scholar Robert Hertz, author of important studies in the anthropology of death and expiation, who was killed in April 1915 as part of an essentially suicidal French effort to retake a position. As Durkheim learned after Hertz's death, the young sergeant had been informed in advance that many of the men in his outfit could be expected to be killed in the attack, and yet he apparently cheerfully assented to the mission. Though this type of suicide can be expected to shrink in modernity, we can find examples in recent news items: a couple who together leaps off a cliff when their young son, who had a serious illness, dies; an ALS patient who swallows an overdose of sleeping pills when he is at the cusp of the point at which he will no longer be able to feed himself; the suicide bomber who willingly gives his life for what he perceives as the war effort of his embattled community.

The third type of suicide Durkheim examines is **anomic suicide**. He begins here with an observation that is quite startling, given our commonsense notion of the relationship between economic well-being and suicide. People commit suicide, we tend to believe, when they lose money quickly (the stereotypical image of the Great Depression is the heartbroken man who has lost his entire savings leaping from a tall building to his demise) or when they do not have the material means to realize their desires—that is, because of negative economic crisis or poverty and/or economic inequality. It is true that negative economic crises, at least, often present an uptick in the suicide rate. Yet, Durkheim tells us, this has nothing to do with poverty *per se,* because we see an even more remarkable connection between sudden economic changes of a positive nature in collective fortunes and suicide (Durkheim, 2006/1897, pp. 264–265). Extensive poverty seems to act as a protection *against* suicide. It is the disturbance in an equilibrium that is the causal agent driving suicide rates up (Durkheim, 2006/1897, p. 267). But why should this be the case?

Durkheim turns here to a discussion of what he sees as some facts of human nature. Humans have a natural tendency toward insatiable desires. Absent regulation, humans will desire things they cannot obtain and thereby be condemned to a perpetual state of unhappiness (Durkheim, 2006/1897, pp. 269–270). There is nothing in our organic or psychological constitution that enables us to regulate ourselves; we need a source outside of ourselves to play the regulatory role required. Only society can fulfill this function, since its moral power is superior to the individual and recognized by the individual as such (Durkheim, 2006/1897, p. 272). In other words, a mere increase in economic growth, which is the constant refrain as the key to happiness in mainstream American politics, would not address the problem of suicide related to unfulfilled desires, because the container to be filled is infinitely large and expands still further whenever more is dumped into it. Poverty, far from operating as a spur to suicide, is actually, so long as it is not sudden but a habitual, long-lasting condition to which the individual inures herself, a practical limitation to desires. One recognizes that one simply does not have the ability to spend endless amounts of time and money in Las Vegas or Atlantic City, and so one does not suffer inordinately from the realization. It is when the normal, external forces that regulate and limit our desires are overthrown by the sudden manifestation of economic and/or prestige resources radically out of line with our customary levels of these resources that suicidal risk is increased. When the norms that govern our desiring are sundered, we are in normlessness, or anomie. Illustrative examples of this type confront us in the entertainment news daily. Some pop star, or actor, or other celebrity achieves success in his industry and then quickly descends into a life of constant partying, unencumbered now by the former economic limits to such activity and surrounded by syco-phantic hangers-on who cannot and will not say "no" to any of the star's desires, and eventually we read of his end in a ritzy hotel somewhere from a drug overdose or a self-administered gunshot wound.

Anomie is also the cause Durkheim finds at the root of the rise in suicide rates associated with divorces and marital separations. He shows that the divorced, both male and female, suffer from suicide rates three to four times higher than those of the married, and their suicide rates are higher also than those of the widowed, and this despite the fact that the latter are generally older and by this fact at higher risk of suicide (Durkheim, 2006/1897, p. 288). Yet divorce, like marriage, affects the sexes differently, and depending significantly on the social context. Men seem to suffer more from divorce and to profit from social policy surrounding marriage that makes divorce difficult, while married women, who, we recall, are more protected against suicide than their unmarried counterparts, do not suffer the same significant rise in proclivity to suicide on the occasion of divorce, and even lose some of the protection against suicide brought by marriage in societies where divorce is difficult to obtain. A practical difficulty is raised for social policy, then, by the fact that men and women experience opposing effects when divorce laws liberalize.

Women generally commit suicide much less frequently than do men, and the reason has to do with the degree to which they are integrated into society and therefore feel positive and negative effects from social sources. The entire array of social facts regarding suicide, marriage, and divorce that Durkheim presents are explained by him in pointing to the greater need men have to counteract the "disease of the infinite" that is caused by insufficient moral regulation. Outside the boundaries of wedlock, men experience a thirst for sexual experience and adventure that cannot be slaked, while women are in less need of such regulation (Durkheim, 2006/1897, p. 301). Marriage, then, which we might believe, in the commonsense vision, to exist for the benefit of the protection of the wife from the sexual aggression of men, actually operates to more effectively regulate the desires of men and to restrict a questionable sexual freedom that, for men, can ultimately only cause suffering (Durkheim, 2006/1897, p. 305).

In a footnote at the end of the chapter on anomic suicide, Durkheim alludes to a fourth type, which maintains the organization of the argument around the two concepts of integration and regulation and the abnormalities of too much and too little of either. **Fatalistic suicide,** which is the form of suicide of men who marry prematurely and of childless married women, is the variety caused by too much regulation (Durkheim, 2006/1897, p. 305). This type, however, consists of few and shrinking examples, so Durkheim feels no need to tarry over it.

It is fairly clear that the connection of marriage to suicide is of central concern to Durkheim. He discusses the complex gendered effects of marriage on suicide rates with respect both to egotistical and anomic suicides, and it is the sole social cause of suicide that is examined for more than one type of suicide. The passages in *Suicide* (as well as those in *The Division of Labor,* discussed in the previous chapter) in which Durkheim describes gendered differences of this sort in what sound like crudely biological terms have been the subject of withering and sustained attacks over the years. As we saw in the previous chapter, Durkheim believed that men and women were different in their propensities and their emotional makeup, although it is not clear that he reduces those differences purely to biology. He believed that these differences were productive for humankind and that both men and women stood to gain from at least some of these differences between them. Ultimately, on the question of gender difference with respect to sexual desire and regulation that he takes up in this final section of his chapter on anomic suicide, those who would challenge him by asserting that there are no differences on this matter between men and women have some considerable contemporary data to explain away. For example, the existing research on the sexually libertarian hookup culture on many college campuses in the United States seems to suggest with some clarity that in liberal sexual marketplaces where most of the traditional cultural barriers to female sexual expression have been significantly weakened if not completely destroyed, women on average still engage in considerably less sexual activity than men, and women themselves act as the primary moral police force with respect to their fellows who are seen as too sexually promiscuous.

In the sixth chapter of book two, Durkheim turns to a discussion of some of the emotional characteristics of the types of suicide he has presented (see Table 4.2), emphasizing that every suicide has its own "personal imprint" but that he is focused on the "general, social cause of the phenomenon" (Durkheim, 2006/1897, pp. 306–307). He begins with egotistic suicide,

Table 4.2	
Type of Suicide	Emotional Content
Egoistic	Apathy
Altruistic	Passionate or willful energy
Anomic	Irritation, disgust

Source: Durkheim, 2006/1897, p. 325.

which can be of two differing types, characterized by different emotional dispositions. In the first, we see "a state of melancholy languor which slackens the springs of action" (Durkheim, 2006/1897, p. 308). Durkheim cites the writer Alphonse de Lamartine's description of this attitude in his character Raphaël, the subject of one of his prose poems. The melancholy figure indicates his weariness of all around him (Durkheim, 2006/1897, p. 309). This, Durkheim notes, is an "intellectual, meditative" kind of egoistic suicide, which has grown in tandem with the heightening of the intellectual and scientific spirit of modernity. The second variety of egoistic suicide, which Durkheim says is more common than the first, is not melancholy in emotional attitude but "cheerful" (Durkheim, 2006/1897, p. 312). Instead of the "philosophic, meditative melancholy" of the first type, it is characterized by "a skeptical and disenchanted common sense" that Durkheim calls "epicurean" (Durkheim, 2006/1897, p. 312).

In opposition to the weariness and indifference of egoistic suicide, altruistic suicide is characterized by an "expression of energy." Here, the suicide actively and avidly pursues his death, often happy to find his end (Durkheim, 2006/1897, p. 313).

Anomic suicide, finally, is, like altruistic suicide, active and passionate, but inspired not by "fanaticism, religious, moral or political faith, or any of the military virtues, but anger and . . . disappointment" (Durkheim, 2006/1897, p. 314). This is the suicide of Goethe's novelistic creation, Werther, hopelessly in love with a woman he cannot have, or Chateaubriand's René, who journeys around the world in search of adventure and the will to live, coming finally to live with the indigenous natives of the New World, only to find that his emptiness and dissatisfaction have accompanied him (Durkheim, 2006/1897, pp. 316, 317). Anomic and egoistic suicide share a "yearning for infinity," the first chasing limitless desire, while the second is consumed by boundless "dreams" (Durkheim, 2006/1897, p. 317). The distinction between the two begins to show some cracks here, and some have argued that the two types are actually only one.

While it might appear to this point that Durkheim is describing categorical types neatly separated from one another in empirical situations, he hastens to assure the reader that this is not the case. Mixed types are perfectly possible, even likely, and he notes that the different causes of different types of suicide (e.g., too little integration, too little regulation) can act at the same time on an individual and thereby produce a mixed variety of suicide (Durkheim, 2006/1897, p. 318).

A question running through Durkheim's mode of analysis in the book has to do with the nature of his data and the ecological correlation fallacy. Is it possible to discuss individual-level facts, as Durkheim does, with aggregate data? His data are not on the suicides of, for example, Catholics and Protestants, but on regions and nations and cities, which he identifies as largely Catholic or Protestant and so forth in order to make arguments about the effects of causal forces on suicide. This kind of inference is tricky, and some have criticized Durkheim's study on these grounds. His response is that he intends to refer the individual events he wants to describe to the facts in the social structure he sees as profoundly affecting if not wholly determining them.

Suicide as a Social Phenomenon in General

The book's final section consists of a sustained insistence that the facts described in earlier chapters are social facts, not mere individual-level phenomena. It is not, Durkheim avers, merely individual psychological makeup that we should look to as an explanation for the statistical data presented earlier; on the contrary, "[i]t is the moral constitution of society that determines at any moment the number of voluntary deaths" (Durkheim, 2006/1897, p. 331). Literally, the acts carried out by individuals are nothing more, and nothing less, than "the outcome and extension of a social state to which they give external form" (Durkheim, 2006/1897, p. 331). Social groups that can be identified along lines of religious affiliation, marital and familial status, occupational identification, and other variables discussed earlier in the book are marked by a collective tendency toward suicides of various types, and this tendency is determined by the currents of egoism, altruism, and anomie existing in the society in question (Durkheim, 2006/1897, p. 332). It is these social currents that give individuals in the affected groups a higher or lower propensity to suicide.

Durkheim addresses here the question of precisely how the statistical regularities should be translated to the individual level, given a properly sociological understanding of suicidal currents. Adolphe Quételet, a Belgian social statistician whose application of statistical reasoning to the human world proved influential on the early social sciences, had argued that statistical regularity could be effectively explained by recourse to the qualities of "the ordinary man"—that is, the typical member of the society in question who would inevitably carry within him the precipitate in individual characteristics of all the phenomena of statistical regularity (Durkheim, 2006/1897, p. 333). But this reasoning is incorrect, Durkheim argues. It is not as though, if 1% of the population annually dies of egoistic suicide, each "ordinary" member of the society will necessarily carry some evidence of the trait. The inclination to suicide is exceedingly rare, so the vast bulk of the population will give no evidence of contact by the forces that move individuals to commit suicide (Durkheim, 2006/1897, p. 335). If, as was so in France in Durkheim's day, there are about 150 suicides per million inhabitants, as a statistical probability for the individual this figure approaches zero (Durkheim, 2006/1897, p. 336). Quételet's "ordinary man" thus cannot show us the presence of the social force produced by insufficient or excessive integration or regulation. We need another framework.

In this initial chapter of the final book, which contains some of the most vivid and powerful sociological theorizing in all of Durkheim's published work, we find Durkheim again targeting Tarde and delivering a steady rain of critical observations on the latter's fundamentally individualist, psychological framework for explanation. The attack on Tarde is a sustained construction of an anti-individual methodology for sociology. Tarde would deny any "trancendency to social phenomena," arguing even that such seemingly transparently collective phenomena as language, moral maxims, or religious rituals are all reducible to the fact of one individual passing it to another (Durkheim, 2006/1897, p. 341). But the evidence of a collective phenomenon when we look at suicide is empirically evident for Durkheim in a powerfully salient way: How can suicide be a wholly individual phenomenon if the individuals making up a society change from year to year, some dying, others being born, and yet the rate of suicide remains unchanged, as it inevitably does, barring some broader social shift (Durkheim, 2006/1897, p. 340)? Tarde's claim that "once you remove the individual, the social is nothing" is true in the sense that social forces must have individuals upon which to act and give evidence of their presence, but this does not mean they can be reduced to the psychological contents of individual minds (Durkheim, 2006/1897, p. 345). On the contrary, social forces are, for Durkheim, "as real as cosmic forces," acting on the individual from outside just as natural forces do, if by different means (Durkheim, 2006/1897, p. 343). He speaks here even of a collective psyche—that is, individuals united together and forming a new kind of "psychic being" with "its own way of thinking and feeling" (Durkheim, 2006/1897, p. 344).

At this point in the text, Durkheim brings in a conceptual term that would emerge as central for him in later work. Social life is, he writes, just as individual psychological life, "essentially made up of representations with this difference: that collective representations are quite different in nature from individual ones" (Durkheim, 2006/1897, p. 346). In a startling passage that reads like a thumbnail summary of the essential argument from his last book, *The Elementary Forms,* he uses religion as an example of the realm of collective representations. Merely "individual states and private feelings" could not produce it as we know it. Religion is our grasping at the reality of something extra-individual: "Never would an individual have risen to the idea of forces that are so infinitely beyond him and everything around him, if all he had ever known was himself and his physical universe" (Durkheim, 2006/1897, p. 346). What is this force so far beyond the individual? Nothing more or less than society itself, which is in fact the gods in all their culturally variable guises in "hypostatic form" (Durkheim, 2006/1897, p. 347). Religion thus is "the system of symbols through which society becomes conscious of itself; it is the way of thinking peculiar to the collective being" (Durkheim, 2006/1897, p. 347).

Collective representations are external to the individual, fixed sometimes in material facts of the social world, such as architecture, which Durkheim classifies as an eminently social thing that demonstrates social life "exteriorized and act[ing] upon us from outside" (Durkheim, 2006/1897, p. 348). Sometimes the representations are not fixed, but "vague . . . free and untrammeled . . . circulating in every direction, crossing and intermingling in a thousand different ways" (Durkheim, 2006/1897, p. 348). Is the argument thus a materialist or an idealist one? The answer seems to be "neither" or "both." What is crystal clear is that Durkheim is arguing for a collection of collectively shared representations of reality that are not reducible to the contents of the individual psyche. Although individuals will inevitably tap into the body of collective representations, and a society is to be defined at least in part by the fact that the individuals making it up share some body of collective representations, each individual consciousness contains but a small piece of this body of representations, and its metaphysical existence, then, can be spoken of only as external to them (Durkheim, 2006/1897, p. 351). This is evident, he argues, in that the collective representations surrounding morality in a given group are reflective of a cultural ideal, and they cannot be found in their entirety in any one member of the group; after all, "the average man is very average when it comes to morality" (Durkheim, 2006/1897, p. 352). Collective moral pressure, however, is exerted on the individual through the collectivity of others. None of them holds the entire contents of the group's morality, but together they are in touch with much more of it than any one individual who strays from its ideal tenets, and they can therefore collectively exercise power to enforce the compliance of individuals (Durkheim, 2006/1897, p. 354). When one healthy youth riding a crowded bus lacks the moral compunction to rise and give up his seat to an elderly woman boarding the vehicle, it is unlikely that all of his fellow riders will be infused with the particular moral representation having to do with proper, expected procedure in such a case, but the more there are of them on the bus, the more likely that sentiment will be found and will express itself.

Suicide has a "double character," at once obviously a phenomenon that strikes individuals but deeply collective in its origins (Durkheim, 2006/1897, p. 357). The same process of "hypercivilization" that produces the anomic and egotistical currents also makes our nervous systems exceptionally sensitive, and this makes it more likely that they will be "less capable of attaching themselves consistently to a defined objective, more impatient of any discipline and more accessible to violent irritation and to exaggerated depression" (Durkheim, 2006/1897, pp. 358–359). So does the social force produce effects at the individual level, effects that may only accumulate in an individual over a lengthy period of time, and hence the higher propensity of suicide among older individuals (Durkheim, 2006/1897, pp. 360–361).

The care to avoid a crudely deterministic theory, precisely the kind of caricature of which Durkheim was accused by Tarde and others in his day, is extraordinary here. In a lengthy footnote at the end of this chapter, Durkheim is clear that his understanding of the force of social currents does not completely determine any outcomes in any specific individuals, who are still free in the classic philosophical sense. Although the sociological approach to suicide states that, once we know the social currents at work in a given group, individuals in given groups will, as an aggregate, kill themselves at a certain rate, no determination can be made of which individuals in the group will do so and which ones will not (Durkheim, 2006/1897, p. 361).

Durkheim then turns to a discussion of suicide in historical relief and in relation to the other major moral transgression involving the taking of human life, homicide. In the classical Greek and Roman world, suicide was illegal only if the State had not given its approval. In Rome, a citizen who desired to take his own life submitted a petition to the Senate, which made a ruling on whether the act could be carried out (Durkheim, 2006/1897, pp. 366, 367–368). Christianity imposed a vigorous criminal ban on all suicide, and some Christian societies went so far as to try suicides after the fact and then hang or drag the condemned body through the streets (Durkheim, 2006/1897, p. 363). Islam too unilaterally condemned the act of suicide (Durkheim, 2006/1897, p. 365). In France, the Revolution removed suicide from the criminal code, but religious morality continued in Durkheim's day to produce in most a sense of repulsion at the thought of suicide (Durkheim, 2006/1897, p. 364).

Why, Durkheim asks, is suicide in the *fin-de-siècle* France of his time still seen as negative despite having been decriminalized? This is due to the triumph of the cult of the human person that is the foundation of all modern morality in Durkheim's view (Durkheim, 2006/1897, p. 371). In this perspective, a suicide does not only harm herself. Society too is attacked and damaged whenever an attack is made on a human individual, which is where modern society's "most respected moral principles rest today" (Durkheim, 2006/1897, pp. 374–375). As the human individual has become a sacred thing, indeed the most sacred value of secularizing late-19th-century Europe, no attack on it can be permitted with impunity (Durkheim, 2006/1897, p. 375).

What is the relationship of suicide to homicide? Some argued for a close connection in origin of the two. Some held to the idea that suicide was simply homicide in altered form—that is, the suicidal, if prevented from killing themselves, would still want to expend the killing energy at the root of their desire, and that would be directed toward others in homicidal acts (Durkheim, 2006/1897, p. 379). In this view, suicide serves, then, as a "safety valve" that perhaps prevents acts of interpersonal lethal violence. But, Durkheim intervenes, if this relationship were so, we should see suicide and homicide rates going up or down in tandem in given societies according to the propensity to this unitary desire for lethal violence. Instead, the statistics indicate that European countries with high murder rates have comparatively low suicide rates (Durkheim, 2006/1897, p. 390). The two vary in opposing manners when seen through a number of other optics as well: Suicide tends to be more concentrated in urban areas, whereas homicide is more prevalent in rural settings. Catholicism seems to protect its members against suicide in comparison with Protestantism, but Catholic areas have higher murder rates. Intense and heavily populated family life reduces suicide but aggravates homicide rates (Durkheim, 2006/1897, pp. 393, 394). Durkheim's conclusion is that the different varieties of suicide he has enumerated have differing relationships to homicide. Egoistic suicide, characterized as it is by depression and apathy, is opposed to homicide, while anomic suicide, which is provoked by "a state of exasperation and irritated lassitude," may be more likely to show a positive relationship to homicide (Durkheim, 2006/1897, pp. 396, 398). Overall, suicide and homicide seem to represent two opposed social trends (Durkheim, 2006/1897, p. 399).

In the final chapter of the book, Durkheim turns at last to considerations of policy that emerge from the scientific examination of what he has argued is an eminently social problem. The first matter to be ascertained is whether it is actually the case that current suicide rates in the West are abnormally high. He refers to the argument in *The Rules,* wherein he had argued that forms of immorality in and of themselves are no proof of social "morbid[ity]" (Durkheim, 2006/1897, p. 403). A certain amount of suicide, as a certain amount of crime, is to be expected and is functional in some ways. Egotism has some social utility, as society would be unable to slough off exhausted traditional ways of life to create new ones without it (Durkheim, 2006/1897, p. 407). Sadness and melancholy too are necessities that human society cannot do without (Durkheim, 2006/1897, p. 408). The emotional concomitants of all three major types of suicide are salutary elements, so long as they are properly moderated: "While a spirit of self-denial [altruism], a love of progress [anomie], and a liking for individuation [egoism] have a place in every kind of society and cannot exist without becoming at certain points generators of suicide, they also necessarily have this property only to a particular degree, which varies from nation to nation. It is only justified if it does not exceed certain limits" (Durkheim, 2006/1897, p. 409).

The evidence, however, suggests that, in Durkheim's analysis at any rate, late-19th-century Europe was suffering from excessive amounts of these social currents and their correlated individual emotions. Durkheim's argument to demonstrate this is not the strongest element of his book. He suggests that simple rapidity of social change in recent years is itself an indicator that suicide rates are abnormally high, as such rapid and massive social change is essentially by definition morbid (Durkheim, 2006/1897, p. 412). More evidence of the pathology of contemporary Europe is to be found in the rise, among the elites, of pessimistic intellectual doctrines like those of the philosophers Arthur Schopenhauer and Karl von Hartmann and, among the masses, of the popular doctrines of "the anarchist, the aesthete, the mystic and the revolutionary socialist" (Durkheim, 2006/1897, p. 413).

The possible policy responses to this problem are, for various reasons, limited. Punishment would serve to reinforce the negative character of the act and perhaps to prevent some motivated to kill themselves from carrying the act through, but such punishment can only be moral and not criminal. The suicide could perhaps be denied an honorable burial, and failed suicides might be denied certain civil rights such as eligibility to stand for election to political office (Durkheim, 2006/1897, pp. 414–415). Education alone cannot solve the problem either, as educators and the educational institutions are deeply influenced by the broader society, and the tendency to avoid condemnation of suicide is so widespread that it has certainly "penetrated" into those institutions as well (Durkheim, 2006/1897, p. 416).

Of the four types discussed in the book, only two contribute to the modern problem of excessively high suicide rates. Fatalistic suicide merits not even a mention in this chapter, and excessive altruism is hardly a problem in the world Durkheim is describing. Egoistic and anomic suicide are the core of the problem in modernity (Durkheim, 2006/1897, p. 417). The question then becomes how to more effectively provide adequate social integration and moral regulation to those at risk of not receiving these required goods. Durkheim bleakly goes down the list of institutional sources we might look to for this task and describes why each cannot do so. The State is too distant from individuals; religious institutions have lost much of their influence under the withering assault of secular republicanism, and in any event can provide support to the individual only by constraining free thought in ways contrary to the direction of social evolution; and, while the family does have "an undoubted prophylactic benefit" and married people enjoy comparative protection from suicide *vis-à-vis* the unmarried, suicide rates for the married have risen historically at the same pace as the rates for the unmarried, and the family in modernity has generally been reduced to a smaller realm of influence (Durkheim, 2006/1897, pp. 417, 419, 420, 421).

The sole institution that might potentially have a real role to play here is the same one we have seen emerging in Durkheim's work elsewhere: the professional group or corporation (Durkheim, 2006/1897, p. 423). Unlike the Church or the family, the purview of the professional group has expanded in modernity, and it potentially provides both social integration and moral regulation (Durkheim, 2006/1897, p. 427).

But the optimism at this policy proposal is vague and quite limited. Durkheim returns to the problem of the seemingly "insurmountable" conflict in the marital institution. The same thing that strengthens men's resistance to suicide, namely reduction of divorce, increases the woman's propensity to kill herself, and the liberalization of divorce that would protect women would open men up to greater risk (Durkheim, 2006/1897, p. 429). Here, Durkheim extends his argument about the nature of this gender divide. Men and women interact with the institution of marriage differently because they "do not participate equally in social life" (Durkheim, 2006/1897, p. 429). Durkheim goes so far as to claim here that men and women will likely never be able to fulfill the same social functions, and he sees value in the functional diversification along gender lines. As, for example, men are largely obliged to absorb themselves in "utilitarian functions" to the exclusion of "aesthetic ones," why should women not be the legitimate rulers in the latter realm (Durkheim, 2006/1897, p. 430)?

Durkheim is a consummate communitarian here, although his argument against too-sudden efforts at overarching social change along the lines of gender equality sounds conservative. Legal equality requires first the reduction of the "flagrant psychological inequality" existing between the sexes, and Durkheim recommends efforts to reduce the latter prior to any moves in the direction of broader legal changes. He ends on a note that is open to the possibility that women and men might be made at least somewhat more alike in terms of their need for the marital institution, and such change would be necessary if marriage can be reasonably considered as an option for reducing suicide rates (Durkheim, 2006/1897, p. 431). It is, to repeat, not a conservative position that emerges here but a carefully historically grounded communitarian one—contingent, open to various possibilities, but concerned that policy options work from reality and not simply from utopian fictions and desires.

   He brings the book to a close by making clear that it is not merely a study of suicide but rather a scientific effort to come to grips with some of the basic social problems wrought by modernity. The emergence of highly individualized, secular, industrialized, capitalist republican societies in the West has wrought massive social and cultural change, much of it obviously historically progressive and even necessary, but it has not offered solutions for repairing the gaping wounds in the older institutions and social bodies rent by the sudden and violent ruptures of the modern world, and there are real and grave issues that must be resolved if modernity is not to reveal itself more bane than boon. The individual is freer; the family and the Church have been weakened, the latter perhaps fatally; and the sole collective entity that emerges stronger than before is the State, which is too distant from us to compel the kind of intense moral and social attachment we require to live balanced and fulfilled lives. Mediating institutions are lacking, and if the professional group cannot emerge to fill this gap, the prognosis is not optimistic (Durkheim, 2006/1897, p. 437).

Conclusion

The results in Durkheim's day of his efforts to contribute to the founding of a new social science with the publication of these two books were mixed. *The Rules* is probably the single most-read work Durkheim wrote, and many summaries of his approach to sociology are based, often inappropriately so, on this book alone, and even on one chapter in the book. Yet, in Durkheim's lifetime, the book received a critical response, even by some of those sympathetic to the effort to make the case for sociology as a unique, empirically based science. One of the closest associates of Durkheim and his students, the philosopher, ENS librarian, and leading figure in Parisian intellectual socialist circles, Lucien Herr, described the book as conjuring up "the ghost of the old realist metaphysics" (Borlandi & Mucchielli, 1995, p. 272). Durkheim himself had the impression that it was largely a failed effort, at least in terms of its effect in proselytizing for Durkheimian sociology. Today, one of the most important commentators on Durkheim's work, Steven Lukes, writing in the preface to a new translation of the book, has bluntly classified *The Rules* as not among his best works, arguing not only that it does not give a good guide to how Durkheim actually did sociology subsequently (i.e., he broke his own rules), but also that it is a good demonstration of "why [the] aspiration [to an objective social science] was, and must remain, frustrated" (Durkheim, 1982/1895, p. 23). Nonetheless, its place among the classics of social science is assured. It was seen by many sympathetic readers of the time as a much-needed assault on dilettantism in sociology, as Durkheim mercilessly criticizes those who would use the term in order to attempt to legitimize impressionistic and unsystematic efforts to examine the social world.

Suicide certainly failed to produce the response Durkheim perhaps, in his heart of hearts, hoped to achieve. In several letters to Marcel Mauss in the wake of its publication, he complained of being caught between two worlds with this book, the specialists finding the book too broadly pitched and the "literary types" disdaining the book's scientific rigor (Durkheim, 1998, p. 48), and he bleakly anticipated a fair approximation of what would turn out to be the book's reception in France: "I feel profoundly discouraged. I thought my *Suicide* was going to dissolve the misunderstandings . . . [but] I have the impression, and it matters little whether it is founded or unfounded, that [it] will be a sword strike in the water" (Durkheim, 1998, pp. 77, 78).

After the book's initial publication in 1897, it was reissued in 1912, the same year Durkheim published *The Elementary Forms,* and thereafter no new editions appeared until the 1960s. In France, the book was almost certainly his least successful. It was largely ignored in the English-speaking world until the 1950s, and it was the last of Durkheim's major works to be translated, in 1950 (Besnard, 2003, p. 231). Yet, despite all this, it is now recognized as a classic text in the establishment of the reasoning of the discipline of sociology.

A few questions

- Why did Durkheim reject methodological individualism? Who comes out looking more "sociologically correct" in today's world, Durkheim or Gabriel Tarde?
- Is a fully objective sociology of the kind proposed in *The Rules* possible?

- Is suicide a social problem of the same sort it was in Durkheim's day?
- What is the evidence that the ongoing increase of social disintegration and decrease of moral regulation that Durkheim essentially predicted in *Suicide* has been borne out?
- Which seems more important and useful as a sociological concept in today's world: social integration or moral regulation?

5

Education as Social Science and Cultural Politics

D urkheim's first position in a university was as a professor of pedagogy and education, though this was due not so much to his pre-existing interest in education *per se* as to the realities of the French educational system in the late 19th century. At the time Durkheim received his first appointment at a university, in 1887, after a number of years in public service as a teacher in a *lycée* (high school), sociology did not yet exist as a discipline in the French intellectual world. Marcel Mauss wrote that Durkheim saw his teaching load in education, which extended from the beginning of his career at Bordeaux through his time at the Sorbonne, as "a weight" that he perceived as a "breaking up of his activity" and an interruption of his sociological work and teaching, which he saw as clearly more important (Mauss, 1925).

But Durkheim, according to Mauss, inevitably brought the same genius and originality found in his other work to his lectures on education, and he even found a way, ultimately, to make his teaching on education and pedagogy into something more than the merely practical task of informing future teachers how to do their jobs. In Durkheim's hands, these courses became a contribution to his broader intellectual concerns regarding the workings of human societies and cultures.

In this chapter, we will focus on the three book-length collections of his writing on education that were culled from his lecture courses after his death. The two topics—sociology and pedagogy/education—were not easily separable in Durkheim's view, since the former presented a view of the human consciousness that was reliant on education as the central engine of the humanizing or making human of the infant and the latter would need to be modified significantly in modernity to reflect current knowledge about the state of things human, which included the new discipline of sociology and its radically innovative way of understanding human phenomena. Debates during Durkheim's lifetime on the establishment of a secular educational system and the role the educational system should play in helping produce citizens of the recently established Republic help situate his work in this area.

The end of the 19th century in France was a period of significant educational reform. In 1868, the minister of public instruction, Victor Duruy, commissioned a large-scale statistical study of the French system of higher education. He championed the German university as a model for imitation by the French, and he advocated increased efforts to study the German system. As a result of his efforts, French scholars (including Durkheim himself) were sent to Germany to study its educational methods in close detail. Duruy was responsible for the creation (in that same year of 1868) of the École Pratique des Hautes Études, an institution for specialized postgraduate study that mirrored important aspects of the coveted German research institute (Weisz, 1983, pp. 60–62). Duruy provided an important ministerial focal point for a more general sentiment felt by many in the teaching profession that major reform was necessary. The coming of the Third Republic pushed educational reform ahead with a renewed urgency, as it now became explicitly linked to political agendas as well as to the professional interests of the class of teachers. There was much evidence of a general fear of national inferiority in light of the overwhelmingly superior performance of the German educational system and the obvious dividends it paid in scientific research, technological advance, and military power. This was linked to the suspicion that such inferiority was an indication of a general cultural decline, so it was widely believed that the malaise in the educational system had to be treated by renewed ideological and pedagogical efforts toward social unity and order.

Some important republican political figures supported reform because they believed higher education could be harnessed to some of the more important political goals of the new regime—that is, social integration and the construction of a secular moral ideology. In line with the dominant political ideology of the early years of the Republic, which was the **solidarism** of Léon Bourgeois and the Radical Party (Hayward, 1961), the advocates of reform in the political classes saw a need for educational change as part of the larger social task of constructing a social democracy that would avoid the Scylla and Charybdis of extremist collectivism (on both the right and the left) and liberal economic individualism of an asocial variety. The solidarist republican politicians sought to enlist the reform movement to the extent possible in their own project, which was itself inspired by the positivist, anticlerical, and social reformist French Revolutionary tradition. This marriage of political and professional goals in the reform movement contributed to making educational debates at the *fin-de-siècle* one of the most explosive cultural powder kegs in the history of the Third Republic.

Attempts to construct a secular morality took on a social and cultural import at the turn of the century that is unmatched in other periods. The very term **morale laïque** (secular morality) is an invention of the Third Republic, intended specifically to refer to the ethical precepts and system taught in the public school system (Stock-Morton, 1988, p. 1). All those who proposed some variation of a secular morality were, though opposed to one another on a range of other issues, united in one common undertaking: the displacement of the ethical and moral authority of the Roman Catholic Church and its largely Jesuit pedagogical institutions.

Durkheim was an important participant in the debates over reform, especially after his arrival in Paris at the Sorbonne in 1902. It was even speculated by some that the reason he was called up to that central post to replace Ferdinand Buisson in a chair in Science of Education had much more to do with his sympathy with the reformers and with the project for a secular ethics than with the actual substance of his work. Once he had moved to the position at the Sorbonne, his course on pedagogy and education became a focal point for the debate around the reform movement. The year of Durkheim's arrival in Paris also witnessed the enactment of several key reforms in the university system that still further emphasized his stature in the reform debates. In 1902, an alternative curriculum, the *enseignement secondaire spécial* (special secondary curriculum), that had been created initially for students destined for careers in industry who were deemed too academically weak to master the traditional French classical curriculum of Greek and Latin and replaced those subjects with applied sciences and a modern foreign language, was formally given equal status with the classical curriculum. This led to calls for changes in the organization of pedagogical study and to the incorporation of the École Normale Supérieure, the elite institution traditionally charged with the education of secondary and university professors, into the University of Paris in 1903. The logical outgrowth of these various moves toward regularization of pedagogical education for those seeking to become secondary and university professors was the move to require all such students in the Parisian university system to attend a core course on the history of pedagogy in France. Who better to deliver such a course than Durkheim? Thus, from the first year of his assumption of the Sorbonne chair, Durkheim's course (first, on moral education; then, beginning in 1904, on pedagogical evolution in France) was the only required course for all candidates for the *agrégation* (state teaching certificate) in the Parisian system. This provided him a tremendous influence, especially given the results of yet another important shift in the educational system that saw a significant increase of the percentage of *lycée* teachers holding the *agrégation,* and therefore made for a much closer flow of ideas from the university level to the secondary educational system and on throughout French society (Weisz, 1983, p. 276).

Education and Sociology

This book consists of four chapters. The first two, titled "Education" and "Pedagogy," were published originally in 1911 in a dictionary of pedagogy and primary education edited by Ferdinand Buisson, whose chair at the Sorbonne Durkheim had taken when Buisson was elected to the French Assembly. The third chapter was the first lecture from Durkheim's first course at the Sorbonne in 1902, and the final chapter was the introductory lecture in the course on secondary education he gave beginning in 1904, the rest of which was published in 1938 as the posthumous book discussed later in this chapter. All four chapters (though not the collected volume) were published in Durkheim's lifetime, and together they provide a broad overview of his thinking on pedagogy and education and their relationship to sociology.

Education: Its Nature and Role

Durkheim begins the first chapter, appropriately given the title, with an effort to define "education." He cites Kant's definition, which tell us that the end of education is "to develop . . . perfection" in an individual to the extent possible (Durkheim, 1956/1922, p. 62). Perfection is here defined as "the harmonious development of all the human faculties," but while this is desirable, Durkheim admits, it is unattainable, and moreover it works at counterpurposes to another common goal of education, which is to teach the required tasks to be performed by each individual who will take up some specific place in a complex division of labor. What then about a more utilitarian definition of education that would, for example, follow the utilitarian philosopher James Mill and set as its goal preparing the individual to add to the overall happiness in society? This falls into the problem of subjectivity, as each will have his own definition of happiness (Durkheim, 1956/1922, p. 63).

Both of these general, abstract definitions of education fail because they do not recognize the historically contingent nature of education. The goals sought by education in Periclean Athens were not those of the Roman Empire, which in turn differed from those of the Middle Ages. There are perhaps as many different kinds of education, with as many different goals, as there are different kinds of societies (Durkheim, 1956/1922, pp. 64, 67). What all varieties of education, in all places and in all times, have in common is the fundamental sociological work of socialization by adults of younger members of the society, whether this socialization is broadly intended for all members of the society in common or directed solely at those members who will go on to perform specific tasks (Durkheim, 1956/1922, p. 71). Education, that is, has a fundamentally social character.

Durkheim then invokes his notion of homo duplex, the idea that the human individual is two beings united in one. The one is purely individual, guided by mental states and life events specific to each of us as individuals, while the other has to do with "ideas, sentiments and practices which express in us ... the group or different groups of which we are part" (Durkheim, 1956/1922, p. 72). He is referring in the latter case to collective representations, whether religious, moral, professional, or some other mode of the collective. The goal of education is to "constitute this being in each of us" (Durkheim, 1956/1922, p. 72). It is, after all, society in us that makes us something more than our animal selves. Someone left only to develop the individual side of her being and not given over to education in the sense that Durkheim defines it would not become a fully human being, as it is this unity of the two sides of our nature that makes us human.

The central and most compelling element of the chapter focuses on the role of authority and compulsion in education. In contemporary American educational culture, the notion that learning should or even must be fun is taken as proverbial, and Durkheim's argument here will perhaps sound like something from another planet for those acculturated in today's educational world. "Nothing," Durkheim writes, "is so false ... as the Epicurean conception of education"—that is, the idea that education can be purely pleasurable (Durkheim, 1956/1922, p. 87). He bases his argument here on the nature of the child. While education cannot create a functioning adult from nothing, it nonetheless begins its work with a creature endowed only with "very general and vague ... innate predispositions" (Durkheim, 1956/1922, p. 82). These basic predispositions can and must be harnessed in such a way as to bring the child into social being. Durkheim uses the analogy of hypnosis to describe the manner in which the educator impresses the lesson upon the child (Durkheim, 1956/1922, p. 85). The child is, necessarily, in a state of passivity, not because he is stupid but simply because he is a child, and a child is a creature with a deep, inchoate, innate desire to be directed and to follow the lead of his elders. Upon this passivity, the educator takes the role of the hypnotist, commanding the subject's response.

Again, it is likely that the contemporary, liberally educated reader will react to such an idea with something approaching shock, if not horror, but Durkheim's argument here can be easily dismissed only by those who do not think seriously about the social and cultural realities that undergird pedagogy. In a smooth dialectical move, Durkheim refuses a simplistic opposition of liberty and authority: "Liberty is the daughter of authority properly understood" (Durkheim, 1956/1922, p. 90). Liberty here is defined not as the ability to do whatever one likes, an impossibility in any event, but as the capacity to master oneself. The discussion here can be made more comprehensible if it is compared in the American context with the clichés about the opposition of freedom and authority so frequently heard in today's political arena. As Robert Bellah and his cowriters pointed out so magnificently in their monumental book *Habits of the Heart* (1985), such a superficial and sociologically incomprehensible definition of freedom cannot be found in the thinking of the American Founders, the wisest of whom envisioned freedom as the capacity of the wise person to choose freely from among the several options which moral code one will adhere to and serve.

The Nature and Method of Pedagogy

In this pithy chapter, Durkheim distinguishes the meaning of the terms "education" and "pedagogy." While the two are obviously parts of a unified enterprise, education must be thought of as the practice and pedagogy as the theory. The role of **pedagogy** is not to "substitute for [the] practice" of education, "but to guide [and] enlighten it" (Durkheim, 1956/1922, p. 107). We must, however, determine first precisely what pedagogy consists of and what it is intended to produce (Durkheim, 1956/1922, p. 92). How do we go about this task? We can study pedagogy scientifically, as we do any other properly sociological object, for the form of education existing in any given society is a social fact in just the same sense that language or the currency system are (Durkheim, 1956/1922, pp. 93, 94). We may believe that we freely choose educational techniques, but these are customs and institutions with a coercive power over us. Simply by virtue of living in a given social environment, we are provided with an educational culture that is essentially inescapable. These collective ideas and sentiments have the same power over us as material laws. The settled opinion of the collectivity, though it be "merely" opinion, nonetheless directs our thought and our action with considerable tenacity (Durkheim, 1956/1922, pp. 94–95). Different societies have different types of education, as they have different familial structures and different religions, but an important commonality of all is their external and coercive nature (Durkheim, 1956/1922, p. 97). This is all quite consistent with Durkheim's arguments in *The Rules* on social facts.

Classifying pedagogy is complicated by the fact that it seems to bridge the gap between theory and practice, as it is a "practical theory" that occupies an "intermediate mental attitude" between the "pure practice without theory" of art and the pure theory of science (Durkheim, 1956/1922, pp. 101, 102). Durkheim compares it in this quality to medicine and politics, which also consist of an admixture of theoretical speculation and practical application. The study of pedagogy accepts two fundamental axioms: It must be a historical inquiry, for the future can be guided only with direction from the past; and it must recognize the tremendous explanatory power of sociology (Durkheim, 1956/1922, p. 110). A classroom, Durkheim writes, is a "small society," and a group of students together "think, feel, and behave" differently than they do when alone (Durkheim, 1956/1922, p. 112).

Pedagogy and Sociology

In this, his inaugural lecture in Paris in 1902, Durkheim summarizes much of the core content of his course on moral education, which he gave for many years between 1899 and 1912. Though intimately aware of the title of his chair and duly praising his predecessor Ferdinand Buisson, who was perhaps the most eminent professor of education in France at the time, Durkheim nonetheless makes clear to his audience that "[i]t is above all as a sociologist that I shall speak to you of education" (Durkheim, 1956/1922, p. 114). It is evident, he argues, that education is a deeply social phenomenon, indeed that it can rightly be defined as "the means by which society perpetually recreates the conditions of its very existence" (Durkheim, 1956/1922, p. 123). As each new generation is born, in cultural terms a *tabula rasa*, society must implant itself anew in each member's deepest being in order to divert them from their natural inclination to egoism and antisociality (Durkheim, 1956/1922, p. 125). In modern societies, education might seem an abstract, formal institution, very distant from the informal techniques and initiation ceremonies of more primitive groups, but the work it does is the same in both kinds of human group: to make the individual a new kind of entity, forcing him to undergo a "second birth" after which he is no longer the same thing he was before but instead now a fully formed social being (Durkheim, 1956/1922, p. 126). Alluding again to the theory of *homo duplex* at the core of his sociology, Durkheim argues that "the best in us is of social origin" (Durkheim, 1956/1922, p. 133).

We can see easily, with but a little examination, that psychology alone is an insufficient tool for the pedagogue. A fully developed psychology (which we do not have even now, a hundred years after Durkheim) would give us insights into the workings of the human mind of eminent practical value in the classroom, but it could not tell the teacher what ends to pursue in that education: "Sociology alone can either help us to understand it, by relating it to the social conditions on which it depends and which it expresses, or help us to discover it when the public conscience, disturbed and uncertain, no longer knows what it should be" (Durkheim, 1956/1922, p. 129). Psychology can show us the proper means of education, but only sociology allows us to investigate the ends it serves. With psychology, we learn how best to get the student to learn X, Y, or Z, but we need a sociology of education to explain why learning X, Y, or Z is desirable and what social consequences such learning can be expected to produce (Durkheim, 1956/1922, p. 130).

Evolution and Role of Secondary Education in France

The final chapter in this brief book is the first lecture in the course on the history of secondary education in France that Durkheim gave in Paris from 1904 through 1913. This course was part of the required lectures for all candidates to sit for the *agrégation,* the examination that permitted university graduates to compete for open *lycée* teaching positions and then perhaps eventually enter the ranks of the professoriate. Though it is a history course, Durkheim proposes, its overarching context and impetus are fully contemporary. Historical knowledge of the French university system, he argues, is required in order to understand what changes in the system must be made in the present. Secondary education was, in the time this lecture was delivered, undergoing a significant period of crisis, and though it was widely recognized that the past system could not be simply reinstated, it was not quite so clear exactly what was to be done going forward (Durkheim, 1956/1922, p. 141). With the two courses on education introduced in these last two chapters of the book, the one historical, the other contemporary, and both deeply meditating on the social context of educational methods and goals, Durkheim was intervening in a major way on the broad debates in France about how to reform education for a secular Republic.

The educational goals of the French university varied historically. In the late Middle Ages, the goal was to make "dialecticians" of students; in the Renaissance, it was to make them "humanists" (Durkheim, 1956/1922, p. 141). The goal today, Durkheim notes, is yet in vigorous dispute, which infinitely complicates the project. Although "no new faith" has yet emerged to take the place of that which has been dismantled, the goal, he asserts to these young men who will become the next generation of teachers, must be to create such a faith: "A teaching body without pedagogical faith is a body without a soul. Your first duty and your first concern are, then, to restore a soul to the body into which you are to enter" (Durkheim, 1956/1922, p. 144). It might sound strange to hear a secular, rationalist sociologist such as Durkheim talking of faith, but he certainly recognized the terms and the register that would be effective for his listeners, and, as we will see in Chapter 6, he also appreciated the limits of purely rational discourse and the emotional power of certain aspects of the religious life.

In order to look ahead, he emphasizes, the students must first be on intimate terms with the history from which they have emerged. Here, and in the details in the full lectures from this course, the blithe criticism one sometimes hears today of Durkheim as an ahistorical thinker is reduced to so much dust. In this course, Durkheim displays all the fine attention to detail of the best historians, combined with a sociologist's eye for broad theoretical principles of causes and effects to bring all that detail together into a coherent image of the past.

The Evolution of Educational Thought: Lectures on the Formation and Development of Secondary Education in France

This book's title is incorrect. Maurice Halbwachs, who edited the French edition, took the title given for the first lecture in the course, which had previously been published in the *Revue bleue,* as the course title. Durkheim had, however, given the course itself the title "History of Secondary Education in France" (Besnard, 2003, p. 122). It is an apt title, since Durkheim plunges deep into the past of secondary and higher education in these lectures.

He begins with a statement of the intellectual principle guiding the course; it is the same intellectual principle he put to work in all of his major studies of specific phenomena, whether the division of labor, or suicide, or religion. Only by a painstaking study of the past, he writes, can we come to firm grips with the present and the future (Durkheim, 1977/1938, p. 9). Too much allergy to history and to sociology and an uncritical reliance on decontextualized reason alone in the study of educational theory and method can produce damaging errors (Durkheim, 1977/1938, p. 13).

The early Christian Church had a fundamental effect on early secondary education. Fundamental among the values it endeavored to impart to students were "contempt for the joys of this world, for material and psychological luxury . . . renunciation" (Durkheim, 1977/1938, p. 20). "[S]imple hearts and minds" were the educational goal (Durkheim, 1977/1938, p. 21). Christian education was intended to shape the moral being of the student as much as or more than his merely intellectual character (Durkheim, 1977/1938, p. 29). The Greeks, by contrast, had not recognized the "deep recesses of soul" that Christian education aimed to shape (Durkheim, 1977/1938, p. 30). Reaching these depths required making the school into a living, moral community.

The Medieval Period: Rise of the University

Durkheim strides briskly through the early Middle Ages in French education, noting which periods were constructive for education (the Gallic, that of the Benedictines and Irish monks) and which were not (the Frankish; Durkheim, 1977/1938, pp. 31–36). The Irish monastic movement contributed greatly to the educational policies of Charlemagne and the Carolingian Renaissance, not least in elevating the monk to the position of key educational figure in Christian Europe. The monk essentially became the "schoolmaster of Europe" in this period (Durkheim, 1977/1938, p. 39). For Christian Europe, truth was a unity, and all pointed neatly to religion. The seven recognized arts were divided into the *trivium* (grammar, rhetoric, and dialectic, which together make up the *logica*) and the *quadrivium* (geometry, arithmetic, astronomy, and music, which make up the *physica*; Durkheim, 1977/1938, pp. 47–48). Much later, these would become the modern equivalents with which we are familiar: the humanities and the natural sciences.

In the Middle Ages, the *quadrivium* was reserved for a small elite, the equivalent of today's higher education students, and the *trivium* made up the general educational curriculum at what we would in the United States today call high school. Grammar became the focal point in the curriculum, as rhetoric and dialectic were viewed somewhat suspiciously by a Christian world with a rigid notion of truth and seen largely only as a means to combat falsehoods (Durkheim, 1977/1938, p. 53). From the 9th to the 12th century, we can speak of the Age of Grammar. All knowledge was seen as residing in texts in this period, and especially in the Bible. The study of grammar was shrouded in Christian mystery, as language was seen as always referring to some religious significance, and though Durkheim recognized this as "an inadequate diet for the mind," he maintains that the study of grammar is an indispensable method for teaching logical thought (Durkheim, 1977/1938, p. 57).

This grammar-centered education of the Carolingian period set the stage for the rise of Scholasticism. The great intellectual problem for Scholastic Christianity of the Middle Ages was that of universals—that is, whether abstract and universal ideas such as "good" or "red" were actually existing realities or merely constructions the mind applies to things (Durkheim, 1977/1938, p. 64). This led from grammar to the study of ontology, or the nature of reality itself.

Social and political events informed Scholastic education as well. The Crusades of the 11th century had as their goal the unifying of Christian society, and the effervescence that infused these military efforts fueled the educational system as well, as more and more desired to become educated to play their part in the struggle for the universal victory of Christianity (Durkheim, 1977/1938, p. 67). Renowned scholars at certain focal points in Europe attracted students from the entire continent.

The beginning of the 12th century marked a critical event in the French educational system. As the Capetian monarchy consolidated itself and established itself permanently in Paris, the latter city became the veritable center of France and the École de Paris became its central educational institution. At this same moment there appeared a charismatic figure who made a crucial contribution to French educational history: Peter Abelard (Durkheim, 1977/1938, p. 60). He was a personification of the intellectual standard of the Middle Ages: "brilliant dialectic, faith grounded in reason, and that curious mixture of religious fervor and a passion for knowledge which was the distinguishing mark of this great era" (Durkheim, 1977/1938, p. 70). When he began teaching at Paris, he made the new capital an intellectual focal point for all of Europe (Durkheim, 1977/1938, p. 71).

Durkheim then describes the creation of the University of Paris in the context of a deeply sociological argument about the university as a corporative body formed by a group of teachers united by a feeling of solidarity and professional interest against the competing interests of the Church. Once again in Durkheim's work we see the emergence of the theme of the corporate professional group as a foundationally important form of social federation and solidarity. Teachers had an age-old custom of conferring authority on their pupils to become teachers themselves by attending the inaugural lectures of the latter and then, at the lecture's conclusion, kissing and thereby giving a blessing to the pupil after the first lesson. This came to be known as the *inceptio,* and it was the mechanism by which teachers themselves protected and reproduced teacherly knowledge and status (Durkheim, 1977/1938, pp. 80–81). The chancellor of Notre-Dame, however, as the leading representative of the Church in the educational system, had asserted the right to award another degree to future teachers, the license or *licentia docendi,* which was a requirement for admission to the *inceptio.* The corporate body of teachers objected to Church control over any significant element of their ability to admit members to their ranks.

These two degrees, and the two corporate bodies behind them (Church and teaching professionals), were in staunch opposition to one another, and the resulting conflict was bitter. Here was the origin of a major struggle of opposing forces in the French university, the "traditional power of the Church" versus the "new power" of the emerging corporation of teachers (Durkheim, 1977/1938, p. 83). Eventually, and with the somewhat surprising aid of the Pope, the teachers obtained substantial gains *vis-à-vis* the chancellor's authority, and the long, progressive march toward the university's establishment of autonomy from the Church began (Durkheim, 1977/1938, p. 84).

In time, the University of Paris grew to have such importance in European intellectual life that it could be fairly said that while the Church had its head in Rome, the intellectual body of European Christendom was in Paris. Yet the question of whether the emerging university was a secular or an ecclesiastical body persisted (Durkheim, 1977/1938, p. 93). Struggles of the faculty against the chancellor, as just described, and their later fight with two monastic orders, the Franciscans and the Domincans, over the teaching of theology made it clear that the university was not a simple organ of the Church, even though the orders eventually won those battles with the faculty (Durkheim, 1977/1938, p. 94). The Church had effectively given birth to the university, but Durkheim asserts that the historical evidence showed it to be neither a purely secular nor a purely religious institution even at this early stage (Durkheim, 1977/1938, p. 95).

Four faculties made up the early university: theology, law, medicine, and liberal arts. As the liberal arts faculty was the only one of these bodies made up of nonspecialist teachers of "general culture," Durkheim restricts his discussion to it (Durkheim, 1977/1938, p. 101).

He makes a compelling sociological sketch of the medieval university student's life. If some contemporary critics of campus life are worried about debauchery and immorality among today's college students, they would be truly horrified at the historical portrait Durkheim provides us here. Students in Paris in the Middle Ages were absolutely steeped in the most dire depravity (Durkheim, 1977/1938, p. 114). They drank constantly and frequented the company of the lowliest criminals, and rape and murder were common offenses in student circles (Durkheim, 1977/1938, p. 115). The practice of boarding students was made obligatory to cut students off from the outside world and moderate these excesses (Durkheim, 1977/1938, p. 116). Durkheim explicitly compares the boarding school system with the cloistering of monks; and, though he recognizes the reasons for its emergence, he sees it as counterproductive, even "morbid" in its overall effects (Durkheim, 1977/1938, p. 124).

What did a day's instruction look like in the Middle Ages? The students of 13th- or 14th-century Paris sat not at desks but on the ground, in order to stifle pride (Durkheim, 1977/1938, p. 132). The teacher then read or dictated to them from a small collection of "great books." All teaching in the university consisted of "commentary on a specific book," and classes were not organized around subjects, as in today's university, but around specific books and their authors. Thus, pursuing a course of study came to be known as "listening to a book," or in Latin, *audire librum* (Durkheim, 1977/1938, p. 133). We see this element of the origins of our contemporary university in the title of "lecturer," which comes from the Latin verb *legere,* "to read."

The Scholastic period of the French university runs roughly from the 12th to the 16th century. For all that one might imagine that an atheist social scientist of the late 19th century must have disdained it, Durkheim insists again that the Middle Ages are badly named. The term would suggest it was merely an intermediate period between the important moments of classical antiquity and modernity, but Durkheim argues it was "admirably fertile," a "period of gestation" of a "new civilization" (Durkheim, 1977/1938, pp. 31, 161). Here, as we have already seen in his lectures on socialism and professional ethics, Durkheim recognizes the important preparatory work that was done in premodern Europe to make possible what came afterward and shows an insight into the complexities of social change that is not often recognized by commentators on his work.

The Renaissance and the Jesuits

With the Renaissance arrives a new epoch in higher education. In the Middle Ages, the task of the university had been to create a foundation for the faith, and so the university took one aspect of Greek knowledge—that is, logic—and made an entire educational system of it (Durkheim, 1977/1938, p. 164). In the 16th century, the European intellectual world turned outside the self to know the external world. But, Durkheim is clear, this was not a merely ideational shift. On the contrary, he writes, significant transformations in educational culture are "always the result and symptom of social transformations" (Durkheim, 1977/1938, p. 166). There was a massive rise of new markets and a rapid growth in towns. The Americas were "discovered," and curiosity about the material world ballooned. Social class distances were shrinking with the successes of early market capitalism, and the slow rise of the bourgeoisie began (Durkheim, 1977/1938, pp. 169–170). Another fundamental change had to do with the fragmentation of Christianity in the wake of the Protestant Reformation and the consequent storm of free inquiry (Durkheim, 1977/1938, p. 171). The material prosperity weakened the ascetic spirit of the Middle Ages, while the schism of the Church withered the power of dogma (Durkheim, 1977/1938, p. 172). In the midst of all this structural change, the goals of secondary and higher education were transformed from the training of Christian logicians to the creation of the "elegant and fluent nobleman" (Durkheim, 1977/1938, p. 171).

Durkheim examines the two chief elements of the new university culture during the Renaissance: the encyclopedic movement, represented by François Rabelais, and the humanist movement, personified by Desiderius Erasmus. In the vision of Rabelais, all of nature and all things natural are good, and all knowledge is good and desirable. An educational theory that sees discipline and restriction of freedom as fundamentally negative and articulates an unquenchable thirst for knowledge driven by what Durkheim calls "the need for infinitude" emerges from this Rabelaisian perspective (Durkheim, 1977/1938, p. 188). The encyclopedic totality of knowledge is the goal here.

Erasmus too perceived education's goal as the making of the student into a "polymath," but there is an important difference with respect to Rabelais (Durkheim, 1977/1938, p. 192). Erasmus stressed not simply knowledge from the reading of texts, but also the method of teaching students the arts of speaking and writing (Durkheim, 1977/1938, p. 194). The ultimate end here is "the art of self-expression," and the means is training and practice in writing and speaking Greek and Latin (Durkheim, 1977/1938, p. 198). Here, Durkheim notes, we are not far from the secondary school practice of the France of the late 19th century (Durkheim, 1977/1938, p. 196). Literature and literary polish are seen as the ends of education, and Durkheim cautions us about the "aristocratic mentality" behind such a vision. Such learning is fundamentally about "luxury" rather than the practical (Durkheim, 1977/1938, p. 229).

In both incarnations, educational theory and practice in the Renaissance fail to reckon with the fact that, in Durkheim's view, education is "first and foremost social, integrally bound up with other social functions, and that consequently it must prepare the child to take his place in society, play a useful part in life" (Durkheim, 1977/1938, p. 229).

At this point in the story, enter the Society of Jesus, or the Jesuits, who exerted great influence over the French secondary education system beginning in the 17th century. This movement was generated by the perceived need in the Catholic Church to challenge the advance of Protestantism, and so the Jesuit educational philosophy was focused on "piety and literature"— that is, a literate culture based in Greek and Latin classicism similar to that professed by Erasmus but with humanism firmly contained by the new goal centered on turning students into "faithful Catholics who respect tradition" (Durkheim, 1977/1938, pp. 243, 254).

The Jesuit system relied on two principles: close and frequent contact between students and their educators, so as to thoroughly immerse the student in the authority and the dogmatic ideas of the system; and stimulation of the students through constant and rigorous competition against one another (Durkheim, 1977/1938, pp. 258, 259, 260). A Jesuit-run classroom would be divided into two warring sides of "Romans" and "Carthaginians" and then set at one another in more or less merciless ways. Durkheim gives an example of having a student's work corrected by another student obviously less intelligent and talented than the first in order to provoke shame and a fierce desire to improve in the first student (Durkheim, 1977/1938, p. 260).

The force that drove the Jesuit revolution was the fact that the individual had in the 17th century begun to emerge in the contemporary form by which we understand the term. An individual who has "acquire[d] self-consciousness" cannot be motivated in an educational setting by the same mechanisms that work in a more collectivist cultural setting, so the competitive methods were devised specifically to speak to the individual's will to excel and triumph (Durkheim, 1977/1938, pp. 263, 264).

The Modern French University

Finally, Durkheim arrives at the last phase in the history of French secondary education, "that improved and more rational brand of Humanism which found its most perfect expression in Cartesianism" (Durkheim, 1977/1938, p. 278). He begins here by describing the educational theory of John Amos Comenius (1592–1670), a Czech by birth who lived in many European cities and made a major contribution to the modern understanding of education. Here, we find an emerging challenge to merely classical culture and a fresh emphasis on "the world of things [and] of reality" (Durkheim, 1977/1938, p. 286). For Comenius, the sciences alone give us accurate knowledge of the world, and education must be according to nature (Durkheim, 1977/1938, p. 287). It took the French Revolution to bring the realist educational vision of Comenius fully into play in France, as its central theorists articulated similar ideas of all knowledge as a unity to be assembled through investigation of the external world (Durkheim, 1977/1938, pp. 292, 294).

The Revolution's educational philosophy emphasized general grammar, history, and legislation in education; history was here understood as the history of the "great ideas" behind the rise of the modern, rational world (Durkheim, 1977/1938, pp. 298, 299). Literature and literary culture did not disappear altogether but certainly took on a less prominent role. The radical changes to education brought about by the Revolution, which Durkheim generally views sympathetically, had a strong effect of effervescence for a short time, but no way was found to effectively institutionalize them over the long term, and the system collapsed in only year 10 of the Revolution—that is, the coming to power of the Consulate headed by Napoléon Bonaparte (Durkheim, 1977/1938, pp. 305, 306).

In 1808, another important event takes place, this one of more lasting significance: the creation of the Université de France (Durkheim, 1977/1938, p. 306). Here, Durkheim describes the emergence of a single, national corporate body, replacing the old system of decentralized local educational institutions and their faculties, that united "all the schools and all the teachers of every type and every level" in the entire country (Durkheim, 1977/1938, p. 306).

Durkheim then briefly describes the part of the educational history of France he had himself lived through. The period of the Second Empire, under Louis Bonaparte, from 1852 to 1870, was one of "intellectual depression," but now, in a Republic, the challenge is to construct an educational philosophy built on the best available historical and empirical facts (Durkheim, 1977/1938, p. 312).

Durkheim pointedly asks his students: What should secondary education today direct itself toward? One thing is certain (and this notwithstanding Durkheim's insistence on the need to prepare students to take up a wide array of different positions in the modern division of labor): It cannot be a *solely* vocational education (Durkheim, 1977/1938, p. 313). Surely, it must impart skills to the student that are useful in his career after leaving university, but "the specific and indispensable object of secondary education . . . [is] to arous[e] the speculative faculties, in exercising them, in strengthening them . . . without however committing them to any vocational tasks" (Durkheim, 1977/1938, pp. 314, 315). It is not a trade the college should teach, but "aptitude in judgment, in reasoning, in reflection" (Durkheim, 1977/1938, p. 315).

There are two basic fields of study for the modern university: the realm of the study of human minds—that is, the humanities—and the realm of the study of the material world—that is, the natural and physical sciences (Durkheim, 1977/1938, p. 334). With respect to the first, Durkheim presents a rigorous criticism of classical humanist education. Rome cannot be presented to students as a utopian moment to which we must always compare ourselves. In fact, the Roman Empire was "creative" only in the realms of law and political organization, and derived much of the rest of its intellectual capital from the Greek civilization that preceded it

(Durkheim, 1977/1938, p. 323). The contemporary university student could certainly gain as much educational value from studying the civilizational history of classical India (Durkheim, 1977/1938, p. 324). Durkheim pushes this **culturally relativist** position still further. We know, he confidently claims, that no one moral system can be posited as optimal for all human societies throughout the history of humankind, and we see with just a little examination that the European moral culture of the late 1800s differs significantly from that of the classical Greeks and Romans, so it cannot be the case that all modern moral truths are present already in Rome (Durkheim, 1977/1938, p. 325).

Forms of knowledge too have a degree of relativity; even methods and systems of logic differ among societies and across times. Then, still more radically, he chastises humanism for attempting to teach a generalized notion of human nature, for this is a nonentity. Human nature, in Durkheim's argument, is an "arbitrary construct [of] the human mind" (Durkheim, 1977/1938, p. 326). What we learn from a careful study of human reality is that a human being, a "man" in the antiquated terminology, was merely an amalgam of the Christian, Greek, and Roman ideals—that is, it is a historical and social construction, not a reality that stands on its own (Durkheim, 1977/1938, p. 326). Contemporary secondary education must propose to the student that the study of human nature requires an acceptance of this relativism.

What disciplines can best present this knowledge to the student? If they were more advanced, Durkheim asserts, "the psychological and social sciences" would be the easy answer, but they are yet in their infancy (Durkheim, 1977/1938, p. 331). We must turn, at least for the moment, to the careful study of history, which in any event is so closely related to the social sciences, in Durkheim's view, that the two will in time come together into a single intellectual project. Historical study should consist of the histories of several different peoples, selected to give the student intellectual experience in understanding the constructed nature of realities he takes as *a priori,* foundational truths. Only by taking the student "out of his own country" can such lessons be taught and learned (Durkheim, 1977/1938, p. 332). This would constitute a faithful continuation of the elements of the humanist project that are valid with necessary "revitali[zation] with new ideas" (Durkheim, 1977/1938, p. 332).

As he turns to education in the natural and physical sciences, Durkheim makes an observation that would sound entirely contemporary to those working today in the burgeoning cognitive sciences: In an important sense, the study of humankind and the study of nature are one, since we can be removed from the natural world only by distorting reality (Durkheim, 1977/1938, p. 337). Consciousness, he goes on, may mark us as distinct from the rest of the material world, but consciousness can arise (to this point, at least!) "only with an organic substratum upon which it is dependent," and it is imperative that the student be made to understand this relationship (Durkheim, 1977/1938, p. 339). There are other ways in which we can observe this symbiotic relationship of the two fields of study: For example, how human groups arrange themselves has a great deal to do with geography (Durkheim, 1977/1938, p. 339).

But if the two can be seen to cover some of the same ground, it is clear for Durkheim that the emergence of the empirical sciences forces literature to give up its claim to be the queen of the university disciplines and forms of knowledge. Scientific thought provides for us something literature cannot: "a kind of exemplary rationality which is the ideal model upon which our individual rationalities should seek to model themselves" (Durkheim, 1977/1938, p. 340).

Language too must be studied in the secondary institutions, as it is the vehicle of our rational consciousness and its study is the best means for teaching the student skills of logical organization of his ideas (Durkheim, 1977/1938, pp. 344, 345). Here, Durkheim, frequently a critic of the old classical model of higher education, argues that the study of Latin and classical Greek is of special benefit in helping the student to see the logic of thought, since they are dead languages removed from us in time and express things differently than we do today. Thus, he writes, somewhat counterintuitively, especially if one expects a crude positivist in Durkheim, it is the "study of style—that is to say of grammar and of language" that makes up the "common basis of all education" (Durkheim, 1977/1938, p. 347). This provides the third piece of what Durkheim classifies as the "triadic culture" of secondary school education: the historical, the scientific, and the linguistic (Durkheim, 1977/1938, p. 348).

He concludes the course by rejecting the idea of trying to turn students into scholars or polymaths. The goal is to "fashion rationalists," by which he means individuals who can organize and express ideas clearly but who recognize and embrace the "irreducibl[e] complex[ity]" of the world; who practice logical and scientific thought and at the same time understand that our knowledge is destined always to be incomplete and imperfect (Durkheim, 1977/1938, p. 348).

Moral Education

This is a version of Durkheim's course on the topic given in the book's title. It almost certainly dates from earlier than 1902, the date Paul Fauconnet gives in the foreword. A better guess, 1899, is given by Philippe Besnard, who shows the great conceptual affinity of these lectures with the theoretical framework of *Suicide:* The three central elements required in education (**discipline, attachment to groups, autonomy**) are Durkheim's solutions to the three maladies that lead to the main currents of suicide (anomie, egoism, excessive altruism, and fatalism; Besnard, 2003, pp. 126–127). Already, in the 1961 introduction to the English translation, mention is made of the particular difficulty of understanding Durkheim on this topic in the United States, where a pedagogical philosophy that has "erred on the side of excessive individualism" is dominant (Durkheim, 1961/1925, p. xiii). Yet this difficulty perhaps also indicates a great utility in his thought on the topic for addressing and potentially correcting this "imbalance" in American educational philosophy and sociology (Durkheim, 1961/1925, p. xiii).

Durkheim begins, as in the second chapter of *Education and Sociology,* by endeavoring to place education among the various forms of human knowledge and endeavor. It is, he argues, "intermediate between art and science," neither unbounded creative expression nor single-minded "expression of reality" as it is, but a form of knowledge designed to rationally understand how best to impart information to individuals so as to effectively guide their conduct (Durkheim, 1961/1925, p. 2). It cannot, as science at times can, formulate "ready made formulae" that then systematically produce useful knowledge, at risk of thereby becoming so much "dead matter" (Durkheim, 1961/1925, p. 2). Instead, it must evolve and change with changing circumstances and contexts. It is therefore not a general theory of education to which Durkheim aims; nor is such a thing even possible. He limits his arguments in the course to those in his own country in his own time (Durkheim, 1961/1925, p. 3). This is a relativizing move that would certainly confound those who would like to condemn Durkheim as an overarching generalizer of social laws and facts.

As the move to a purely secular education was at the time of this writing recent in France, Durkheim understood he was dealing with a subject that generated passionate opinions and debate. Opposition from traditionalists notwithstanding, he intends to argue that a fully rational moral education is conceivable, even if he accepts that rationalism is not the proposition that science will ever achieve perfect knowledge of everything (Durkheim, 1961/1925, pp. 4, 5). A science of morality may seem impossible to some, but so too did a physical science appear hopelessly unattainable in the past (Durkheim, 1961/1925, p. 5).

What is the object of morality to which a **moral education** would orient itself? In primitive societies, the answer was the gods. Even in ancient Greece, where the forms of reason we recognize as fundamentally modern were being born, impiety was punished more severely than murder. Christianity, however, begins to move morality toward the object of one's fellow humans, albeit indirectly and in a complex manner historically (Durkheim, 1961/1925, p. 6). The Christian law of "love thy neighbor," motivated primarily by love of God, to be sure, shows a shift in the directed end of morality from the supernatural to the social. The Protestant revolution in Christianity furthered this attention on the human as a sacred end, diminishing the role of ritual and elaborating the requirements of Christians to their fellows (Durkheim, 1961/1925, p. 7). This is the point at which Durkheim believes contemporary moral education must take over from the Church. The Christian sacralization of the human person indicates the proper end of moral culture. There is a "transcendent reality" behind moral order, though it is not the supernatural world envisioned by Christians but the human person itself that Durkheim so frequently discussed (Durkheim, 1961/1925, p. 10). Morality, thus, inevitably must become rationalized in modernity, but it must retain the foundation in the sacred human person or it loses its foundation. Secular education then does not simply remove elements from the old educational culture but is called on to replace them with rational ends. Durkheim is confident that morality can be taught in the schools in its "rational nakedness . . . without recourse to any mythological intermediary" (Durkheim, 1961/1925, p. 11).

Such secular moral education must be more than simply rote learning of past moralities; nor is it enough simply to warn students away from the grossest transgressions. A truly human society "must . . . have before it an ideal toward which it reaches" (Durkheim, 1961/1925, p. 13).

The Spirit of Discipline

Durkheim then turns to the first element of which this secular education consists: the spirit of discipline. Moral education, he notes, is legitimately a part of the elementary school, even if the family might want to claim sole right to this form of training (Durkheim, 1961/1925, p. 18). Such education will consist not simply of the teaching of many specific virtues but rather of "those general dispositions" that enable the child to act morally in a wide range of situations (Durkheim, 1961/1925, p. 21).

What is moral behavior? It is in all cases behavior that "conforms to pre-established rules," as "morality is a totality of definite rules" (Durkheim, 1961/1925, pp. 23, 26). These rules pre-exist transgressions, so there is no need to deduce them from general principles. On the contrary, they already exist in our everyday world (Durkheim, 1961/1925, p. 27). Morality therefore is designed to shape conduct by eliminating the arbitrariness of individual and unique responses. Learning to act morally is fundamentally about learning to develop habits that produce adherence to the moral rules (Durkheim, 1961/1925, p. 27). This places us firmly in the domain of duty.

But regularity is only one element of morality, and if this were the only source of morality, then strong custom would be the only necessity (Durkheim, 1961/1925, p. 28). Custom, however, is internalized in the person, while morality necessarily comes from a source external to us. Beyond regularity, morality also requires the idea of **authority**—that is, an external moral power to which we are obedient and that sets up "a system of commandments" to which we subordinate ourselves (Durkheim, 1961/1925, pp. 29, 30). This source of authority is not merely rational, as it is, for example, in medical authority. Moral acts are not undertaken for solely utilitarian reasons, and if they are, they are not moral: "[O]ne must obey a moral precept out of respect for it and for this reason alone" (Durkheim, 1961/1925, p. 30).

But we can perhaps hear a contemporary reader (and especially an American one) ask, How can discipline be a *good* thing in education? When we limit or restrain the student, this must surely be a bad thing by definition if the goal is to instruct him. Thus certainly believed Jeremy Bentham and the other utilitarians who saw law and morality as involving "a kind of pathology" (Durkheim, 1961/1925, p. 35, 36). The leftist tradition in education, for its part, pointed to a society with minimal or no regulation as a desirable and achievable goal. These thinkers would unite in seeing discipline as merely a police action with no conceivable positive consequences (Durkheim, 1961/1925, p. 37). But they fail to reckon fully with a central fact of human life, which has to do with the incredible difficulty of constant improvisation. We simply cannot expend the energy that would be required to face all experience anew without debilitation. The regularity of norms makes everyday relationships manageable.

Aspirations too must be restrained, for unrestricted they accumulate to infinity and bring on "pessimism" and "anguish" (Durkheim, 1961/1925, p. 40). Durkheim turns to literature for one of the standard examples of the overambitious man brought low by his desires: Goethe's Faust (Durkheim, 1961/1925, p. 40). This is also the anomic individual examined so carefully in *Suicide*. Moral regulations form "an imaginary wall" around us that shows the limits of desires and passions and prevents us from experiencing the vertigo of seeing only "boundless, free, and open space" (Durkheim, 1961/1925, pp. 42, 43). Again, in contemporary American society, it is hard even to hear such claims properly without prejudgment and dismissal even before we have understood the argument, and yet the news carries the dire consequences of boundless, unregulated aspiration every day, in stories of stock market gamblers destroying their own futures and those of their companies and stockholders; figures in the sporting world crashing to their deaths in cars, on skis, and so forth as they pursue ever more unreachable speed records; and myriad other such examples. In Durkheim's view, a properly moral education would impart to students the comforting idea that limitations are necessary if we would be happy and in sound moral health (Durkheim, 1961/1925, p. 44).

But this is a *subordination* of the will, Durkheim knows the critic will respond. Yes, it is, he acknowledges; but the alternative is *not* self-sovereignty, for when we are freed of morality, we are still not our own masters. Instead of being subject to morality, we are then subject to our desires, which dominate us still more mercilessly and lead us away from healthy collective life to disaster (Durkheim, 1961/1925, p. 44). "Self-mastery," Durkheim argues, "is the first condition of all true power, of all liberty worthy of the name," and such self-mastery requires a willful decision to subjugate oneself to a moral system (Durkheim, 1961/1925, p. 45). We cannot set our own limits, for obeying limits requires understanding their reality, and the force of those limits comes from outside us. Moral education must show the child that there are boundaries that are established in "the nature of things"—that is, which are out of his control—but this does not mean "insidiously inculcating a spirit of resignation [or] curbing his legitimate ambitions [or] trying to hide the injustices of the world" (Durkheim, 1961/1925, p. 49). Durkheim certainly recognizes the existence of injustice, but he also recognizes the reality of differences of temperament and aptitude. Moral education should direct the child to seek goals that are within the realistic reach of his abilities (Durkheim, 1961/1925, p. 49). In reading this section of Durkheim's argument, one might perhaps think of the spectacle in American society of popular television programs such as *American Idol,* on which people with little or no obvious talent in some realm of activity nonetheless vigorously pursue the goal of a career in that field, disdaining the well-intentioned criticisms of those who attempt to dissuade them and turn them instead to some more appropriate trajectory. There is room for moral innovation, and Durkheim names the examples of Jesus and Socrates, but we must be careful to avoid confusing "the need to substitute a new regulation for an old one . . . and the impatience with all rules, the abhorrence of all discipline" (Durkheim, 1961/1925, p. 53). Neither Jesus nor Socrates advocated the dismantling of all moral codes and the reign of moral anarchy, but instead each established new moral codes to replace older, dated ones. At the end of the day, arguments in favor of unrestricted freedom are little more than "apologies for a diseased state" (Durkheim, 1961/1925, p. 54). Real freedom and moral regulation are not opposed terms. Liberty is only possible as a consequence of the disciplining of the will.

Attachment to Social Groups

The second element of morality is attachment to social groups. All human behavior has either personal or impersonal ends, and Durkheim suggests that acts with merely personal ends cannot by definition be called moral. They are always directed toward either self-preservation or self-aggrandizement (Durkheim, 1961/1925, pp. 55–56). All moral acts must be impersonal, and even action in normally impersonal spheres of action can be morally perverted by personal motivations—for example, the scientist or artist who pursues his craft merely for self-aggrandizement through fame, wealth, or some other form of power is not morally revered. No society, Durkheim claims, has ever existed that saw egoistic action as moral (Durkheim, 1961/1925, p. 58). So what is the object of the impersonally motivated moral act? Durkheim's answer is crisp and clear: "[T]he domain of the moral begins where the domain of the social begins" (Durkheim, 1961/1925, p. 60). He returns here to his argument concerning the *sui generis* nature of society. Society as the object of moral action cannot simply be the liberal economist's vision of the sum of all individuals making it up, for if we act motivated by our feeling for others, whether the limited number of our own families or the large number of those who together with us make up our nation, we are still acting from self-interest in the desire to aid discrete individuals who matter to us. The social end of morality must therefore be an entity other than the sum of all the members of society. It must be a being having its own independent existence "distinct from that of its constituent individuals" (Durkheim, 1961/1925, p. 60). When we combine the two separate, malleable elements of tin and copper, we get a new substance, bronze, that is not simply the sum of its parts, for it has a characteristic, hardness, not present in the two precursors. Such is the nature of the relationship of society to the individuals who make it up (Durkheim, 1961/1925, p. 61).

But why should we subordinate ourselves to society if it is so separated from us as individuals? The answer has to do with the fact that the individual is only able to realize her true nature in society. Durkheim here gives examples, directly from the research for *Suicide*, of how marital status, children, and social crises that are collectively felt reduce the suicide rate (Durkheim, 1961/1925, pp. 68–69). The best in human beings (language, religion, and science are among the examples he gives) comes from our collective existence (Durkheim, 1961/1925, p. 69). The egotistical individual would like to see herself as a whole, but we cannot deny the bonds that tie us to others (Durkheim, 1961/1925, p. 71).

All social groups do not, however, occupy the same position in the hierarchy of moral action. The family, the nation, and the human community each "represent different phases of our social and moral evolution, stages that prepare for, and build upon, one another" (Durkheim, 1961/1925, p. 74). We need to be encompassed in the moral regulation provided by orientation to all three, but there is a hierarchy among them. The family is closer to the individual and therefore less impersonal than the other two (Durkheim, 1961/1925, p. 74). The moral community of humankind is loftier and its goals higher than those of any nation, but there is yet the problem, in Durkheim's day as well as our own, that there exists "no constituted society" at the global level (Durkheim, 1961/1925, p. 76). But Durkheim believes this is a contradiction that can be resolved by nations committing themselves to altruistic, international goals—that is, refusing simply to "expand . . . to the detriment of its neighbors" and committing instead to "justice . . . a higher morality" (Durkheim, 1961/1925, p. 77). Here, he is echoing remarks from his lectures on civil morals that we discussed in Chapter 3.

Charity is a profoundly collective and moral value. One who feels morally united with countrymen, or with other humans in general, cannot bear to watch them suffer without endeavoring to do something to stop that suffering. Charity points to self-sacrifice and the ability to go outside the boundaries of self-interest (Durkheim, 1961/1925, p. 83). Those who feel no compassion for others who suffer are insufficiently tied to the moral system. Durkheim makes a powerful argument here for the need for collective responses to problems created by too little collective pity and compassion. If problems such as "social vagran[cy]" or "alcoholism" are on the rise (as they were in the France of Durkheim's day), this is because there exist varieties of intense social stress against which the individual is helpless (Durkheim, 1961/1925, p. 84). Only a collective solution in the form of social policy, and not simply individual acts of charity, will constitute an effective response.

There is a close connection between the two elements of moral education so far discussed. The being best constituted to take up the position of authority is "the collective being," and thus discipline and attachment to groups turn out to be two sides of the same reality (Durkheim, 1961/1925, pp. 85, 88). Each society has the morality it requires—that is, moral ideals are socially and historically variable (Durkheim, 1961/1925, p. 87). The greatest historical figures are not artists, statesmen, or scientists but men who brought great "moral triumphs" such as Moses, Socrates, Confucius, Buddha, Mohammed, Luther, and Jesus (Durkheim, 1961/1925, p. 93).

Society is spoken of by Durkheim here in a language that we will see again in the discussion in the next chapter of *The Elementary Forms*—namely, religious language. Society is none other than the actual God to which we orient ourselves when we believe we are pledging faith to a supernatural entity, and the moral system prevalent in our social world is the content of God's commandments to us:

> On the one hand, [society] seems to us an authority that constrains us . . . and to which we defer with a feeling of religious respect. On the other hand, society is the benevolent and protecting power, the nourishing mother from which we gain the whole of our moral and intellectual substance and toward whom our wills turn in a spirit of love and gratitude. In the one case, it is like a jealous and formidable God, the stern lawmaker allowing no transgression of His orders. In the other case, it is the succoring deity to whom the faithful sacrifice themselves with gladness. (Durkheim, 1961/1925, pp. 92–93)

Secular morality owes most of its content to religious morality, as Society transforms into God in this vision with only minimal revision. As was the case for God, Society not only commands obedience and love from us, but it is an ideal toward which we strive (Durkheim, 1961/1925, pp. 103–104). Later, in *The Elementary Forms,* Durkheim will provide more detail to this argument about the reality of religion.

The Autonomy of the Student

The third and final element of moral education is what makes Durkheim's vision as complex as it is. In the first two elements, the individual is required to subject herself to an external entity. In this third element of autonomy of the will, or self-determination, the individual is put back into the equation as an active agent. Durkheim turns here to the limits of Kant's conception of morality. Kant had recognized the need for obligation in moral behavior, but he also believed that the autonomy of the will had to be acknowledged. The way in which he manages to arrive at a conjunction between these seemingly conflicting facts is to argue that the fully rational person would come to see the necessity of obedience through pure reason. Against this conception, Durkheim argues that reason comes up against one of its stark limits here, for "we are not beings of pure reason [but also] have sensibilities that have their own nature and that are refractory to the dictates of reason" (Durkheim, 1961/1925, p. 109). The authority of moral law, which again is the collective being at bottom, requires deference even from reason itself (Durkheim, 1961/1925, p. 110). Human reason, Durkheim argues against Kant, is not transcendent but "implicated in society and consequently conforms to the laws of society" (Durkheim, 1961/1925, p. 110). Our reasoning nature has limited power to move us in this realm, as we are also emotional creatures, and our emotions push us toward individualistic, irrational, and ultimately immoral ends. In short, humans are "complex and heterogeneous being[s] divided against [themselves]" (Durkheim, 1961/1925, p. 113). We are able to act morally only if reason can act in a constraining manner on the passions. Kant's view of reason in human nature is too idealist, too disembodied, and ultimately unsustainable precisely because such a view of human autonomy is simply utopian.

Nonetheless, Durkheim wants to salvage some notion of human autonomy, though it cannot be some merely abstract truth of the nature of Kant's reasoning (Durkheim, 1961/1925, p. 114). Autonomy emerges progressively, he argues, as a result of our growing knowledge of the various forces that limit and define our choices. In the physical world, there are many forces that control our actions in significant ways, and we cannot undo the laws that determine that control. We can, however, gain a "first degree of autonomy" by coming to understand the physical forces acting on us and accepting this as a part of our natures and the nature of the world. Autonomy in Durkheim's sense, then, consists of learning why things are as they are and coming to see and accept this reality as desirable. He is clear here: There is "no better alternative" and "wishing freely is not desiring the absurd" (Durkheim, 1961/1925, p. 115). It is understanding that liberates us, not becoming autonomous in some more ambitious, utopian sense. Whatever we might will, we remain subject to many things beyond our control, not only in the physical realm but in the moral order as well. Of course, in the moral realm, there is room to criticize when the moral order is not based on "the order of things" but instead comes to be "abnormal" (Durkheim, 1961/1925, p. 117). Generally speaking, though, the moral and physical orders affect us in similar ways and autonomy with respect to both requires a conscious understanding and acceptance of their workings.

Thus is Durkheim able to reconcile autonomy and obedience to authority. As finite beings, we recognize limits and we remain essentially passive before the rules that order our actions. Yet we assert freedom in actively coming to accept the obedience as inevitable and, finally, good (Durkheim, 1961/1925, p. 118). This is "an enlightened assent" and not a mere resignation (Durkheim, 1961/1925, p. 120). A secular morality distinguishes itself from other kinds of morality in this third element, which is wholly absent in religious morality. Merely religious moral orders can simply subjugate even the unwilling, but the teaching of a secular morality requires moving beyond preaching and indoctrination to explanation (Durkheim, 1961/1925, pp. 120, 121). Secular morality is defined by Duty and the Good, as are all moral systems, but it adds Reason to the other two (Durkheim, 1961/1925, p. 122). The child must be instructed on how to take on an unselfish demeanor and adopt a "preference for moderation . . . which is the necessary condition of happiness and health" (Durkheim, 1961/1925, p. 124). A human subject becomes fully such only through the rational decision to submit to rule and devote herself to the group, thereby achieving a melding of "subordination and power, of submission and autonomy" (Durkheim, 1961/1925, p. 124).

Thus ends the part of the course dedicated specifically to the theoretical explication of secular morality. In the book's last section, Durkheim provides more practical information on the methods for imparting these secular moral principles to the student.

Discipline: Punishment and Expiation

Discipline is a required element in education in Durkheim's estimation. Moving a child into the social order necessitates getting him to adopt regular habits and exercise self-control over individual desires—that is, teaching him to distinguish what is possible from what is not (Durkheim, 1961/1925, p. 130). The child is to be taught that society is larger and ultimately more important than he is, and so he must conform to it in at least some basic ways. Durkheim compares the child to the "primitive" who simply fails to understand the idea of limits: "when he is fond of something, he wants it to satiety" (Durkheim, 1961/1925, pp. 131, 132). Fortunately, two innate qualities in the child provide a way into this necessary moral training: (1) the child is a creature of habit, and (2) the child is accessible to "imperative suggestion" (Durkheim, 1961/1925, p. 134). It seems a contradiction, but the child is at once anarchic and massively repetitive and habitual. She hates change; for example, she wants to eat always the same things she likes, be read the same books over and over again, and so on. A parent wearing a strange outfit can cause significant emotional distress in young children (Durkheim, 1961/1925, p. 135).

Durkheim posits that the child already has an innate notion that there is one true, natural order, and this can be used as a stepladder to get the child on the road to greater self-moderation and submission to the rule of the group (Durkheim, 1961/1925, p. 138). The goal is to get the child to accept the reality of moral forces to which submission is the only response. Echoing the same metaphor from the first chapter of *Education and Sociology*, Durkheim argues that the moral training of the child at these early stages has some of the appearance of hypnosis. He is relatively passive and his mind is blank, and he is given to credulity, docility, and good will (Durkheim, 1961/1925, pp. 139, 141). The educator must make the child feel that refusal is simply out of the question (Durkheim, 1961/1925, p. 140). It is of paramount importance in Durkheim's view for the moral educator to establish authority over the child assertively and early. The educator's authority is constructed through suggestion. For example, when the child has eaten and desires more, the response should be something along the lines of the assertion "you have eaten enough" (Durkheim, 1961/1925, p. 141).

Order in the classroom is essential, and not simply in order to maintain the peace but because it expresses the moral discipline of the "small society"—that is, the school class (Durkheim, 1961/1925, p. 148). The children need to feel restrained in order to avoid "a state of ferment that makes them impatient of all curbs" (Durkheim, 1961/1925, p. 150). Discipline in education was already under attack from the individualist left in Durkheim's day, and he recognized that the program he was suggesting was in some ways not consistent with the cultural political winds of the day. He was careful in the lectures to note that discipline cannot be unrestricted, and the teacher's disciplinary powers should be constrained in specific ways (Durkheim, 1961/1925, p. 153). Yet the secular educator is in Durkheim's vision something like the priest; as the latter is "interpreter of God," the teacher is "interpreter of the great moral ideas of his time and country" (Durkheim, 1961/1925, p. 155). However, as the authority of the educator comes from an "impersonal source," it should not be accompanied by "arrogance, vanity, or pedantry" (Durkheim, 1961/1925, p. 155).

The classroom should not be presented as a military barracks, but it is nonetheless true that the child must be made to undergo strenuous efforts and hardships. The mere fear of punishment is insufficient for moral discipline, and a disciplined class is one that does not require much punishment (Durkheim, 1961/1925, p. 160). Punishment must be understood not as intimidation, but, at least in part, as a kind of expiation that "makes amends . . . for the offense" (Durkheim, 1961/1925, pp. 164, 165). The moral order in the classroom should be understood as something sacred and outside the control of the student. When a rule is violated, it begins to lose its appearance of inviolability, and any sacred thing that is transgressed against loses its sacredness if nothing is done to restore it to its previous state: "One doesn't believe in a divinity against which the vulgar lift their hands with impunity" (Durkheim, 1961/1925, p. 165). Violations of the rules tend to damage the child's "faith in the authority of school law," which is seen as possessing a certain force and prestige (Durkheim, 1961/1925, pp. 165, 166).

So the expiation of punishment is designed not simply to cause the guilty to suffer or to threaten other potential transgressors but simply to reinforce the sense in the other students that the sacred rules in which they have such confidence cannot be undone by violations (Durkheim, 1961/1925, p. 167). It is, in other words, not the guilty party but the rest of the class that is centrally aimed at in punishment, as their faith in the rule must be sustained by sanctions being brought against its transgressors.

In practical terms, what methods will school punishment take up? Some (Rousseau, Spencer, and the Russian writer Leo Tolstoy are named by Durkheim as examples) supported the idea of punishment as simply allowing the guilty party to suffer the consequences of his misdeeds. For example, if Émile breaks his window, we leave it in that state and let him get cold at night to see the negative effects of his act (Durkheim, 1961/1925, p. 168). Durkheim is critical here, arguing that it is not even clear that the child will realize the connection between the ill effects and his own deed. When a child overeats and gets indigestion, it is not a given that she will accurately connect the two events and understand her culpability in bringing on the malady (Durkheim, 1961/1925, p. 171).

Punishment, as we have already seen, is directed in large part at others in the classroom, but there is also a motivation to express disapproval to the offender (Durkheim, 1961/1925, p. 181). Nonetheless, however serious the offense might be, corporal punishment in the schools is under an "absolute prohibition" because it collides with the sacred respect commanded by the human person: "By virtue of this respect, all violence exercised on a person seems to us, in principle, like sacrilege" (Durkheim, 1961/1925, pp. 182–183). Within the family, mild physical correction can be effective when the child is too young to be educated and can only be trained. But there the harsh effects of corporal punishment can be softened by displays of tender affection, while at school, no such moderating measures exist (Durkheim, 1961/1925, p. 183).

Durkheim then briefly explores the history of corporal punishment in education. We might tend to think it originated among primitives, but ethnographers have revealed that the simplest cultures do not physically discipline children, but instead often indulge them in ways moderns would find extravagant (Durkheim, 1961/1925, pp. 184–185). Corporal punishment was rare in the ancient Roman world and only became truly widespread in the Christian Middle Ages (Durkheim, 1961/1925, pp. 185, 186). It was the Christians who perfected the use of "the lash, the rod, and fasting" in schools (Durkheim, 1961/1925, p. 187). Generally speaking, disciplinary measures in education increase as civilization progresses, and this is because life is simpler and the body of material required to be learned by the young lighter in earlier societies. In the modern world, we are required to learn a great deal in the way of moral and intellectual culture, and this education cannot be left to chance, as the functioning of the society depends on it, and thus exacting educational processes are required (Durkheim, 1961/1925, p. 189). This produces an inevitable "darken[ing of] the child's life" as civilizations grow more complex, far from the happy utopia of education seen by thinkers such as Tolstoy (Durkheim, 1961/1925, p. 191).

Punishment must be exacted on a graduated scale (Durkheim, 1961/1925, p. 198). Once it is applied, punishment begins to lose some of its force as a matter of course. It is the anticipation of blame that gives it power, and once we have braved the transgression and faced the punishment, our sensitivity to shame is blunted (Durkheim, 1961/1925, p. 199). The child must therefore not be administered punishment in heavy amounts, and it should be resorted to only as a last resort, after trying all other means of dissuasion and disapproval, and only after a period of reflection by the educator to avoid acting in haste or anger (Durkheim, 1961/1925, pp. 199, 201).

Durkheim argues that rewards for correct moral performance in the classroom should be avoided, as the child is doomed to experience a "great disenchantment" when he learns that simply doing what is expected of him is not so gratuitously rewarded in the world outside school (Durkheim, 1961/1925, p. 205). The child should be led to understand that adherence to the moral system is something expected of him. Here, as in many other occasions in these lectures, Durkheim runs quite counter to the received wisdom in the American educational system, where punishment is increasingly frowned on and rewards are given to students for virtually every kind of "good citizenship" imaginable.

Duty in the child can be shaped by the effective use of punishment. Getting her to move toward the Good requires moving her in the direction of "empathy [i.e.,] those tendencies that we call altruistic and disinterested" (Durkheim, 1961/1925, p. 207). But is there anything in the child naturally on which to build a sense of altruism? We often tend to think of egoism as the primary orientation of the child and altruism as only a relatively late element of the child's character entirely produced by the effects of socialization (Durkheim, 1961/1925, p. 208). But Durkheim argues that it would not be possible to get the child to behave in a particular way if there were no seeds already there predisposing him for it (Durkheim, 1961/1925, p. 209). Egoism and altruism are more complexly interrelated in the child, and in adults, than is commonly recognized. The child has different kinds of interests and urges: those that are clearly directed to her individuality (having to do with her "body . . . health . . . fortune . . . social condition . . . reputation") and others that are directed to things external to her individuality that nonetheless still "touch [her] personality"—for example, "things of all sorts that are familiar to us," things still further beyond us and all connected to us, and finally the social groups to which we belong (Durkheim, 1961/1925, pp. 213, 214). Though it seems these latter kinds of things are external, we necessarily internalize them in making them matters of importance; representations of the things have to be taken inside of us. So, for example, we suffer at the death of someone else because a representation of that person has become a part of our own self and we experience "a painful void in our consciousness" (Durkheim, 1961/1925, p. 215). This reduces the difference between egoism and altruism a great deal, as we now see that the one is embedded in the other, and that our individuality is made up of elements that reach us from outside ourselves. Thus, pure egoism and altruism are mere abstractions and one is always implicated in the other (Durkheim, 1961/1925, p. 217). In this manner, Durkheim arrives at the core of altruism in the child needed to reach and extend it in education.

Drawing that root out into a flourishing growth of attachment to the group requires giving him a strong sense of the social groups of which he is a member (Durkheim, 1961/1925, p. 228). On entering school, the child knows only two groups: the family and groups of friends and acquaintances (Durkheim, 1961/1925, p. 230). The school itself can and should become another social group of reference for the child, an important intermediary society, like the occupational group invoked by Durkheim so frequently, between the family and the State (Durkheim, 1961/1925, p. 231). The class is a much more concrete and lived form of social existence than the more abstract national identity that might unite students, and ideas of the spirit and honor of the class should be repeatedly imprinted on the student's mind (Durkheim, 1961/1925, p. 241). Making some punishments and rewards collective rather than individual is one effective way of awakening solidarity in the class (Durkheim, 1961/1925, p. 244).

Curriculum and Moral Education

Durkheim finally turns to some remarks on curriculum. There is a danger, he argues, in "oversimplified rationalism" in pedagogy (Durkheim, 1961/1925, p. 250). A certain perverse reading of Descartes might bring the educator to believe that what should be privileged in elementary education is the "perfectly simple," which can be comprehended by reason immediately as a "luminous representation" (Durkheim, 1961/1925, p. 250). The tendency in French education is to seek out such pristine and pure elements and view the complex as superficial. But stripping away to get to the general requires stripping away parts of reality as well (Durkheim, 1961/1925, p. 254). The child must be immunized from this oversimplified Cartesianism by being led to understand the provisional nature of scientific knowledge: "[T]omorrow, perhaps, a new fact may be discovered that may put everything into question again" (Durkheim, 1961/1925, p. 262). Biology can be used to show the child complexity; the cell seems a perfectly simple object, but examination reveals this is not the case (Durkheim, 1961/1925, pp. 263–264). The child must be shown that we will perhaps never know everything we want or need to know, though we nonetheless progressively reduce the expanse of our ignorance (Durkheim, 1961/1925, p. 265). While science and rationalism do not promise an end point of our knowledge, at which time we will know all that can be known, the child should neverthe-less be shown that "there is no reason to set a limit to the progress of sci-ence" (Durkheim, 1961/1925, p. 265).

Education in aesthetics is of particular use in moving the child away from narrow egoism, as the cultivation of a taste for art helps open the student to selflessness and sacrifice (Durkheim, 1961/1925, p. 269). Aesthetic educa-tion, however, points away from reality to the ideal, which puts it in contrast with moral education. Both art and morality draw the individual out of himself, but one links us only to images, while the other grounds us in the real (Durkheim, 1961/1925, p. 271). Nonetheless, Durkheim is not dismiss-ing art here. It may well be "a game; but games are a part of life" (Durkheim, 1961/1925, p. 273).

He closes with some remarks on the teaching of history. History instruc-tion must emphasize not great individuals but the dependency of each gen-eration on those that preceded it (Durkheim, 1961/1925, p. 276). A proper understanding of the French Revolution, for example, must describe how those who lived under the Old Regime prepared the way for it.

Conclusion

The sociology of education in the English-speaking world has, by and large, and at least until recently, paid surprisingly little attention to the work Durkheim did in this area. In the United States, this likely has much to do with the historical emphasis on educational theories and pedagogies informed much more by psychology and other individual-centered disci-plines and forms of knowledge. As a kind of impromptu experiment, I looked over the list of courses in my own university's department of educa-tion and found many with the word "psychology" or some derivative of same in the title but not a single course with the word "sociology" in the title, and no mentions of Durkheim anywhere in course titles or descriptions.

Yet, as is evident in the material summarized in this chapter, Durkheim's thought on education is fundamentally imbued with the spirit of his sociology, and he constantly brought to bear a singularly sociological vision in all of his writing on educational matters. These educational writings and courses offer a vision of the eminently practical and activist spirit of Durkheimian sociology, as this was a realm of cultural and social life that Durkheim considered of tremendous importance in effecting changes and directing the future of entire societies, and he vigorously advocated making use of this realm to directly put the new sociological way of knowing to work in creating the future France. If moral solidarity had suffered in France during Durkheim's lifetime and the old discourses for generating it that were centered on institutions (the Church, the Army) that were themselves weakened proved ineffectual at addressing the problem, new secular, scientific, and democratic solutions had to be implemented, and a sociological transformation of the French educational system was something Durkheim tirelessly presented as a necessary element in this project.

A few questions

- What is the evidence for the existence of *homo duplex*?
- How does Durkheim's definition of the autonomy of the student compare to those of other important thinkers on educational matters?
- What contemporary educational debates could be informed by Durkheim's thinking on education?
- What is the evidence that psychological theories of education are more or less viable than theories such as Durkheim's?
- Why does Durkheim believe it is so important to carefully balance the unavoidable element of preparation for career in education with loftier goals?

6

The "Revelation" of Religion

In 1894 to 1895, Durkheim gave his first course on religion at Bordeaux. It was at this point, he later claimed, that he first realized the importance religion has in the study of human society and culture, and he began to formulate a framework to study it sociologically. He classified this moment as a "revelation" (Lukes, 1985, p. 237). As we have already seen, the middle 1890s were a period of immense creative energy for Durkheim. Just a year previously, he had published *The Rules,* and a year later, in 1896, he would launch the effort to create the first sociological journal, *l'Année sociologique,* and then in 1897 *Suicide* appeared. But all along, while he was publishing this other material, Durkheim was working feverishly on a grand study of religion that ultimately did not see the light of day for almost two decades after the first course on religion.

Durkheim had convinced his nephew Marcel Mauss (who was Durkheim's junior by 14 years) to forsake the prestige of Paris as a university student and come instead to study with his uncle in Bordeaux. Later, once Mauss had gone off for graduate study in Paris, Durkheim, who was already preparing his nephew to join his sociological research team, coached him to take up the study of religion more or less exclusively so as, in Mauss's words, to "put his force in the best place to render service to the new-born science" of sociology (Mauss, 1979, p. 214). Mauss, in tandem with Henri Hubert, another key member of the *Année* team, began during the period of the mid 1890s to produce a large body of work on the topic, including long essays on sacrifice (in 1899) and magic (in 1904) that appeared in the *Année.* From correspondence, we know that Durkheim played a significant part in the discussions and writing of the essay on sacrifice (Durkheim, 1998, pp. 95–96), and he made significant use of the results of the essay on magic in *The Elementary Forms of Religious Life,* as we will see.

Durkheim was also publishing material on religion and the related topic of collective representations himself beginning in the late years of the century, with most of it coming after he had moved to Paris in 1902. In 1899, his first, tentative attempt at an explication of the sociological significance of religion appeared in the *Année.* The year before, he had written an essay on individual and collective representations that formally laid out his thinking on this topic. In the 1902 and 1903 editions of the *Année* appeared lengthy essays on totemism and categories of classification in primitive societies, the latter cowritten with Mauss. In 1906 and 1911, Durkheim published important essays on morality that were tightly connected to his developing argument concerning religion and the social foundations of knowledge. Finally, in 1912, only a few years before his death, the massive *chef-d'oeuvre* that was *The Elementary Forms of Religious Life* emerged.

In this chapter, we will look carefully at his thinking concerning religion and the sociology of knowledge, with an especially lingering discussion of what should be considered his masterwork and the most enduring work in his corpus, *The Elementary Forms.* This is an immense book, in pure length but also in argumentative expanse, and a good deal of the chapter will be taken up dealing with it.

On the Definition of Religious Phenomena

In this initial effort to sociologically take on religion, Durkheim proceeds in a manner that will, in some of its elements, at least, look familiar to readers of *The Elementary Forms,* although his thinking here is still clearly a work in progress. He looks first at, and rejects, several definitions of the basis for religion that compete with the one he will propose. Max Müller and Herbert Spencer see the desire to plumb the depths of mystery and the incomprehensible in the world through systems of belief and practice that postulate an omnipresent force beyond our reasoning (Durkheim, 1969/1898, pp. 142–143). Durkheim dismisses this idea because the most primitive religions have no notion of the supernatural world required for such mysteries. Another competitor sees the search for an ethic that ties us into relations with divinities at the heart of religion (Durkheim, 1969/1898, p. 145). But, Durkheim argues, one can easily find religions in which the divinity is engaged in a crudely contractual way little befitting an entity who is supposedly adored. In a passage that will be taken up in the later book on religion, he asserts that there are even some religions without divinities (Durkheim, 1969/1898, p. 146).

The true definition of religion, he concludes, has to do with the obligatory nature of the beliefs associated with the religion and the collective rites that are connected to the beliefs (Durkheim, 1969/1898, pp. 159–160). Discussion of religion that would begin from the standpoint of individual beliefs misses the fundamentally social nature of religion and thereby radically misunderstands the phenomenon in question. It may be that individual faiths or individualized variations on established faiths exist, Durkheim allows. But in human history the overwhelming majority of religious practices consist of collectively held beliefs and rites with a public aspect and a force of obligation fringing on and often becoming coercion (Durkheim, 1969/1898, p. 162). Where else could the obligation in religious belief and practice come from, if not from society? In many cases in which an individual element of a religious faith is present, he argues, this easily coexists with a broader, collective framework (Durkheim, 1969/1898, pp. 164–165). In the end, all individual religious beliefs must, in a historical sense, derive from those that are collectively generated and held.

Durkheim also briefly takes on the distinction between sacred and profane things and symbols that will play such a crucial role in *The Elementary Forms*. The difference between the two is cut and dry in this essay: Sacred things are those the representations of which society itself has created, while profane things find their representations in the meanings and experiences of individuals. The distinction of sacred and profane is thus neatly parallel to the distinction between society and the individual or between sociology and psychology (Durkheim, 1969/1898, p. 162–163).

Primitive Classification

This lengthy article was cowritten with Marcel Mauss and published in the *Année* in 1903. The argument is straightforward and electrically provocative, especially in its historical context. Durkheim and Mauss set out to demonstrate that the **classificatory systems** humans have devised to organize their knowledge of the world cannot reasonably be thought of as the mere achievements of individual psychologies, and, moreover, that they cannot be reasonably understood as the context-independent products of individual minds grappling directly with the world. Logicians and psychologists approach the human cognitive capacity according to these unreasonable principles, and they are therefore unable to comprehend the actual origins and source of complex human thought. The upshot of this set of claims is radical. Complex human knowledge is inevitably a social product, and it originates in the group's reflection on its own organization and form and not in any independent and objective perception of the reality of things in themselves. A radical sociology of knowledge that would examine even the seemingly most objective forms of human knowledge as deeply determined by the social situatedness of all human activity thus finds its first major work in *Primitive Classification*. It is also, as Rodney Needham points out in his critical introduction to the English translation, a less systematic precursor to the argument of *The Elementary Forms*, and its argument must be contended with because of its place in the evolution of Durkheim's thought.

How then do humans classify things in the world? As a merely experiential fact, Durkheim and Mauss argue, all things encountered in reality are different, and generally radically so, and relations among them are far from self-evidently demonstrable. No two leaves or snowflakes or dogs or trees or people are precisely the same, and the process by which we come to understand individual phenomena as members of groups that can be classed in structured relations with the members of other groups is one of the hoariest objects of philosophical inquiry. All societies classify. They put the living and nonliving things of importance to their daily lives into hierarchically arranged groups that cannot be reduced to mere resemblances of the things thus classified. In his story "The Analytical Language of John Wilkins," the Argentine writer Jorge Luis Borges illustrates the relativity of such classificatory schemas by imagining a bizarre system in which some of the groups would include animals of the following types, among others: those belonging to the Emperor, those that are trained, those that are fabulous, and those that resemble flies from a great distance. How could such groups make sense? Durkheim and Mauss suggest a revolutionary solution to the problem of how such classificatory systems arise: *They are all, in their origins, rooted in the structure of the classifying group itself.*

Methodologically, the study proceeds just as Durkheim would later in *The Elementary Forms*—that is, in a search for the most primitive, basic, unadorned societies and an examination of their forms of classification that will, given Durkheim's assumptions about the traces of evolutionary origins in even the most advanced forms, inform us about all human classification and not just the primitive forms themselves (Durkheim & Mauss, 1963/1903, p. 9). This most primitive form of classification is to be found in Australian aboriginal totemism, although that choice is only inadequately defended here (Durkheim would return to it with greater focus, albeit without eliminating the main criticisms of the method, in *The Elementary Forms*). Here, in social orders in which the social groups transparently identify themselves with totemic entities in the natural environment (whether plants, animals, or natural phenomena such as wind or fire), one finds a clear parallel between the classification of things and the classification of groups of people (Durkheim & Mauss, 1963/1903, p. 11). Australian aboriginal tribes are divided into smaller units known as **moieties**, themselves further delineated into separate clans, and a specific organizational, classificatory hierarchy places each clan into a specific set of relationships with the others. Members of one moiety may be required to marry members only of the other, and particular rules may apply among the clans as to what can and cannot be done with the totem entity of each clan. As go these collective mental maps of the relationships of the human groups, so go the classificatory schema by which all entities in the world are classed. In the Mount Gambier tribe in Australia, the two moieties are each divided into five totemic clans, among which are the pelican, the black cockatoo, and the kangaroo. The different groups are interrelated by stringent rules of intermarriage and commerce. Attached to each clan totem are particular seasons, elements, and celestial objects (e.g., the white cockatoo and the summer, wind, and sun; the black cockatoo and the moon and stars). Other animals and plants are identified and classed with the various totems (Durkheim & Mauss, 1963/1903, pp. 20–21).

After examining the Australian totemic examples that they feel are the most primitive and illustrative of their theory, Durkheim and Mauss briefly argue for the subsuming of some more peripheral Australian data into the argument as well before turning to examples in indigenous North America, specifically the Zuni and the Sioux. Then, in perhaps the essay's most startling turn, they discuss two cultural examples far removed from those presented previously in both historical stage and cultural geography. The "astronomical, astrological, geomantic and horoscopic divinatory system" of China, rooted in the ancient past and in Durkheim's time (i.e., pre–Communist Revolution) still a cultural system of immense purview in China, and the classificatory system of classical Greece are described as later variations on the systems examined earlier in which the connection to social structure has already been effaced. Nonetheless, Durkheim and Mauss contend, the neat delineation of groups of items of a vast variety (time, space, living entities, celestial objects, colors, emotional qualities) seen in the totemic systems can be seen here as well. It is doubtless true that there is much ground for criticism in the details here. The peoples described in the course of the article have had many careful pages dedicated to their various cultures, and Durkheim and Mauss play fast and loose with data, generalizing readily from cherry-picked examples and overlooking material that is unhelpful to their case.

The causal arrow is not unidirectional in the relationship between the social structure of the group and the set of classificatory ideas that emerge from it. Although Durkheim and Mauss argue that the social structure provides the initial impetus to the emergence of classification schemas, once the schemas emerge, they can act back on the group's form and change it (Durkheim & Mauss, 1963/1903, p. 32).

Individual and Collective Representations

Durkheim begins the 1898 piece by this title with a sustained attack on radically materialist psychological theories of cognition, which endeavor to reduce the content of our ideas to the physical state of the brain at the time the idea is conceived. If such theories were true, he argues, the study of human ideation would consist solely of the study of "the anatomical conditions of which [ideas] are the more or less faithful reflections" (Durkheim, 1953/1924, p. 9). Durkheim is trying to set the ground for an argument about collective representations by demonstrating the separability of representations and the neural material that is their biological condition:

> If representations, once they exist, continue to exist in themselves without their existence being perpetually dependent upon the disposition of the neural centres, if they have the power to react directly upon each other and to combine according to their own laws, they are then realities which, while maintaining an intimate relation with their substratum, are to a certain extent independent of it. (Durkheim, 1953/1924, p. 23)

After a lengthy argument about the psychological aspects of the representation, Durkheim arrives finally, near the end of the essay, at the real core of his argument. The case he has made for the distinction between representations and the biological material that is their ground is the same made in his previous work for the distinction between social facts and the individuals that are their ground. As individual representations cannot be reduced to merely physical events in the brain, neither can collective representations be reduced to a combination of interactions between individual minds (Durkheim, 1953/1924, pp. 24–25). If psychology is allowed to persist in the face of the materialist arguments about the possibility of reducing individual representations fully to neural states, then it must be recognized that sociology has a legitimate area of its own study, which is that of social facts and collective representations. Collective representations are, in their most typical forms at least (e.g., religion, morality, law), "expressly obligatory" and originate in a moral power outside of and superior to the individual, "which the mystic calls God or which can be more scientifically conceived" (Durkheim, 1953/1924, p. 25).

Is Durkheim a monist or a dualist on the venerable mind/body question in the philosophy of mind? It is not altogether clear. He certainly rejects the claims of reductive physical monists to fully explain all representations as ultimately and fully physical states, but he does not clearly take up a dualist position, either, hedging between dualism and a kind of nonreductive physical monism.

The Determination of Moral Facts

This paper, which was given as an address to the Société française de philosophie in 1906, begins with a restatement of some basic principles on morality and its study that we discussed in Durkheim's lectures on moral education. Morality can be looked at in two ways: in an evaluative and subjective way or in a scientific, objective way. It is the latter approach Durkheim intends here (Durkheim, 1953/1924, p. 35). It is through the results of a scientific study of morality that we can hope to change morality, to "modify the real and to direct it" (Durkheim, 1953/1924, p. 60).

He then reiterates the description of morality that had emerged in the course on moral education: Morality consists of three elements, which are obligation, desirability, and a connection to social groups (Durkheim, 1953/1924, pp. 36–37). All three are indispensable. Mere subjugation to authority, as we saw earlier, cannot produce moral action (Durkheim, 1953/1924, p. 38). The relationship of the social group to morality is complex in his argument. We cannot be merely compelled by the group to morality, and yet the morality posited by the group is the only one to which we can possibly direct ourselves. The object of moral conduct is not the empirical society in which we live, with all its moral flaws and inconsistencies, but the ideal that society posits for itself (Durkheim, 1953/1924, p. 38).

It is also important to recognize the relationship of morality to sacredness. It is almost impossible to understand morality if we fail to see its relationship to religious life. Both consist of "the same duality" of obligation/duty and attractiveness/desirability, and each necessarily contains within itself at least some elements of the other (Durkheim, 1953/1924, pp. 36, 48). Durkheim recognizes a point of similarity between his argument and that of Kant on the relationship between morality and religion. Kant argued that the existence of God must be postulated because there is no other way to make morality intelligible, and Durkheim will simply substitute Society for God. "The Divinity," he writes, "[is] only society transfigured and symbolically expressed" (Durkheim, 1953/1924, p. 52). Society both compels, as a force outside us, and attracts, as something in our interior (Durkheim, 1953/1924,

p. 57). Following Rousseau, humankind without what society has given us is nothing more than instincts and crude sensory experience; we are essentially animals without it (Durkheim, 1953/1924, p. 55).

He returns yet again here to the idea of the human individual or person as a sacred object. This is, he argues, not something inherent in the individual but something conferred on her by the society, and thus "moral individualism, the cult of the individual" becomes itself a social and cultural phenomenon: "It is society that instituted it and made of man the god whose servant it is" (Durkheim, 1953/1924, p. 59).

After delivering his talk, Durkheim was then permitted to reply to several questions posed by members of the learned audience. We no longer have the questions, but Durkheim's replies point to them in elaborating on the argument of the paper. In the first, on the topic of "The Feeling of Obligation: The Sacred Character of Morality," Durkheim begins by showing why he cannot be labeled a simple moral conservative. The contemporary moral landscape has been shaken, he writes, and it is not clear what the consequences will be or what will emerge to replace what has been destroyed, and yet there is no way to go back into the past. We are forced to find solutions from where we are (Durkheim, 1953/1924, p. 68).

He turns back to the sacred character of morality, which he reemphasizes while also clarifying that he believes this sacred character of morality can be expressed in secular terms (Durkheim, 1953/1924, p. 69). He defines the sacred in a manner directly anticipating the definition in *The Elementary Forms*: Sacred things are those that have to be kept apart from the profane or else they lose their basic nature (Durkheim, 1953/1924, p. 70).

We must study morality with a "moral sociology," which he argues is based not in the study of social structure as an always determining fact but in the study of representations and of systems of ideas and beliefs. This is a Durkheim who seems quite distinct from the author of *The Rules* and of some other earlier texts in which a sense of the relative determination of representations from facts of social structure can be found. He is clear that he is not arguing that the study of social structures or the political and economic systems can hope to explain moral systems in their complexity. What can produce such explanations? Only "the special science of moral facts," which must be sociology, but "it is a very particular branch of sociology" (Durkheim, 1953/1924, pp. 71–72). Moral phenomena are "*sui generis*," clearly involved in complex relationships with other aspects of society, but constituting "a distinct sphere" (Durkheim, 1953/1924, p. 72). Durkheim here sounds much like a contemporary cultural sociologist in the vein of Jeffrey Alexander, arguing for the autonomy of culture from social structure.

He then returns to the idea of society's act of making the individual a sacred object. There is a powerful dialectic involved in our submission to society, which is certainly a kind of submission, but one that simultaneously emancipates us. Freedom is nothing more than escape from determination by blind physical forces, and this is achieved by opposing "the great and intelligent force which is society" to those forces (Durkheim, 1953/1924, p. 72). Society covers us in its embrace, making us dependent on it, but it is a strange kind of dependence that also frees us.

In a second response, titled "Philosophy and Moral Facts," Durkheim turns still more minutely to the issue of the method of this moral sociology he proposes. What precisely will sociologists of morality study, if it is not primarily the social structures that some would argue must be its cause? There are a number of sources of such study, and we do well here to allow him to speak for himself:

> There is first of all a considerable number of ideas and moral maxims that are easily accessible, those that are written down and those that are condensed in legal formulas. In law the greater part of domestic morality, the morality of contract and obligation, all the ideas relating to the great fundamental duties, are translated and reflected. . . . When we have broken this new ground we will pass on to another. I do not deny that there are duties and moral ideas that are not formulated in law, but these must be reached by other methods. Proverbs, popular maxims and noncodified customs are no less sources of information. Literary works, the conceptions of philosophers and moralists (you observe that I do not exclude them), direct our attention to aspirations that are only at the stage of attempting self-realization. . . . It may seem that these are clumsy methods that stand little chance of discovering all the subtleties and shades of moral reality, but this is a difficulty that faces all science at the outset. (Durkheim, 1953/1924, p. 77)

Here, again, we see what looks unlike most textbook caricatures of the methodological beliefs of the great founder of French sociology. He sounds again like a cultural sociologist, who freely recognizes that we can study the texts that human beings produce as a form of evidence of the meanings behind them that are informing human life in various ways.

He closes with a comment on the idea of individual morality, acknowledging that in some sense each individual has his or her own morality and reiterating that no individual contains the entirety of the collective morality of our society, which exists in holistic form only externally to real individuals who endeavor to realize it in their imperfect ways. This latter point indicates that, in the logical sense of the definition, we are all immoral in some ways, as the perfect and ideal morality is present only in that collective representation that eludes each one of us in its perfection (Durkheim, 1953/1924, p. 78). It may well be that the individual aspects of morality could be studied, but this is not the task of the moral sociologist. It is the more important task of studying the collective moral conscience to which she must turn, and it is this that will be encountered in the sources Durkheim has just delineated.

Value Judgments and Judgments of Reality

Durkheim intervenes in this 1911 paper on a philosophical question to attempt to show how it can be resolved with the use of sociology. Throughout his career, Durkheim, who was trained as a philosopher, never lost sight of the organic relationship of philosophy and the social sciences and made frequent efforts to illustrate the ways in which sociology could speak to philosophical issues, and often with greater precision and accuracy than philosophers could. What is the difference between **value judgments** and judgments based on a scientific examination of reality? The latter are purely descriptive of either objectively observable external facts (e.g., the mass of bodies or physical laws) or preferences with respect to certain external objects of the person speaking, who can be taken to be a trustworthy source on the matter (e.g., "I prefer beer to wine"; Durkheim, 1953/1924, p. 80). Value judgments, on the other hand, are statements that allude to external things in a manner that "attribute[s] to the people or things an objective character quite independent of my own individual feelings"—for example, stating that a certain painting has high artistic quality (Durkheim, 1953/1924, p. 81).

Evaluation, then, entails an individual's account of the worth of something according to his own individual sensibilities, and at the same time it presents the value of the thing evaluated as in some sense existing objectively. This is a contradiction to be resolved.

Durkheim next presents a number of the efforts at resolution in the philosophical literature. He describes three competing theories: In the first, value is inherent in some important characteristic of the thing valued; in the second, value is determined by the effect it has on "the average individual"; in the last theory, value is intrinsic in the effect something has on "the collective subject" rather than the individual (Durkheim, 1953/1924, pp. 82–85). The first theory is a kind of philosophical idealism, often argued by religious philosophers, and it is invalidated, argues Durkheim, because there are individual differences regarding value—that is, some people do not value things that are argued by this theory to have intrinsic value in themselves. The second and third theories are versions of utilitarianism, which defines morality as the course of action that yields the greatest good for the greatest number. The second is invalid because the average individual has only a "mediocre" capacity for evaluation, and the third because, although it makes the promising move toward a social theory of value, its utilitarian premise cannot account for the fact that some collective values with low utility are nonetheless held in great esteem—for example, artistic values (Durkheim, 1953/1924, pp. 83, 85).

All three, in Durkheim's view, go astray in trying to locate value in the thing valued rather than somewhere outside it. A little empirical investigation shows the folly of this presumption: Great paintings that compel the admiration of millions are nothing more in themselves than a wood frame, some canvas, and splotches of linseed oil with pigment, and the flag the soldier dies for is a mere scrap of cloth (Durkheim, 1953/1924, p. 87). He refers to the Kantian notion that humans have the faculty to transcend experience and invent ideals. It is these ideals that are at the root of values, not real, empirical objects (Durkheim, 1953/1924, p. 88).

The ideal is, however, culturally relative—that is, it changes from one social group to the next (Durkheim, 1953/1924, p. 89). Although ideals are not simple empirical objects, there are empirical measures of them, and so the social scientist can speak of them in a way that is not simply evaluative. All human societies hold to some ideal concerning marital coupling; the sociologist can investigate the power of that ideal by looking at the rate of adultery, divorce, separation, and other similar empirical phenomena (Durkheim, 1953/1924, p. 89).

Durkheim is now ready to posit his alternative, sociological theory of value. As he had already noted, the last of the three philosophical theories he had shown to be incorrect had taken a sociological stance on value, but he now shows that the notion of sociology behind it was incapable of appreciating the cultural construction of the ideal. The view of society in that rejected theory is simplistic, a vision of "a system of organs and functions" striving in struggle against external enemies in the same crude struggle for life of a biological entity reacting blindly as a stimulus-response machine. It is striking that the sociological perspective he is attacking is remarkably similar to the caricature of Durkheim's own view by those who have badly understood him! His own sociological perspective on value and ideals again sounds much more like a precursor to today's cultural sociology as articulated by Jeffrey Alexander's Yale School. Against this crude model in which ideals would be mere epiphenomena of the physical morphology of the society, he argues that a proper sociology of value will have to understand society not as a mere collection of "organs and functions" but as "the centre of a moral life of which the strength and independence have not always been fully recognized" (Durkheim, 1953/1924, p. 91).

Here, values are seen to emerge from ideals generated in social groups in "moments of collective ferment . . . period[s] of creation or renewal," when the members of the society are drawn into more intense relations with one another and the circulation of ideas is frenzied. Durkheim cites the period of the birth of Scholasticism in the 12th and 13th centuries, the Reformation, the Renaissance, the French revolutionary period, and "the Socialist upheavals of the nineteenth century" as examples of such morally intense times (Durkheim, 1953/1924, pp. 91–92). In these periods, society experiences exaltation and continued collective effervescence, and the ideal becomes so powerful and real to members of the group that they may believe that they are experiencing the emergence of utopia, whether explicitly religious or secular. In time, the fervor climaxes, and the level of collective energy returns to normal, and it is in this moment that the distinction between the here and now on the one hand and the ideal on the other emerges. The ideals are recalled to the collectivity at periodic intervals during festivals, ceremonies, and other public ritual settings when people come together in "intellectual and moral communion" (Durkheim, 1953/1924, p. 92).

The argument here sounds much like that in *The Elementary Forms* regarding how religious symbols come to be permeated by force. As in that later book, Durkheim stresses the importance of collective representations, ideas, and ideals charged up with the memory of the collective effervescence experienced when they were generated and collectively celebrated. Again, Durkheim seeks to elude the simplistic categories of materialism and idealism altogether by transcending them. Society is not simply material forces, and the ideals that power it are not ghostly "abstractions" from "cloud cuckoo land." These ideals are natural forces that can be observed empirically in the material objects that represent them ("[d]rawings, symbols of all sorts, formulae") and the collective phenomena that demonstrate their power (Durkheim, 1953/1924, pp. 93, 94). His theory, in short, explains how a scrap of cloth compels men to kill and die. It is because society has put in the place of the world of the senses a new world of the values collectively made and constantly reproduced by the group of which he is a member (Durkheim, 1953/1924, pp. 94, 95). His effort to transcend the established binary categories here is vigorous. Society itself, he concludes, is a natural phenomenon that has managed to transcend and dominate the nature from which it springs (Durkheim, 1953/1924, p. 97).

In the end, then, the distinction between value judgments and judgments of reality breaks down, since values inhere in ideals, which are themselves objective creations of a social group that exists in the real world. In this sense, there are not as many differences separating moral values and scientific concepts as we might like to believe. Both are products of the human mind, and both are necessarily collective products insofar as they are transmitted in the collective medium of language (Durkheim, 1953/1924, p. 95). For the actual differences, Durkheim rehearses the argument on the distinction between religious and scientific knowledge he would make in *The Elementary Forms* only a year later. If both concepts (i.e., scientific judgments) and values (i.e., collective ideals) are in fact "species of ideals," the former stop at merely "express[ing] the reality to which they adhere," while the latter exalt and glorify it (Durkheim, 1953/1924, p. 95). Here, as in *The Elementary Forms* later, it is unclear if this argument is successful at rescuing objective, scientific evaluation of reality from the radical sociology of knowledge Durkheim had just constructed.

The Elementary Forms of Religious Life

In this, the final of the three book-length empirical studies he published in his lifetime, Durkheim followed the same structural framework of the first two: The book is divided into three lengthy subsections, which he calls "books" (*livres* in French). The first is dedicated to preliminary questions of the definition of religion and the method of the study, and the other two have to do with a careful consideration of the nature of the beliefs and practices, respectively, that make up religion.

He begins with a statement of a clearly evolutionary perspective. It is a fundamental theoretical presupposition of the book that the complex can be understood by reference to its more primitive predecessors (Durkheim, 1995/1912, p. 3). Religions are, in Durkheim's view, all basically different species of the same genus. He uses a biological analogy that he made much use of in his various writings, the study of unicellular organisms as a way to know fundamental things about more advanced life forms, to illustrate his perspective (Durkheim, 1995/1912, p. 6). It is not an actual starting point for religion that we can hope to locate, as this is forever lost in the mists of history, and perhaps there never was a single moment and place when religion started (Durkheim, 1995/1912, p. 7). Sociology is in any event not coming at religion from the same standpoint as history or ethnology, which are interested in, respectively, actual past events and the peculiarities of primitive peoples (Durkheim, 1995/1912, p. 1). It is the present that sociology wants to account for, but (and this is a crucial point for Durkheim) we cannot hope to do that in a careful way without some knowledge of the historical and comparative ethnographic data on the topic at hand. It is not the origins but the "ever-present causes on which the most basic forms of religious thought and practice depend" that we want to find, and this is easier to see in simpler social forms; hence the desire to track the most primitive forms of religious life (Durkheim, 1995/1912, p. 7).

Much of the scientific attempt to understand religion, before Durkheim and in our own time, starts from an assumption that religion is based on falsehood. This is not Durkheim's perspective. Something that has existed for so long, in every form of human social life of which we are aware, must be based in some aspects of reality, for "[a] human institution cannot rest upon error and falsehood [or] it could not endure" (Durkheim, 1995/1912, p. 2). He is attempting to take up a position between the standard options of defender or attacker of religion. It may well be that what the religious them-selves believe to be taking place in their worship is mistaken, but it is unques-tionably the case that something real is happening there, even if the believers are unaware of what it is, and we can find it with scientific method (Durkheim, 1995/1912, p. 2).

This is a book about religion, but it is also, by virtue of that fact, a book about the forms or categories of thought by which humans understand the world, since the first such categories originate in religion (Durkheim, 1995/1912, p. 8). In one succinct passage early in the book, he summarizes its argument:

> [R]eligion is an eminently social thing. Religious representations are collective representations that express collective realities; rites are ways of acting that are born only in the midst of assembled groups and whose purpose is to evoke, maintain, or recreate certain mental states of these groups. (Durkheim, 1995/1912, p. 9)

In other words, at their origins, our ways of understanding the world are social and religious. We understand time in units (days, weeks, months, years) that map directly to recurring religious "rites, festivals, and public ceremonies" (Durkheim, 1995/1912, p. 10). We parse space, which modern physics has certainly shown us consists of no objective standpoint from which to evaluate position, according to "different affective colorings" (Durkheim, 1995/1912, p. 11)—that is, as one of Durkheim's students and *Année* collaborators Robert Hertz showed brilliantly in a 1909 essay, the right is associated with the good, and the left with the sinister. Even princi-ples of logic such as identity and contradiction have social elements, in Durkheim's view (Durkheim, 1995/1912, p. 12). The sociological study of religion can thus address philosophical problems of the origins and nature of knowledge, as it is clear that it is religion that has formed the intellect.

Durkheim now describes the two mainstream approaches in philosophy to the problem of knowledge, which he intends to leap over toward a more appropriately sociological solution to the problem. The *a priorists*, represented by Kant, propose that the categories of knowledge are given by human nature, while the **empiricists**, represented by David Hume, argue that we come into the world without such categories of knowledge and that they emerge through our experience in the world (Durkheim, 1995/1912, pp. 12–14). Durkheim painstakingly shows how both approaches fail to adequately explain the categories. They are necessary and, within limits, universal, so experience, which is varied, cannot explain them. Durkheim even characterizes the empiricist approach as ultimately irrational (Durkheim, 1995/1912, p. 13). Yet there is some social variation in the categories that we can easily see if we look comparatively across cultures, so no crude *a priorism*, which unduly privileges the mind as having the capacity to transcend experience completely, will suffice either (Durkheim, 1995/1912, p. 14).

Durkheim solves the problem by meeting each in the middle, in a sense. There must be some way in which the categories are rooted in "the nature of things," but experience clearly does cause them to differ. The level at which we must examine experience, however, is not individual but social. It is immersion in different social groups, each of which has its own way of parsing up the world, that causes individuals to come to different ways of knowing that carry a moral obligation of participation. This is a kind of sociologically critical Kantianism, wholly compatible with the revision of Kantianism found in Durkheim's great philosophical teacher, Charles Renouvier.

Now we get a statement of the core of Durkheim's sociological vision, in a famous phrase often repeated in the textbooks: "Society is a reality *sui generis*" (Durkheim, 1995/1912, p. 15). It is, in other words, not reducible to anything else; it is a singular phenomenon that must be examined apart from our investigations of other levels of human nature and experience. Human nature is dual: We are at one and the same time individual beings and social beings, and the two levels are separable, with the latter level necessarily constituting the most important element in our makeup (Durkheim, 1995/1912, p. 15). Being human means existing within the collective representations or categories of knowing that are present in the society that contains us. Such categories are translations of states of the social group and we transcend our individual selves in participating in them. In a wonderful footnote, Durkheim summarizes how the three different approaches to knowledge view the categories of knowledge: For the empiricist, they are "artificial"; for the *a priorist*, they are "natural"; and from Durkheim's perspective, they are "works of art, in a sense, but an art that imitates nature ever more perfectly" (Durkheim, 1995/1912, p. 17).

Definition of Religious Phenomena and of Religion

In the first chapter of book one, Durkheim endeavors to define the central topic of the book. What exactly do we mean to indicate when we say "religion"? Several contending definitions from scholars already exist, and Durkheim addresses, and rejects, each of them in turn. Herbert Spencer and Max Müller argued that religion is rooted in beliefs about the supernatural world, and others see it rooted in an attempt to understand mysterious, chance occurrences in nature such as solar eclipses, but Durkheim shows that a conception of the supernatural would logically entail a conception of the natural order defined by immutable physical laws, which is a modern concept not found in any of the primitive societies Spencer and Müller purport to be describing (Durkheim, 1995/1912, p. 24). Moreover, if religion were motivated only by the desire to explain mystery, why do we see it so often turning to explain the normal, everyday workings of the universe as well (Durkheim, 1995/1912, p. 26)? Finally, there is the argument that religion is defined by beliefs in a divinity or divinities, but Durkheim points to major world religions that have variants with no gods—for example, Theravada Buddhism and Jainism (Durkheim, 1995/1912, p. 31).

Now, having rejected his competitors' definitions, Durkheim gives us his own. Religion must be understood as consisting of two elements: beliefs, or ideas, and rites, or actions (Durkheim, 1995/1912, p. 34). Religious rites can only be understood by reference to the ideas that motivate them, since without them as a code to translate, the actions can appear indistinguishable from other actions; so, Durkheim logically proceeds, we must examine beliefs first.

The central characteristic of religious beliefs is the presence in them of a fundamental dichotomy, the **sacred** and the **profane** (Durkheim, 1995/1912, p. 34). These two concepts are the most radically opposed of all categories, and we must be careful not to confuse them with other important but less universal opposing binaries such as good/evil, superior/inferior, or God/Devil. The sacred cannot be equated to divinity, again, since there are religions without gods but none, according to Durkheim, without the sacred (Durkheim, 1995/1912, p. 35). There is a dangerous possibility of contagion between the two, and sacred things must at all costs be kept protected from the profane with prohibitions and barriers (Durkheim, 1995/1912, p. 38). Durkheim saves fuller descriptions of these core elements of the book for later in the argument.

Defining religion requires separating it from some phenomena too commonly taken to be reducible to it. Magic too has rites and beliefs, but the relationship of religion and magic is characterized by hostility, as magic is frequently oriented to "profaning holy things" (Durkheim, 1995/1912, p. 40). More importantly, religion never exists without a Church—that is, "a moral community made up of all the faithful, both laity and priests"—while magic has no such social group bound together by moral commitments on which to rest (Durkheim, 1995/1912, p. 42). There may be brotherhoods of magicians, but they are merely professional groups, from which nonpractitioners of magic are excluded.

So the definition of religion rests on these two central elements: It is a system of beliefs and rites oriented to the sacred/profane dichotomy that unites a social group into "one single moral community called a Church" (Durkheim, 1995/1912, p. 44). Durkheim emphasizes that all currently existing and historical religions are Churches in the sense he has just argued. There are, he acknowledges, some who see the future direction of religion as the expansion of a purely individual cult in which the social nature of religion is curtailed or even eliminated, but Durkheim puts this speculation aside, at least for the moment. It is the scientist's task to describe what has been and what is at present, not to speculate prematurely about what is to come (Durkheim, 1995/1912, p. 43).

Now, in keeping with his evolutionary framework, once we have a definition of religion in hand, we want to locate the most primitive forms of religious life. The argumentative style here is just what we saw in the previous sections: lay out and examine contending arguments prior to rejecting them and then suggesting his own alternative. There are two main arguments about the nature of the earliest religions. **Animism** presents primitive religion as focused on spirits, which take myriad forms as souls, demons, and deities. **Naturism** is the theory that early religion was based in worship of natural phenomena—that is, the winds or the sky or natural objects such as plants and animals (Durkheim, 1995/1912, p. 45). In animism, the idea is that primitives experience a double of themselves in dream life, which they extrapolate into a notion of the soul (Durkheim, 1995/1912, p. 47). They then further speculate that, at death, the soul is separated from the body, to which it had previously been inextricably attached, and becomes an independent spirit. So here, death is seen as the crucial event that transforms the soul into a full-blown spirit; thus, the first religious rituals involved funeral and mortuary rites (Durkheim, 1995/1912, p. 49). In time, this animistic framework produces a cult of the deceased ancestors of the primitive group. E. B. Tylor suggests that this leads directly into naturism later because primitives are, much like children, unable to distinguish animate and inanimate things and assumed the latter too had souls since the former did (Durkheim, 1995/1912, p. 50). Spencer, on the other hand, believes that over time primitives confused the naming of individuals after, for example, an animal with a historical origination of the human line in that animal. So an individual is given the name "Tiger," and eventually the primitive group comes to believe that the now-deceased person really *was* a tiger, and the ancestor cult dedicated to him is dedicated to the animal as well (Durkheim, 1995/1912, p. 51).

Durkheim recognizes the advance of looking at the concept of soul historically that is achieved by the animists (Durkheim, 1995/1912, p. 52). Ultimately, however, animism assumes too much gullibility and conceptual naiveté on the part of primitives, who Durkheim believes are not so unsophisticated as to need to "objectify all [their] sensations" (Durkheim, 1995/1912, p. 54). It is also not at all clear why the problem of the double would have needed a resolution of this type, since, after all, for centuries people believed the sun was an object only a few feet in diameter, and no one struggled to get to the bottom of it for a long time (Durkheim, 1995/1912, p. 54). There is also no evidence that the cult of the dead is the most primitive form of religious belief, for no traces of this kind of cult exist in Australia, where we find among the aboriginal natives some of the simplest forms of religious life (Durkheim, 1995/1912, p. 61). Finally, if religion is the basis for so much ("law, morals, and scientific thought"), how could it originate in a mere empty "phantasmagoria" such as the double/soul/spirit (Durkheim, 1995/1912, p. 66)? On the contrary, Durkheim, in a firmly materialist statement, believes that a scientific study of religion ought to presume that religion "expresses nothing that is not in nature" (Durkheim, 1995/1912, p. 66).

Animism tends to be proposed by anthropologists, who specialize in the study of simple societies. Naturism, on the other hand, is generally a theory proposed by scholars of the history and origins of the major European and Asian civilizations (Durkheim, 1995/1912, p. 68). Max Müller, who did crucial work on the study of the Indo-European origins of European culture and translated important texts produced during this period of historical origins such as the Vedas, was a central figure in this camp in Durkheim's day. For Müller, religion originates in actual experience, not in the "confused dreaming" of the animist theory (Durkheim, 1995/1912, p. 70). The first deities, he argued, were natural phenomena because nature was a constant source of wonder and fear for primitive humans (Durkheim, 1995/1912, p. 71). Religion is born in the transformation of these phenomena into anthropomorphic agents (Durkheim, 1995/1912, p. 72).

Müller attempted to trace this historical process linguistically—that is, he wanted to see if European and proto-European languages demonstrated a common original conception of natural things as personal agents. Some of what might appear to be evidence of this type can still be seen today in Latin-originated languages that unfailingly assign gender to inanimate things; for example, in French and Spanish, a house is gendered female (*la maison, la casa*), while its roof is male (*le toit, el techo*; Durkheim, 1995/1912, pp. 73, 74).

Durkheim notes that criticisms have been made by linguists of Müller's argument, but, lacking the requisite linguistic training himself to effectively discuss them, he moves to criticize Müller more broadly. If, as Müller presumes, religion emerged as an effort to explain the natural world and orient our relations to it systematically, it would not have been able to survive the clear falsehoods of the naturist perspective. After all, he writes, even unsophisticated primitives could not have taken long to discern that, for example, categorizing the rain as a god who can be invoked or placated by sacrifices or collective rite is inconsistent with reality. They would have noted the many times that the sacrifices and other rites failed and the rain came or did not come despite the rites (Durkheim, 1995/1912, p. 77). Naturism, like animism, would have religion born out of mere "hallucinatory images" (Durkheim, 1995/1912, p. 78).

If these options are indefensible as theories of the origins of religion, where should we next turn? Durkheim comes at this point to totemism. Both animism and naturism seek to explain religion by rooting it in our experience of natural phenomena, in the one case physical, in the other biological (Durkheim, 1995/1912, p. 84). The two are united in their rooting of the sacred/profane opposition in the natural world. But since neither human individuals nor objects in nature are sacred in themselves, their sacredness must come from elsewhere, and thus beyond both naturism and animism, there must be some more primitive religious form (Durkheim, 1995/1912, p. 85).

Totemism, a social/religious system based on divisions of human groups into clans that are conceived as members of a common family, was initially believed to be a religious form specific to the indigenous natives of North America (Durkheim, 1995/1912, p. 85). But William Robertson Smith was the first to see clearly how important totemism actually was, and, relatively recently at Durkheim's writing, W. B. Spencer and F. J. Gillen had discovered a variety of totemism that seemed simpler and much more archaic than the North American variety in Australia (Durkheim, 1995/1912, pp. 86, 88). A study of the meaning of totemism, then, must take the Australian cases as its primary data. Durkheim invokes the principle enunciated in *The Rules of Sociological Method* that the best-case scenario is to compare societies that are of the same social type in order to study a particular social fact in incarnations that are structurally similar (Durkheim, 1995/1912, pp. 90, 91, 93). At the same time, he admits, he will invoke some data on indigenous American totemism as well, while keeping the Australian cases as the primary example of the model, because this will allow some comparison of "two varieties of the same type" (Durkheim, 1995/1912, p. 93).

The fact that *The Elementary Forms* essentially swims in ethnographic data from premodern societies is an indication of a major methodological shift in Durkheim's sociology. In the middle 1890s, when Durkheim purported to have had his religious revelation, he was methodologically suspicious of the utility of ethnographic material in sociology. This is plain in *The Rules* but even more directly expressed in a lengthy review of a book on the origins of marriage by the Finnish thinker Edvard Westermarck (which will be discussed in Chapter 7), in which Durkheim argues that relying too heavily on ethnographic data without any historical data to undergird them exposes the researcher to the risk of failing to understand what she observes locally and, worse still in especially primitive societies, attributing its causes to psychology and biology alone. By the preface of the first volume of the *Année*, however, in 1898, Durkheim had begun to change his mind on this question. He now admitted ethnographic data fully to the table (Besnard, 2003, pp. 87–96, 94). By the time of *The Elementary Forms*, ethnographic data had become the central source on which he drew.

The Elementary Beliefs

The clan is the core of totemism, and two central principles of definition are involved here: The members are understood as united by kinship of name, and each clan has its own totem, unique to it (Durkheim, 1995/1912, p. 100). A **totem** (the word comes from an Algonquin Ojibway term) is an entity in the animal or plant world, and sometimes from the variety of inanimate natural things in the environment (Durkheim, 1995/1912, pp. 101, 102). There are at least three differing forms of totemic system defining how the child inherits a totem: It can come from the mother, from the father, or from a mythical ancestor (Durkheim, 1995/1912, pp. 104–105). There are larger social groups, known as **phratries**, made up of groups of clans, which can also have totems, but, Durkheim notes, they are diminishing and clans have taken on primary importance in the social organization of Australian aboriginal society (Durkheim, 1995/1912, pp. 106–107).

The totem is more than just a name. More profoundly, it is "an emblem, a true coat of arms," and Durkheim directly compares it to the heraldic coats of arms displayed by European feudal lords on their castles and weaponry (Durkheim, 1995/1912, pp. 111, 112). Clan members not only wear the image of the totem on their bodies in the form of drawings, tattoos, and scarrings. They also seek to resemble it themselves, and hence bodily modifications of a specific variety with that goal are often obligatory. When the totem is a bird, the men may wear its feathers, and in the tortoise clan, the men may shave their heads and leave six curls at appropriate angles to mimic the legs, head, and tail of the animal (Durkheim, 1995/1912, pp. 114, 115).

In clan society, the totem is the primary sacred entity, "the very archetype of sacred things" (Durkheim, 1995/1912, p. 118). It manifests itself in three different forms: the plant or animal itself; its representation or image, and the clan members themselves, who are understood as family members of the totem. Durkheim gives a number of compelling examples of the sacred power of the totem image, largely drawn from the groundbreaking ethnographic work of Spencer and Gillen. In central Australia, there is frequently found an object called a *churinga* (Durkheim notes that similar objects exist in the north—the *nurtunja*—and in the south—the *waninga*), which is a piece of wood or polished stone, usually oval or oblong in shape (Durkheim, 1995/1912, pp. 123–125). In some cases, it produces noise when whirled through the air and is then referred to as a bull roarer. The totemic group generally has a collection of these objects.

They are kept in a special location, the *ertnatulunga*, generally a cave in some remote location unknown to the profane—that is, women and boys who have not yet been initiated into manhood, who are not permitted to touch or even see them (Durkheim, 1995/1912, p. 119). The *ertnatulunga* itself is made sacred by the contagious touch of the *churinga*, so a man in danger of any sort who runs there is safe from harm. The *churinga* heals wounds and sickness by the merest touch, yet the only thing distinguishing it from other objects of wood and stone is the totemic mark it bears (Durkheim, 1995/1912, pp. 120, 121).

The relationship between the totem animal and the clan member is complex and exacting in specific rules of contact and avoidance. You may not ingest or kill the totem of your clan (Durkheim, 1995/1912, p. 131). There are some exceptions and mitigations for this harsh rule. For example, in cases of extreme hunger, or danger from the totem animal, one may break the rule, but subsequently one must excuse oneself for the offense (Durkheim, 1995/1912, p. 131). In certain clans that have the water totem, obvious difficulties are presented; clan members will die without water, but they nonetheless cannot drink it unassisted but only from the hands of someone in another phratry (Durkheim, 1995/1912, p. 130).

This may seem contradicted by the obligation of the clan member to wear the totem, or at least its image, especially once we realize, Durkheim notes, that prohibitions regarding the *image* of the totem are yet more stringent than those surrounding the totem animal or plant itself, which indicates that the representation of the totem is more sacred than the actual thing itself (Durkheim, 1995/1912, pp. 132, 133). Still more complexity is seen in the fact that clans consider human beings by nature to be profane, and yet clan members are believed to *be* the totem (totem myths frequently have original humans born surgically, by axe blows, etc., from animal ancestors), which is sacred (Durkheim, 1995/1912, pp. 133, 135). Yet humans in general have sacredness concentrated in certain parts of their bodies, especially the hair and the blood (Durkheim, 1995/1912, p. 136). In ceremonies, the *nurtunja* is anointed in human blood, and the Arunta draw the totem during religious rites on soil that is soaked in the blood of clan members.

The details of these practices and beliefs make it clear that totemism is not at all a species of animal or plant worship, since the clan member is himself the totem and the image is considered more respected than the actual entity (Durkheim, 1995/1912, p. 139). A central practical object of totemism, which is true of all religions in Durkheim's view, is the production of a system of ideas that will represent and classify all the objects in the known world (Durkheim, 1995/1912, p. 141). In totemism, all things are seen as related in some way to the clan, whether by familial affinity or profane antagonism. Durkheim here refers directly to the argument in *Primitive Classification* and provides a chart showing two phratries, with their constituent clans, and the material things in the world that can be classified as familial relations of the clan. For example, in the Kumite phratry, one of the clans is the fish-hawk totem, which obviously places that animal in connection to the clan, and also classes smoke, honeysuckle, and certain trees, among other things, as clan identified (Durkheim, 1995/1912, p. 143). Totem systems of classification such as this are the first classificatory systems we find in human history, in Durkheim's argument, and they are "modeled on social organization"—that is, as we saw in *Primitive Classification,* the clan is classing all things in the universe in a manner parallel to the classification of human groups with respect to one another (Durkheim, 1995/1912, pp. 143, 145).

Since the phratry, a two-fold division of the tribe, is the fundamental division of the human social world in Australia, it results that binary, opposed categories are basic. Durkheim is here suggesting an origin of binary thinking in social organization. He even argues that the scientific classification of living things into the basic unit of the genus should be seen as a logical development from these early classificatory efforts based on the empirical reality confronting primitives of their own social organization (Durkheim, 1995/1912, p. 148). The scientific classificatory method for the natural world is also hierarchical; the species is more basic than the genus, which is more basic than the family, and so forth. Where else, Durkheim asks, could we have generated this mode of classification if social organization, which is the location par excellence of organization into "superiors, subordinates, and equals," were not the primitive model (Durkheim, 1995/1912, p. 149)? Raw sense data show us that the phenomena in the world are "disparate and discontinuous," and yet we created categories of common, related things. It was religion that began this process, and even logic can be traced to these social roots (Durkheim, 1995/1912, pp. 238–289).

Durkheim then moves to a discussion of different facets of totemism. In addition to the collective level of totemic identity, where clan is the operative group, there is a sexual level, where men and women, respectively, share a totem that opposes them to the members of the other gender, and an individual level, where an individual acquires a personal totem in addition to his or her clan totem (Durkheim, 1995/1912, p. 158). Durkheim argues that the collective, clan totem is more primitive than the individual one, which is not imposed structurally but "acquired by a deliberate act" (Durkheim, 1995/1912, p. 163). He shows that in Australia the collective totem is nearly always present, while there are no examples of tribes where only the individual totem is present. Meanwhile in North America, where totemism is less archaic, the individual totem is stronger, and the collective totem is "in full decline" (Durkheim, 1995/1912, p. 181).

In a key chapter in the book, Durkheim addresses the totemic principle— that is, the source of its sacredness and its power. It is important to understand precisely what is being claimed when, for example, a member of the crow clan claims to be the totem. He does not mean he is literally a bird but that both he and the crow are animated by the same fundamental source of power (Durkheim, 1995/1912, p. 191). Totemic societies see the whole universe as powered by forces that with a few exceptions take the forms of animals and plants. This force that resides in the totem is a moral force, and it arouses both fear and respect (Durkheim, 1995/1912, p. 192). Durkheim summarizes an account he cites from a member of a North American totemic group, the Dakota, regarding the nature of this "diffuse power," which the Dakota call *wakan*, as follows: "[W]akan . . . goes and comes through the world, and the sacred things are the places where it has alighted" (Durkheim, 1995/1912, p. 201). In other words, throughout the universe, the totemic principle, which is given different names by different primitive groups, flows hither and thither, occasionally focusing itself in particular objects, which thereby acquire power and the consequent sacred status that humans award to powerful things. As a general term, Durkheim adopts the same Melanesian word for such power that was utilized by Marcel Mauss and Henri Hubert in their 1902 *Année sociologique* essay on magic: *mana*. This idea, whatever the term used to express it, is the historical predecessor to the scientific concept of "force" (Durkheim, 1995/1912, p. 205).

The totem is essentially a representation or a symbol of something beyond it. What is the thing standing behind the totem? It is this power of *mana*, to be sure—that is, the totem being or god in its abstracted form—but it is also something else. The clan—that is, the social group or society—is also what is symbolized in the totem, which means the social group and the totemic principle are essentially one (Durkheim, 1995/1912, p. 208). This stands to reason, argues Durkheim, as society is eminently in possession of everything required to "arouse the sensation of the divine": It forcibly compels us, it crushes opposition, and it is the object par excellence of authority (Durkheim, 1995/1912, pp. 208, 210). It works on us mentally in such a way as to give us the sense that there are moral powers outside us that command us. Yet this power is not solely coercive; it also undergirds our own power and instills us with confidence and energy when we are in its grip (Durkheim, 1995/1912, p. 211).

We come now to another key term in *The Elementary Forms*: **collective effervescence**. When human groups are assembled together and driven by common aims, they become filled up with a certain kind of energy. Durkheim describes the example of the man speaking to a crowd, who, when he is really in "communion" with the group to which he is speaking, and when his words begin to take on a palpable power greater than his own physical forces, begins to feel delirious with this power and can readily "slip . . . into every kind of extreme" (Durkheim, 1995/1912, p. 212). This kind of phenomenon can be transitory, as in this example, or it can be more sustained, such as during "some great collective shock," such as the Crusades or the French Revolution (Durkheim, 1995/1912, p. 213). Even in more mundane moments, we can see this force at work, in the "lift" we feel from the "esteem" given us by others when we fulfill some moral duty. Consider a scene on a crowded city bus. There are no empty seats when an elderly woman, burdened with bags, shakily makes her way up into the bus. A lone man who stands to offer her his seat is rewarded with the thanks of the woman, but also with the admiring, approving looks of others.

A description of the typical cycle of life in a totemic society is essential for a full understanding of the fundamental facts of their religious experience. Such clans typically divide the calendar into two broad periods: In the first, the clan population is fragmented into smaller units for hunting, gathering, and familial life; in the second, it is concentrated together for periods of religious festival in which only the men participate or a universally attended collective celebration called a *corroboree* (Durkheim, 1995/1912, pp. 216–217). In the part of the calendar when the clan is broken apart into smaller units, economic life predominates and collective energy is minimal. In the other part, religious life predominates and there is a much greater level of collective energy. This energy derives largely from the act of congregating itself (Durkheim, 1995/1912, p. 217). During a *corroboree*, the clan members are caught up in a collective frenzy, as they emit cries and violent gestures and then focus the collectively generated "electricity" into rhythmic avenues of dance and song. As emotional intensity rises, the energy produced provokes powerful sexual desire; wives may be exchanged, and even incest may occur (Durkheim, 1995/1912, p. 218).

Durkheim gives a lengthy description from Spencer and Gillen of an Australian tribe, the Warramunga, in their collective celebration dedicated to the totemic snake Wollunqua. The rites go on over several days, but Durkheim concentrates on the events of the fourth day, when the two phratries of the tribe gather around a mound of sand bearing the emblem of the snake. Once darkness falls, they begin to sing, and then the members of one phratry bring their wives up to offer them to the members of the other phratry, who immediately have sexual intercourse with them. As one might imagine, everyone is in an excited state at this point! Fires are lit, and then the members of the first phratry begin to writhe rhythmically around the mound, in unison, giving off shrill cries, while the members of the second phratry clang their boomerangs loudly. The first phratry goes around the mound twice, then resumes singing. This continues throughout the night. Finally, when dawn nears, the mound is violently attacked by the members of the first phratry and torn to pieces (Durkheim, 1995/1912, p. 219). "It is not difficult," Durkheim notes, "to imagine that a man in such a state of exaltation should no longer know himself" (Durkheim, 1995/1912, p. 220).

The experience of this dual world of time spent in quiet isolation and time spent together and filled to bursting with energy and emotional power gives the clan member to understand that there are two neatly separated worlds: the world of the sacred and that of the profane. In Australian societies, as according to Durkheim they are the most primitive societies of which we know, the boundary between the sacred and the profane is the starkest. In the modern world, on the other hand, we have intermingled the two more fully, and a great deal of the intensity has therefore gone out of the sacred and collective effervescence (Durkheim, 1995/1912, p. 220–221).

Another important question remains to be answered: How does the idea of this emotional, collective power get transferred to the totem symbol? It is, after all, as is made clear in Durkheim's description, generated by the phenomenon of the collectivity in proximity, ritually focused on rhythmic and intense activity—that is, by what might seem a purely material, physical set of facts. But for the member of the clan, the feeling of effervescence and the totem symbol are united by the omnipresence of the totem image at the moment of the experience of effervescence. That which generates the force—that is, society itself and the experience of collective exaltation—is a complex, difficult thing to comprehend (Durkheim, 1995/1912, p. 221). The symbol of the totem simplifies and crystallizes this

complex reality and comes to replace it. Durkheim returns here to the idea
he had earlier presented of the totem as an emblem. When a soldier at war
is killed, he is often said to have "died for his flag," by which we mean that
he died for his country. We moderns might think ourselves perfectly capable
of sorting the two out and recognizing their distinction. After all, the flag is
not the country, but only a scrap of cloth. And yet many soldiers in societies
much more advanced than the totemic clans of Australia have perished in
combat while attempting to reclaim an actual flag abandoned in territory
lost to the enemy, despite the fact that it is perfectly clear that the country
will not perish if that one flag is lost, and the war will not be won simply
by reclaiming it. Just as the clan member with his totem, the soldier "forgets
that the flag is only a symbol that has no value in itself but only brings to
mind the reality it represents [and] treat[s it] as if it was that reality"
(Durkheim, 1995/1912, p. 222).

The clan member, then, during the *corroboree,* fails to see that what he
experiences is coming from the group itself. He feels himself swept up in a
powerful sentiment, and he wants to connect this experience to a cause.
When he looks around him at the exalted moment, it is the symbol of the
totem, engraved on the *churingas,* that he sees. He is mistaken in the source
of the power, but not in the recognition of the power, which, Durkheim
asserts, is real and comes from society (Durkheim, 1995/1912, pp. 226–227).
A certain "delirium" is the hallmark of such experiences, and Durkheim
writes that all collective representations are "in a sense delusive" (Durkheim,
1995/1912, p. 228). The state produced here is literally "ecstatic," and
Durkheim gives the Greek term, εκστασις, *ek* "out of" and *stasis* "stand,"
literally *to stand outside of.* Such experiences are not merely imaginary; their
reality is why they affect us so dramatically. If the clan member rubs himself
with the *churinga,* he feels stronger, and "he *is* stronger" (Durkheim,
1995/1912, p. 229, emphasis added). Durkheim sounds like an idealist here
when he describes the social world as "a realm of nature in which . . . far
more than anywhere else, the idea creates the reality . . . and the role of matter is at a minimum" (Durkheim, 1995/1912, p. 229).

Another classic phrase from the book turns up here: "[S]ocial life is
only possible thanks to a vast symbolism" (Durkheim, 1995/1912, p. 232).
He gives intriguing examples involving tattooing and the social symbolism
of collective membership it conveys. The sharing of some common life
often moves certain individuals to mark that collective identity on their
bodies (Durkheim, 1995/1912, p. 233). The first Christians, he writes,
tattooed themselves with Christ's name or the image of the cross. Soldiers,
sailors, prisoners, and today even members of the same pledge class in a
sorority or fans of the same professional football team will do the same

(Durkheim, 1995/1912, pp. 234–235). This is a powerful way of illustrating one's membership in the group and constantly making available to oneself a symbol of the group that can enable a limited tapping into the energy of collective effervescence stored up in it.

There is a brief discussion of the soul in chapter eight of book two. It is not a concept of central importance in totemism, but Durkheim feels it necessary to explore its origins given the importance it will take on in later religious forms (Durkheim, 1995/1912, p. 242). There is a soul in totemism, and it consists of the substance of the totemic principle. Indeed, we are told that it signifies the totemic principle "incarnated in each individual" (Durkheim, 1995/1912, p. 251). The totem is closely associated with the ancestors, and Durkheim has already explained that many totemic myths describe the origins of the clan from the proto-totem entity (Durkheim, 1995/1912, p. 258). The totem can thus be thought of as the collective body of the ancestors, and the individual bears his slight piece of this identity in the soul. The soul, then, is the social in the individual, the "best and most profound in us" (Durkheim, 1995/1912, p. 251–252).

Durkheim uses his notion of *homo duplex* to discuss the relationship of the individual, the soul, and the clan. The truly individual side of us is the material body, which is profane. The collective side of us, represented in totemic societies by the clan, is the sacred. The soul, then, is the element of the spiritual and collective sacred that resides in the person (Durkheim, 1995/1912, p. 266–267). The belief in the immortality of souls was a primitive way of explaining the continuing existence of the group despite individual death: "The individuals die, but the clan survives" (Durkheim, 1995/1912, p. 271).

When the individual dies, the soul that had until then been bound to the body is now a freed spirit that may come and go from particular material places (Durkheim, 1995/1912, p. 276). Each individual in a clan is understood as the double of an ancestor, as it is understood that there is "an original fund of fundamental souls from which all the others derived" (Durkheim, 1995/1912, p. 280). Durkheim returns to the notion of the individual totem, believing this discussion of the soul has enabled him to tie it more firmly to the collective totem. The individual totem has the same characteristics as the protecting ancestor whose soul is a double of that of the one he protects. In both the individual totem and the protecting ancestor, Durkheim claims, we see manifestations of the soul. In the case of the totem, it is the soul "externalized and invested with greater powers than those it is believed to have while inside the body" (Durkheim, 1995/1912, p. 283). The individual totem thus is both our personality and something external to us.

Durkheim turns next to a discussion of totemic conceptions of god, and finds, startlingly, that there is evidence of the birth of the conception of god that is found in the world's historical monotheisms (Judaism, Christianity, and Islam) in totemism (Durkheim, 1995/1912, p. 298–299). Some Australian tribes have arrived at a basically monotheistic conception of the god, or at least of a god who is supreme among others (Durkheim, 1995/1912, p. 288). This god's characteristics are always the same: He is immortal, eternal, a creator, "the father of men" (Durkheim, 1995/1912, p. 290). Durkheim recounts one totemic myth of the god making a clay statue and breathing life into it. This monotheistic Australian god is considered an ancestor and is viewed as a man who has lived a man's life on earth, albeit one who has special powers (Durkheim, 1995/1912, pp. 293–294). There is a great unity in the totemic system: The monotheistic god is an ancestor who achieved extraordinary things. The spirits of the ancestors are "forged in the image of the individual souls," which are "the form taken by" the totemic principle (Durkheim, 1995/1912, p. 299).

The conception of god described here is much like that of Yahweh for the ancient Israelites. For the Australian aborigines, other gods exist, as was true for the Israelites, but their tribal god is supreme over these other gods, and it is "tribal feeling" that drives the members of the clan to unite the various cults inside the clan into a unified whole with a supreme god at the top (Durkheim, 1995/1912, p. 299).

The Principal Modes of Ritual Conduct

In the third and final book, Durkheim takes on the two aspects of ritual: the negative and positive cults.

He begins with the **negative cult**—that is, the ascetic rites. These are concerned with taboos and interdictions, with protecting the sacred from the profane, and sometimes also with keeping sacred things of different species apart from one another (Durkheim, 1995/1912, pp. 304, 305). There can be no positive cult without the necessary prior intervention of the negative cult (Durkheim, 1995/1912, p. 320). Taboos of contact are important here. The profane must literally be prevented from touching the sacred, and one sacred entity must not be allowed to touch another of a different species (Durkheim, 1995/1912, p. 306). The uninitiated may not touch the *churinga*, and blood should not be touched (Durkheim, 1995/1912, p. 307). Food taboos are frequent. Profane persons may not eat sacred things, and sanctified persons may not eat profane foods—for example, young initiates may not eat foods designated as women's foods during their initiation (Durkheim, 1995/1912, p. 308).

One may come into contact with something merely by being breathed on by it, by hearing it, or by looking at it. Women should never see the tools of the religious cult, and a dead man's face is covered so it may not be seen (Durkheim, 1995/1912, pp. 308, 309). There are taboos of naming; for example, the names of the deceased are not to be invoked, nor are the names of sacred entities. Women must not hear certain ritual songs, and a special, sacred language is sometimes required, which only men know, to keep them from learning them. Men also have secret names that women may not even know and that are never used in ordinary life (Durkheim, 1995/1912, p. 310). Clothing and food are profane, so nudity and fasting are often needed to enter the realm of the sacred (Durkheim, 1995/1912, p. 311).

Economic activity is also generally profane, and feast days and special places of worship arose to help remove the individual from the need for mundane economic and other such transactions (Durkheim, 1995/1912, pp. 312–313). Versions of quasimonastic retreat may be necessary to prepare for engagement with the sacred. Durkheim describes the preparation for initiation, in which the initiate must "live in the bush, far from his peers," avoid women, abstain from eating, sleep little, refrain from bathing, speak no more than required, and sometimes even abstain from all bodily movement (Durkheim, 1995/1912, p. 314, 315).

Asceticism is the core of the negative cult, and pain is its "necessary condition" (Durkheim, 1995/1912, pp. 315–316, 317). He provides vivid examples: the Arapaho torturing themselves in advance of war to obtain protection in the coming battle, the Hupa swimming in freezing water and then lying on the shore as long as possible in order to gain favor in some endeavor or another (Durkheim, 1995/1912, p. 317). Perhaps the most spectacular example is of the "cruel rites of circumcision and subincision," where the genitals are mutilated in order to give them the power of generation. In such societies, Durkheim writes, sexual intercourse is stamped with religious power: "It is thought to bring into play awesome forces that man can approach without danger only if he has gained the requisite immunity through ritual procedures" (Durkheim, 1995/1912, p. 319). The belief is that the painful procedure makes the organ capable of standing up to the powerful sacred forces of sex, which it would be unable to weather in an unprotected state. Pain is a symbolic indication for the Australian aborigine that he has moved out of the profane and into the realm of the sacred. He proves he is "stronger than nature" in enduring the pain, and the pain stands for him as the undeniable evidence that he is not mistaken about his change of status and his ability to access the powerful resources of the sacred.

This ascetic suffering of the negative cult is entailed by the nature of sacredness, which works by contagion and represents literally "a world apart" (Durkheim, 1995/1912, p. 322). Such ideas of the contagiousness of sacredness are to be found not only among primitives. Modern Christians believe it too, and hence, for example, the host at a Catholic mass cannot be touched improperly or by just anyone. This is all, in Durkheim's view, not simply irrational, for scientific logic itself is born in this sense of the importance of contagiousness in nature (Durkheim, 1995/1912, p. 329).

Now he turns to the **positive cult**. First there is the rite of sacrifice. Durkheim uses as an example a ceremony of the Arunta in the witchetty grub clan known as the *intichiuma* (Durkheim, 1995/1912, p. 331). The *intichiuma* is the ceremony designed to ensure the reproduction of the grub (which is a large, white moth larva) totem. At its start, the men of the totemic group gather at the main camp, while others keep their distance. All but two or three then depart, and those left, naked and weaponless, walk silently to a place where a block of quartzite has been inserted into the ground and surrounded by small stones. The quartzite block is the symbol of the adult witchetty grub (Durkheim, 1995/1912, p. 332). The leader of the ceremony, known as the *Alatunja,* then hits the block with a wooden plate while imploring it in a chant to lay eggs (Durkheim, 1995/1912, pp. 332–333). He rubs one of the stones on the stomachs of the others present. They all then move to another, nearby stone representing the grub, and the *Alatunja* strikes this too with the plate. This action is repeated at many different similar locations, perhaps as many as 10, up to a mile apart. The meaning of the striking of the stone is to detach some dust, which is understood to be the eggs of the grub, and their goal is to spread the dust out as widely as possible to ensure the reproduction of the totem force (Durkheim, 1995/1912, p. 333).

In some clans during this sacrificial rite, the blood of the members is mixed with the totem dust or remnant to make the operation even more fertile (Durkheim, 1995/1912, p. 334). In a fish clan, the leader sits in a pool and pierces his scrotum, and the blood that emerges is believed to engender the new fish (Durkheim, 1995/1912, pp. 335–336).

Then, to return to the Arunta, in the next act of the rite, they gather grubs and cook them. The *Alatunja* eats a small amount of the totem animal as the initiation of the ceremony, and he gives a small amount to others as well. He may not eat a lot but is required to partake of at least some of the grub in order that he be properly fertilized for the operation (Durkheim, 1995/1912, p. 339). This, Durkheim tells us, is a primitive sacrificial rite (Durkheim, 1995/1912, p. 340). He invokes William Robertson Smith in arguing that **sacrifice** is not about tribute or homage but about a communal repast in which the god and the worshipper become one flesh and "tie a knot of kinship between them" (Durkheim, 1995/1912, p. 341). A sacrifice properly defined, then, is far from the sense it has tended to take on in the vernacular English today of a renunciation or a giving up of something desirable. It is an act of "alimentary communion" (eating of the god) and offering (scattering the dust of the grub to propagate the totem; Durkheim, 1995/1912, p. 346). After approvingly citing Robertson Smith's definition, he then challenges his belief that sacrifice in its proper form is really only present in the great world historical religions, firmly asserting its presence here in totemism (Durkheim, 1995/1912, p. 345).

In communion and offering, we see the dialectic of the human and the god. Humans make gods, but gods also make humans. Man endures only because of the gods, but the gods also endure through the actions of human beings at the *intichiuma* (Durkheim, 1995/1912, p. 345). This is directly analogous to the individual's dialectical relation to society; neither can get along without the other (Durkheim, 1995/1912, p. 351).

Mimetic rites are the next aspect of the positive cult Durkheim discusses. These are the part of the positive rites that consist of imitation of the totem—for example, members of the kangaroo clan hopping about like kangaroos or those in the frog clan croaking like frogs (Durkheim, 1995/1912, p. 357). In the Arunta witchetty grub clan whose sacrificial rite Durkheim had just recounted, there is a set of mimetic rites that consists of the members, in the wake of the sacrifice just described, imitating the process by which the grub enters the chrysalis stage and subsequently emerges in a metamorphosed form (Durkheim, 1995/1912, pp. 355–356). Two principles drive these rites, and this is true of all sympathetic magic: "Whatever touches an object also touches everything that has any relationship of proximity or solidarity with that object" and "Like produces like" (Durkheim, 1995/1912, p. 360). The member of the totem clan imitates the totem because he really believes the same substance inhabits him, and he desires to imitate the totem principle just as, for example, the Christian wants to imitate Christ (Durkheim, 1995/1912, p. 362). Mimetic action of this kind creates moral power, and Durkheim argues that the actual justification for such rites is not the pursuit of "kangaroo-ness" but in the actual force they exercise over the individual's mind. The real moral power of the rite is what produces belief in the sympathetic magic.

The principle of causality is at issue here. Mimetic rites are believed to effect changes in things, and as *mana* is the primitive idea of force, Durkheim believes mimesis is the primitive idea of cause (Durkheim, 1995/1912, p. 367). The first thing implied by cause is efficacy, or force. Just as Durkheim traced force back to the social as its source, so too he traces causality back to the totemic principle, which is nothing more than society (Durkheim, 1995/1912, pp. 367–368). Force and cause come to us through "inward experience," and yet they are external in origin. They are a power from outside us that nonetheless works on us as a moral, and thus internal, force (Durkheim, 1995/1912, p. 369).

In mimetic rites, the belief is that the acts undertaken in imitation of the totem are a further contribution, in addition to the sacrifice, to the propagation of the totem. It is easy to see how such processes would be marked by the utmost gravity. If the totem is not reproduced, the clan members are doomed. They all act together, performing identical motions that they take to be the efficacious cause of the regeneration of the totem. There is nothing of the sort going on, but what *is* going on is that they are building up collective effervescence (Durkheim, 1995/1912, p. 371).

Unlike the rites previously discussed, **representative or commemorative rites** are not understood by members of totemic groups to have actual physical effects on the world. They are celebrated in a gesture of "faith with the past" and in order to "preserve the group's moral identity" (Durkheim, 1995/1912, p. 375). Durkheim's first example here is of the Warramunga and their ceremony of the Black Snake, which is the equivalent of the Arunta *intichiuma* and reenacts the mythical history of their ancestor, Thalaualla. It consists largely of "rhythmic and violent trembling of the entire body" in mimesis of the ancestor's shaking the seeds of life out of himself (Durkheim, 1995/1912, p. 376). However, in this ceremony, unlike in the witchetty grub example, the movements made are not seen as actually causing the totem to be reproduced. It is pure commemoration, recalling of the memory "to revitalize the most essential elements of the collective consciousness" (Durkheim, 1995/1912, p. 379). Another example given is of the Warramunga celebrations in honor of the snake Wollunqua, which is not an actual empirical variety of snake that exists in the world but rather a unique, mythological monster snake (Durkheim, 1995/1912, p. 380). In both cases, the "recreational and aesthetic element" of these rites is of great importance, and they are likened to "dramatic performances" (Durkheim, 1995/1912, p. 383). These rites certainly are intended to remind the individual of his connection to the collectivity and to its past, but they do so through entertainment (Durkheim, 1995/1912, p. 384). Durkheim makes the profound observation that games, sport, and "the principal forms of art" would appear to be practices that derived from originally religious rites such as these, and, more, those realms have "long maintained their religious character" (Durkheim, 1995/1912, p. 385). All festivals and similar great public celebrations, even the most seemingly secular, retain some of the elements of religious ceremony (Durkheim, 1995/1912, p. 386). The chief consequence of all such events is to unite groups of people and, through song, dance, music, and other such rhythmically charged and dramatic material, not to mention "stimulants that increase vitality" to "put the masses into motion" (Durkheim, 1995/1912, p. 387).

The last subset of the positive rites Durkheim takes on is **piacular rites.** These are group-imposed rites of mourning, and the moral necessity at their core is to show the continued strength of the group in moments of weakness—that is, the death of its members (Durkheim, 1995/1912, p. 400). Durkheim asserts that the traditional ethnological answer to why these rites exist is the same one provided by the clan members themselves: that is, the dead want to be mourned and they threaten to haunt the living if mourning rites are not carried out. But why, Durkheim asks, would the dead want the living to beat themselves, sometimes even to death, as is frequently observed in piacular rites of totemic groups (Durkheim, 1995/1912, p. 402)?

Durkheim offers another explanation. In intense, emotional, collective suffering, the group members demonstrate how deeply they feel the loss of their clan member (Durkheim, 1995/1912, p. 403). Moreover, the blood they shed in their mourning is a veritable sacrifice to the dead man (Durkheim, 1995/1912, p. 406). Finally, there is exaltation in suffering, as Durkheim showed in his discussion of the rigorous ascetic practice of penile subincision: "When one feels life in oneself—in the form of painful anger or joyful enthusiasm—one does not believe in death; one is reassured, one takes greater courage, and, subjectively, everything happens as if the rite really had set aside the danger that was feared" (Durkheim, 1995/1912, p. 411).

It is not only death that is the occasion for piacular rites. They may also be called for when, for example, a sacred relic is lost or stolen, in response to an insufficient harvest, or during drought or famine (Durkheim, 1995/1912, pp. 406, 407).

Durkheim then proceeds to a crucially important aspect of the sacred that he had numerous times earlier alluded to without full explanation. Robertson Smith, he recalls, had recognized that the sacred was actually a binary concept—that is, there were two kinds of sacredness. These are the **pure sacred** and the **impure sacred** (Durkheim, 1995/1912, p. 413). In English, the dual meaning of the term "sacred" has disappeared, but it is still present in some other languages. In Durkheim's French, for instance, the term *sacré* (which comes from the same Latin root as the English) can refer both to the holy—that is, that which is venerated—and to the blasphemous—that which inspires horror. So in French one can produce *la musique sacrée* and *un sacré menteur*, the English translations of which ("holy music," "a damned liar") require other terms to preserve the meaning. Note that the impure sacred is *not* comparable to the profane, which is merely anything not sacred. Both pure and impure sacred are collective in their very essence (Durkheim, 1995/1912, p. 417). Piacular rites deal with the impure sacred, while positive rites deal with the pure sacred (Durkheim, 1995/1912, pp. 415–416).

Religion's Future; Science and Religion

In the book's brief concluding remarks, Durkheim reiterates or restates much that has gone before, but he also provides insights not present in the earlier pages of the book. Although early religious systems were the first efforts to systematically know the world, religion in its present incarnations derives its staying power not from any contributions it makes to knowledge but from what it provides in increased energy and vitality to act (Durkheim, 1995/1912, p. 419). Collective effervescence is a vital element of any society, and there is "something eternal in religion which is destined to outlive the succession of particular symbols in which religious thought has clothed itself" (Durkheim, 1995/1912, p. 429). Here, he seems to be saying that, if given religions come and go, we can expect new ones to continue to arise to meet the symbolic and experiential needs they meet, or at least we can expect some new cultural forms of life that are able to produce the same real results in terms of collective effervescence and symbolic integration of the individual into a life larger than her own to do so. Durkheim presents to us as essentially comparable three different phenomena: Christians celebrating the life of Christ, Jews celebrating the Exodus, and citizens celebrating a "great event of national life" (Durkheim, 1995/1912, p. 429). He refers briefly to the ultimately unsuccessful efforts of the French Revolution to create new, secular forms of collective effervescence and communal celebration, and one cannot help but imagine that he might have been thinking of the real possibility of the emergence of a renewed such cult in the French Third Republic.

The conclusion also expands on the relationship of religion and scientific thought to which he had made tantalizing but brief sketches earlier. Scientific thought, far from being radically different than religious thought, is a member of the same family; religion is a distant ancestor without which science could never have been born (Durkheim, 1995/1912, p. 431). Science does differ from religion in that it is more distanced from action, while religion is necessarily drawn to it (Durkheim, 1995/1912, p. 432). But like religious concepts, and indeed all human concepts, scientific concepts must be collectively shared to have efficacy. The lone scientist may crow about truth all he likes, but if he cannot convince the rest of the scientific community at some point that his ideas merit attention, he will not be published, and he will have no position and no laboratory, and he will produce no results and be forgotten. So science too has some social element that must be considered in understanding its nature. Though scientific representations of the world are more subject to systematic criticism than those representations (such as religious ones) that derive *all* their authority from being collective, ultimately,

Durkheim suggests, the differences are less great than we might imagine. Faith still plays a role in the scientific world we inhabit, and not just because religion still exists. Witness the unquestioning faith many citizens, most of whom have not had even high school biology or chemistry, have in every pronouncement on dietary knowledge made by the scientific world, and then in the next pronouncement that nullifies the one just made, and so on, and so on (I am thinking of the constant stream of scientific reports on the dangers or benefits of caffeine, but the reader can plug in a dozen other examples easily enough). The faith the public has in science is, Durkheim notes, not fundamentally different from the faith the religious have in their gods, as the value the public ascribes to science is reducible to "its nature and role in life," which makes it a "state of opinion" (Durkheim, 1995/1912, p. 439).

Scientific concepts are rigorously debated and criticized only in a tiny minority community, and yet science is, like religion, a fully public form of knowledge. Durkheim sounds much like numerous writers in the contemporary constructionist sociology of science (e.g., Bruno Latour, David Bloor, or Steven Shapin) in passages like this one:

> To be believed, it is not enough that [concepts] be true. If they are not in harmony with other beliefs and other opinions—in short, with the whole set of collective representations—they will be denied; minds will be closed to them; as a result, they will be and yet not be. (Durkheim, 1995/1912, p. 439)

Even when Durkheim concludes by giving science the advantage over religion, it is not because of its epistemological superiority but for sociological reasons. If scientific classifications have become more powerful than religious ones, this is at least in part because of a new social referent for those representations: Whereas in the past all representations were limited to the boundaries of one tribe, clan, nation, or another, scientific representations increasingly have the ability to reach a social group constituted by the whole planet (Durkheim, 1995/1912, p. 446).

Conclusion

Durkheim was attacked in his work on religion and knowledge from both sides of a charged cultural debate in France at the time. The religious intellectuals, Catholic and Protestant, denounced his "atheistic" effort to reduce religion to a merely social fact, while rationalists and materialists often equally vociferously rejected him for purportedly muting his criticisms of religion by admitting that it served positive social ends.

The Elementary Forms thus received something of a hostile reception. The Société française de philosophie organized a discussion of the book in February 1913, and Durkheim gave a short summary of its argument and then addressed questions. His interlocutors showed themselves largely incapable of understanding or following the basic argument of the book, insisting on asking questions that had to do with matters not addressed in the book. Among anthropologists and historians of religion, the reception was frequently focused on the specifics of his characterization of totemism—for example, on whether Central Australian totem societies, which Durkheim emphasizes in examples in the book, are representative of totemism in Australia—and failed to engage the larger issues of the book. Even Alfred Radcliffe-Brown, the British anthropologist who was among the most central in introducing Durkheim to the British scholarly world, wrote to Mauss that he found *The Elementary Forms* a "disappointing" book (Fournier, 2007, p. 803). E. E. Evans-Pritchard, another giant of British anthropology who was greatly influenced by Durkheim, rejected the centerpiece of the book's argument in pronouncing, "It was Durkheim and not the savage who made society into a God" (Durkheim, 1982/1895, p. 15).

Though *The Elementary Forms* was the last book he wrote, this was the first of his books to be translated into English, in 1915—that is, only a few years after its original publication. Though initially it did not approach the influence in the English-speaking world attained by his other books, more recently it has been avidly taken up both by cultural sociologists, who have used the book's argument to discuss cultural phenomena seemingly widely separated from religion (e.g., sport and popular culture), and sociologists of scientific knowledge, who have read the book's approach to the social construction of knowledge, as well as Durkheim's other efforts in the sociology of knowledge discussed in this chapter, as a fruitful boost to their own efforts to sociologically describe the activities of scientists.

It is fairly clear that we miss many things if we look at *The Elementary Forms* solely as an ethnographic study of Australian totemism, and not simply because at least some of what Durkheim knew about Australia has been overtaken by more recent and careful ethnographic research than that on which he relied (Lukes, 1985, p. 477). The book remains a powerfully important study for broader reasons of its contribution to sociological theorizing about religion, culture, and knowledge.

A few questions

- Does a theory of religion like Durkheim's constitute a refutation of the metaphysical claims of religion?

- What kinds of contemporary popular cultural phenomena might be studied using Durkheim's argument from *The Elementary Forms?*
- How does Durkheim manage to preserve the status of science as a uniquely accurate form of knowledge, given his arguments about value judgments and the origins of scientific schemes of classification in religion?
- How, if at all, did Durkheim's own personal experience of religious faith and its loss affect his research on religion?
- What is the case that Durkheim can accurately be considered a cultural sociologist, that is, one who understands culture, or the ideal realm of human activity, to have at least a relative autonomy from material causes?

7

Unfinished Business

La Morale, the Family, and the War

By his mid-fifties—that is, into the second decade of the 20th century—Durkheim had already produced a vast body of work. When war came to Europe again in the summer of 1914, he and his allies jumped into the French war effort. During the Great War, France suffered horribly, and the *Année sociologique* group was especially hard hit. In 1915, one of Durkheim's strongest and most promising young students, Robert Hertz, was mowed down during a suicidal advance on German lines in Lorraine. Later that same year, Durkheim's only son, André, was killed in battle at the Bulgarian front. Durkheim learned the crushing news only several months later, in February 1916. Grieving terribly, he attempted to continue working and was able to find energy to continue to contribute to the war effort on the home front. But an undetermined illness weakened him and finally ended his life, before his 60th birthday, in November 1917.

This chapter describes Durkheim's war efforts in light of his intellectual work, and especially with respect to his thinking about the political engagement of the scholar. It also considers the plans he had for two more major works (on morality and the family) that he was unable to finish in his lifetime, and reviews the work on these two topics that we have not already discussed.

The Work on Morality and the Family

In a melancholy essay memorializing his deceased uncle and summarizing the unpublished material that had fallen into his hands at Durkheim's death,

Marcel Mauss argues that two particular areas of study were Durkheim's "most cherished work": morality/ethics and the family (Mauss, 1925).

Durkheim managed to work briefly during the summer of 1917 on the book on morality that was his next planned project, completing a brief sketch of an introduction (fewer than a dozen pages in the English translation) that was subsequently published in 1919 in the *Revue philosophique*. Incomplete as it is, it is scintillating in what it promises in this tragically unfinished book.

Durkheim considered the study of the family a logical extension of his interest in social solidarity and collective human nature, as the family is the human social group with the longest history. Mauss writes that, toward the end of his life, his uncle desired to "dedicate the rest of his life to [a study of] the natural and comparative history of the family and marriage up to the present," with materials he had used for years in his courses on this topic as the starting point (Mauss, 1925, p. 12). Durkheim's thought on this subject has been perhaps more widely misunderstood and misrepresented than his work in any other area, maybe at least in part because of the pronounced rise in the past several decades of intellectual perspectives on gender and the family with a pronounced impatience for contextualized historical understanding of earlier intellectual perspectives on these matters. Although little has been published, Durkheim wrote a good deal on this topic, much of it in the form of book reviews in the *Année sociologique* (Durkheim took chief responsibility for reviews in this area) and in course lectures that were, apparently according to his wishes, not published in his lifetime and subsequently lost, probably during the German occupation during the Second World War.

In the following sections under this heading, we examine the introduction to Durkheim's study of morality and some of the most important work he produced on the family in his lifetime.

La Morale

La morale in French (translated into English as either "morality" or "ethics") can refer either to the actual moral judgments humans make in their dealings with the world and one another or the "systematic speculation about moral matters" (Durkheim, 1978c/1920, p. 192). In the first case, it is a question of human actors following moral rules they have set for themselves; in the second, it is the scientific study of that activity. Such study faces what might seem a dilemma, since science is a form of knowledge in principle separable from action, while morality is inevitably geared to action. This means that the study of morality must also necessarily be concerned with "the question of action" (Durkheim, 1978c/1920, p. 194). Durkheim writes in a remarkable passage, "[t]here is no science worthy of the name which does not end in art; it would otherwise be a mere game, an intellectual distraction, pure and simple erudition" (Durkheim, 1978c/1920, p. 194). Here, at the end of his life, we find yet more evidence of the eminently practical and political motivation of much of Durkheim's intellectual project.

The study of ethics, in Durkheim's argument, cannot proceed from merely psychological bases, for psychology assumes everywhere and always the same basis for its facts—that is, the human mind. We know, however, that morality and ethics change cross-culturally and even from one historical period to another in the same culture (Durkheim, 1978c/1920, pp. 195–196). History is essential in the study of morality, for the morality of every human group is "a product of its history" (Durkheim, 1978c/1920, p. 196). Morality and ethics must be properly defined in order to separate this study from the study of other aspects of human activity that are in principle unrelated to ethics—for example, the cognitive and aesthetic sides of human life. Morality is an essential aspect of human life, but it is not *all* of human life, so we must carefully understand what specific aspects of human life are affected by ethics and morality.

The study of morality is made difficult precisely because of its self-evident nature. Everyone assumes they know all they need to know about its workings, because as moral beings they can respond appropriately to the moral questions posed in their world. Some philosophers even argue that a moral sensibility is simply an inherent given of the human condition, which we all have at birth and which requires no further cultivation. But, Durkheim argues, science can take nothing for granted. If scientists stopped at mere sense data and asked no more questions, we would never have inquired deeply into the nature of light or electricity (Durkheim, 1978c/1920, p. 197). It is undoubtedly so that morality works in human society as axiomatic—that is, as a member of a moral culture, one simply "automatically" knows what to do and what not to do. But the sociologist must get to the bottom of this "automatic" behavior. Morality, like religion and science itself (as we saw in Chapter 6), relies on collective representations. It is a certainty that the assumptions the moral actor must make in acting morally are not completely in keeping with the actual realities of the world, and the sociologist wants to discern the relationship between that reality and the moral representations that have been created out of it (Durkheim, 1978c/1920, p. 198).

The goal is to class moral facts as we class all other "natural things" in scientific examination (Durkheim, 1978c/1920, p. 199). This classification will rely on a careful study of the representations of the moral order, to be sure, but not only that. The institutional spaces within which moralities emerge and function will also need to be studied, as well as their histories.

So if we want to understand the morality operative in the familial setting, then the constitution, functions, and history of the family are necessary parts of that study (Durkheim, 1978c/1920, p. 200). It is, he writes, a "Science of Moral Facts" that he is proposing (Durkheim, 1978c/1920, p. 202).

Durkheim left a brief outline of further elements of the book on morality that Mauss used to complete the introduction. He was apparently intending to include chapters on traditional morality, the idea of subjective morality, Gabriel Tarde's theory of morality, and Kantian morality, as well as discussions of judgments of value and ideals and a comparison of individual moral consciousness and objective morality (Mauss, 1925).

On the Origins of Human Marriage

In 1891, the Finnish-born ethnologist Edvard Westermarck, who lived and worked for long periods in London, published a study in English on the history of marriage that brought him considerable academic fame. When the book was translated into French a few years later, Durkheim promptly addressed a lengthy critical book review to it, which was published in the *Revue philosophique* in 1895.

Durkheim crisply attacks the methodology of the study and many of its results. The fundamental criticism had to do with the fact that, in Durkheim's view, the ethnographic data from primitive societies mobilized by Westermarck simply did not allow him to make the arguments he desired to make about the entire history of the institution. Historical facts—that is, information about early marriage in more advanced societies in the form of laws and customs—are needed in a discussion of an institution that, as Durkheim would argue, is fundamentally defined by legal structures. Law does not exist in these societies in any sense that would allow us to compare merely customary practices to the legally sanctioned institutions of more advanced societies (Durkheim, 1975d/1895, p. 72). Recall from the previous chapter that Durkheim had not at the time he wrote this review yet made the turn he would make in the mid 1890s to a fuller appreciation for ethnographic facts.

Durkheim also attacks Westermarck's crude evolutionary stance. Sociology in Durkheim's view cannot be based in any simplistic way on Darwinian evolutionary biology. Westermarck wanted to move from instincts to institutions in a straightforward manner, and he argued that marriage, which he defined simply as a more or less stable union of male and female that extends beyond the simple act of procreation, essentially exists in all "superior vertebrate" animals (Durkheim, 1975d/1895, p. 76). The evidence for marriage, Westermarck insisted, is greater the higher up on the evolutionary chain of being we look.

Durkheim would have none of this. At the simple factual level, this does not hold up; many species of bird, he notes, have more stable unions than many mammals (Durkheim, 1975d/1895, pp. 77–78). But beyond this, Durkheim was troubled by the insinuation that there is no important sociological distinction between animal and human sexuality. That both are means of reproduction biologically is clear enough, and on that ground they are comparable. But for Durkheim the real action in a sociological discussion of marriage is in the territory of the moral—that is, in how sexual commerce is thereby taken out of the pure realm of reproduction and subjected to regulation and normalization by a social institution. Westermarck's definition of marriage was too loose, and virtually everything counted. Durkheim recognized two different schemas for sexual coupling in human societies: On the one hand, there is **free union**, or concubinage, and on the other, legal marriage. What distinguishes them is basic and obvious: Free union exists outside the notion of law, while marriage is defined by juridical structures that assign to it certain rights and duties that are enforced by legal sanction (Durkheim, 1975d/1895, pp. 78–79). So what defines marriage in Durkheim's argument is not mere durability but legal structure and regulation. Westermarck effectively defined these two radically distinct forms of practice with one term, which is the kind of terminological error that in Durkheim's view would "condemn us to never know what we are talking about" (Durkheim, 1975d/1895, p. 79).

On Marriage, Motherhood, and the Law

Marianne Weber was the wife of Max Weber, one of Durkheim's great contemporaries, and herself a writer of considerable talent. In the 1906 to 1909 issue of the *Année*, Durkheim reviewed her book on the legal history of marriage and motherhood.

Durkheim accuses Weber of constructing a "simplistic" history of the family in which only two familial forms are recognized, the communistic clan and the patriarchal family, which lends itself to greater individuation. But this forced her to crush disparate historical family forms into these two boxes (Durkheim, 1978d/1906–1909, p. 141). He does note that she was "wisely conservative" to reject the idea, common among feminists in their day, that the elimination of the institution of marriage would undo the vestiges of female subjugation (Durkheim, 1978d/1906–1909, p. 142). But she was, in his view, insufficiently aware of the complicated value of marriage as an institution and of the need to oppose its weakening. Weber advocated that marriage be dissolvable solely at the discretion of the involved parties—that is, divorce by mutual consent—which, for Durkheim, indicated a trivialization of the social value of the marital bond. The fundamental problem with Weber's book was that "her entire theory rests on the principle that the patriarchal family has brought about a complete enslavement of women" (Durkheim, 1978d/1906–1909, p. 143). This is entirely too simplistic, argues Durkheim. Certainly, legal inequality has resulted from the dominance of this familial form, but other social benefits have accrued, for women specifically and for the larger society. Women have come to occupy an exalted position at the control of the hearth, their roles as caregivers and nurturers widely recognized and respected. Family and spousal relations have grown closer and more intimate than in earlier historical periods. The "religious respect" inspired by the institution of the family has much to do with the strength of the marital bond and the difficulty of easily undoing it. This would be damaged by weakening the institution (Durkheim, 1978d/1906–1909, pp. 143–144).

The Conjugal Family

Durkheim published the essay with this title in 1892 in the *Revue philosophique*. The **conjugal family** is the typical modern form, consisting only of husband, wife, and their unmarried children. It results from the "contraction of the paternal family," which includes the spouses and all their descendants with the exception of adult female children who have been married off into other paternal lines (Durkheim, 1978e/1892, p. 229). The central result of the rise of this familial type, in which the children are increasingly independent of the parental pair, is that "the old familial communism has been shaken apart to an extent that we have never before encountered" (Durkheim, 1978e/1892, p. 230). The paternal family first removed the collective entity of the family as the central actor and gave this honor to the father, and now progressively in the conjugal family, each member is made an autonomous entity. All that remains in the conjugal family of the former communism is the restriction of rights of the school-age child (Durkheim, 1978e/1892, p. 231).

It is plain to see that the evolutionary process, still early in Durkheim's day, has today advanced much farther. Durkheim suggests a "law of contraction or progressive emergence" wherein "more and more restricted groups . . . tend to absorb the whole of family life" (Durkheim, 1978e/1892, p. 232). Today, this contraction is arguably reaching its mathematical limit with the precipitous rise of the "family of one" so much discussed in contemporary media and scholarship. This familial contraction follows the extension of the "social milieu" outward. As the boundaries of the social groups with which individuals have some investment are pushed back to the global level, the family can be expected to continue to shrink (Durkheim, 1978e/1892, p. 233).

A central question then is how this affects "domestic solidarity" (Durkheim, 1978e/1892, p. 234). In familial communism, Durkheim argues, solidarity comes from relations both to persons and things that can be provided by the family—for example, domestic property. In the conjugal family, attachment is only to persons, and this entails a *de facto* weakening of solidarity, which troubles Durkheim. However, this also means a movement in the direction of the dissolution of the father's right to leave his property to his children, a privilege cherished by conservatives but, as we saw in Chapter 3, rejected by Durkheim in the interest of greater economic equality. So Durkheim takes a complicated position on this issue, as an advocate of both close-knit families with mutually interdependent members and economically progressive social policies such as the revision of inheritance law (Durkheim, 1978e/1892, p. 235).

Some in Durkheim's day argued, a century before the articulation of the same claim by today's advocates of a more individualist definition of the marital institution, that personal, conjugal love between two people is more than enough to maintain familial solidarity. Durkheim strongly disagrees (Durkheim, 1978e/1892, p. 237). Citing the statistics on marriage, family, and suicide that he would later mobilize in his book on suicide, he notes that suicide rates in the family are kept low, especially for the wife, not simply by the conjugal love of the marital couple but by the increased solidarity of the collective hearth that is produced by the procreation of children (Durkheim, 1978e/1892, p. 238).

Durkheim suggests, in consonance with many of his other writings, that only one other social group can provide the solidarity lost by the weakening of the family: the occupational group, or the guild. The essay closes with a sociological attack on "free unions"—that is, childrearing out of wedlock. A moral society requires that "members have obligations toward one another," and in his view such free unions are not cemented by any formal bonds and therefore lack the requisite moral glue to actually hold the participants together in any real way (Durkheim, 1978e/1892, p. 239).

On Divorce

Durkheim wrote the essay "Divorce by Mutual Consent" in 1906, and it was published in the *Revue bleue*. Even in Durkheim's day, any intellectual who dared to criticize the increasing fragility of the marital bond and to call for its strengthening risked being labeled a reactionary *a priori*. Durkheim attempts to dissuade those critical of his position from doing just that to him by remarking that the sociologist must be willing to subject *all* institutions, "even . . . those which pass for being the most sacred," to questioning and critical analysis, but he must also recognize that it is not intellectually sound simply to yield in all cases, with no debate, to those who desire rapid and radical change (Durkheim, 1978f/1906, p. 240). Ideological partisanship cannot be allowed to replace cautious and thorough sociological analysis.

It is perhaps difficult for a contemporary reader to fairly understand Durkheim's position in this and some of his other interventions on matters concerning marriage and sexuality precisely because the century since his death has seen an acceleration of just the kind of increasingly radical social change represented in his time by the movement for divorce by mutual consent. The supporters of divorce by mutual consent claim it is clearly in the interests of both parents and frequently of the children involved as well, but Durkheim notes that there is another aspect of the question to be considered: "the interest of the institution of matrimony itself, which the system of divorce cannot fail to affect" (Durkheim, 1978f/1906, p. 241). He hastens to add that it is clear that divorce cannot be universally prohibited, and there are cases in which the dissolution of a marriage is a desirable thing for both spouses, but there are facts that would suggest that this liberalization of divorce law would significantly harm the institution of marriage.

He first recalls some of the data on the effect divorce rates have on suicide rates he had discussed in detail in his book on suicide. In that book, he showed that marriage is, generally speaking, a significant factor in reducing the likelihood of suicide. He is able to augment that observation here by presenting data that show that in parts of France in which divorce is more common, the protection marriage provides against suicide is weaker; it is in Paris, where divorce is most common, that the effect is weakest (Durkheim, 1978f/1906, p. 244). He had noted in *Suicide* that the protective power of marriage was greater for men, while women were only protected if their marriage had yielded children. He had even argued then that the suicide rates of married women seemed to be lower compared to their unmarried counterparts in Paris, that is, where divorce was frequent, than in the provinces, where it was not. But here he takes back that claim, arguing instead that the comparative advantage of married women in Paris is an effect not of the ready availability of divorce but of the peculiar stresses facing unmarried young women in Paris that significantly raise their suicide risk compared to young unmarried women in the provinces (Durkheim, 1978f/1906, p. 246). Divorce, he summarizes, seems not to affect the female suicide rate much one way or the other.

The effect on the *male* suicide rate is, however, pronounced. He recapitulates some of the reasoning given in *Suicide* on why men derive protection from suicide in marriage. Absent an exterior regulatory force or presence, individual men are not effective at moderating their sexual energies. If their desires are not regulated, emotional distress and dissolution tend to be the results. The marital institution provides the necessary regulation. However, "[r]egulation from which one can withdraw whenever one has a notion is no longer regulation," Durkheim argues (Durkheim, 1978f/1906, p. 248). Removing the role of the agent who stands in for society, the judge, from the decision-making process of divorce is a step that will inevitably weaken the regulatory force of marriage (Durkheim, 1978f/1906, p. 248).

Those who supported divorce by mutual consent contended that, since marriage is a contract, it should be dissoluble on the agreement of the involved parties. But Durkheim insists that the effects of a contract can be felt on parties beyond the two spouses. Children are the most obvious such party. They change the marital relationship so compellingly that the end of the marriage is altered once they exist; the couple itself, once the end, is now but a means to the end of the family for which the couple is responsible (Durkheim, 1978f/1906, p. 249). There is thus a clear obligation for spouses in marriages with children that invalidates a merely mutual consent model for divorce.

Even the partners themselves may well benefit from marriages that they seek to escape in a fit of anger or spite. Certainly, there are marriages in which disharmony between the spouses is so great that separation is the only reasonable path, but there are many, many more "simply mediocre marriages," imperfect, inconstantly exciting and joyous, that nonetheless produce "sufficient feeling for . . . [the] duty . . . to fulfill [one's] function" and thereby provide a not insignificant social good (Durkheim, 1978f/1906, p. 250). This is a communitarian statement of the sociological value of even unspectacular marriages and criticism of too-easy divorce that merits a serious reading by anyone who takes marriage seriously.

On Sexual Education

Durkheim took part in a public debate in 1911, published in the *Bulletin de la Société française de philosophie,* on the topic of what and how the schools should teach youth about sexuality. His opponent was a physician and an advocate for a purely "scientific" approach to sex in the French school system, a Dr. Doléris. Durkheim begins the discussion by agreeing that education on the importance of sexual hygiene and health is paramount in the schools and that all societies have some such education (Durkheim, 1975b/1911, p. 241). Doléris, however, fails to understand the difference between hygiene and morality, and he does not understand why the latter is of such great social importance. From a moral perspective, Durkheim argues, the problem is how to impart to the young person the idea that continence is a duty (Durkheim, 1975b/1911, p. 241). Doléris acknowledges the possible physical and moral "worries" produced by "free" (that is, unmarried) sexual activity, among the chief of which are unwanted pregnancy and the spread of disease, but he does not take on the larger question of how sexual education would get at the difficult moral imperative, for Durkheim, of making the student understand the deep moral significance and indispensability of the institution of marriage in regulating sexual behavior. If we can be excused a pun, nakedly biological information about how the sex organs and reproductive process work will not suffice here.

Durkheim accepts the idea that sex has a "mysterious character" in "public opinion and religious belief" and, as he would do with religion in the book on that topic that he would publish in the following year, he classifies it as something much more complicated and profound than a "simple prejudice" (Durkheim, 1975b/1911, p. 242). Although religious ideas may be weakening in modern France, Durkheim notes that it is nonetheless the case that a "collective sentiment" that is present and upheld over virtually the entire span of humankind on the planet must be rooted in something concrete and not in mere superstition. All religion, he claims, sees human sexuality as something "grave" and "solemn" (Durkheim, 1975b/1911, p. 242). The moral sociologist's task here, as in the case of religion, is to find the kernel of truth in sexuality that is expressed by this universal sense of seriousness in the act.

The sex act is universally understood as having something mysterious about it, which means it cannot be easily and unproblematically made part of "vulgar life"; sex is "exceptional," "troubling and disconcerting," and it "awakens in us contradictory sentiments"; it "shocks, offends, repels" us at the same time as it "attracts"; it violates our sense of modesty more effectively than any other act, and yet it also is the act that most strongly connects human beings (Durkheim, 1975b/1911, p. 243). It should not be surprising, then, that such an "ambiguous" phenomenon troubles our moral consciousness, which can finally neither simply "condemn" nor "praise" sex and finds a compromise position: Sex is acknowledged and accepted as a reality, but one that must be occluded and removed from public view and discussion (Durkheim, 1975b/1911, p. 243). In this, sex reveals a unique role in the moral life that is unlike any other act or aspect of our nature.

Sexual education, therefore, in Durkheim's view, must include this conflicted and complex aspect of sex and its role in our moral culture. In arguing, as Doléris does, that sexual education should simply treat the sexual act as "an ordinary act of physical life," sex is robbed of its fundamentally cultural character (Durkheim, 1975b/1911, p. 244). Sex is *not* just any other biological process, such as digestion or circulation, and the moral problem of trying to treat it as though it were should be self-evident (Durkheim, 1975b/1911, p. 244). Durkheim carefully notes that he is not by any means arguing here for the victory of "bourgeois prudishness," but to ensure that students understand the sound moral basis for sexual modesty and restriction (Durkheim, 1975b/1911, p. 244).

Doléris responds in a manner that rings consistently with what many an advocate for relatively morally unrestricted sexual education in schools today would likely have to say. He makes the rhetorical ploy of claiming to desire to stick solely to "the terrain of science," which requires a rejection of all moral claims like those made by Durkheim (Durkheim, 1975b/1911, p. 244). But Durkheim recognizes that there is not only one scientific discourse involved in this topic—that is, that of biology; there is also that of *social* science. Doléris insists on seeing in sex "a very clear and simple reality," and he charges Durkheim's field, sociology, with the task not of actually trying to understand the bases for sexual morality but only of understanding why religions insist, in his view foolishly, on shrouding it in mystery. He also insinuates that Durkheim speaks under the influence of the "education . . . of a particular milieu"—that is, his Jewish heritage—which has apparently filled him with irrational sexual taboos and prevented him from accurately understanding sexuality (Durkheim, 1975b/1911, p. 245). Doléris's perspective on the degree of complexity of human morality is fairly well summarized in an example that he believes shows how little human morality is affected by the complete demystification of human sexuality: He alludes to the young female medical students who dissect cadavers and know how the human body is put together, and who nonetheless are still "decent" (Durkheim, 1975b/1911, p. 246). He seems, in short, determined to avoid seeing morality as a delicate, complex structure that can be disrupted in many ways.

Durkheim's response is that the mysterious aspects of the sex act were revealed to him not by his religious background but through his research into historical and ethnographic data on human societies (Durkheim, 1975b/1911, p. 246). He speaks, he says, not as a man but solely as a sociologist. Reason is the core of sexual education, but this must not be a reason that would limit itself to the "exterior gestures" studied by the "physiologist" but one that would also explore the "sentiments, ideas, and institutions which give these relations their specific human form" (Durkheim, 1975b/1911, p. 247). Sex has a dual nature in the human world that must be taught to the child if she is not to come away with an oversimplified view of things.

Durkheim then sketches briefly his vision of a sexual education curriculum. This would be integrated into a sociological discussion of the entirety of "domestic morality"—for example, the institution of marriage and its history and sociological bases (Durkheim, 1975b/1911, p. 249). He cites Kant in describing the basic immorality of sexual commerce. Kant had seen that the reason sex is so immediately morally troubling for us is that if it is not properly circumscribed by institutions that require mutual consideration and respect, it is an act in which an individual simply uses another as an instrument of pleasure, which is contrary to the dignity of the human person (Durkheim, 1975b/1911, p. 249). This respect for the individual is, as we saw in his response to Ferdinand Brunetière that was discussed in the second chapter, the very basis for modern morality for Durkheim, so anything that potentially compromises or challenges it must be questioned. This respect for the human person is what leads us to keep a certain distance from others, to avoid any contact that can be seen as too intimate with anyone with whom we are not sufficiently acquainted, to shield our bodies from the "indiscrete looks" of others: in short, to "isolate ourselves" in many ways. All this indicates that we are in the realm of the sacred (Durkheim, 1975b/1911, p. 249).

He then borrows heavily from the theoretical argument of the book on religion that he was in the process of finishing: If we attempt to come into contact with the sacred—in this case, the person of the other—without proper ritual preparation and purification, we commit a "sacrilege" (Durkheim, 1975b/1911, p. 249). In sex, the profanation is particularly intense, as bodily integrity is fully breached through penile penetration of the vagina. Again, the shattering of the sacred boundary of the person is great here, but at the same time this "constitutional immorality" is counterbalanced by "the most intimate communion that can exist between two conscious beings" (Durkheim, 1975b/1911, p. 250).

In this communion, two people literally become one and "a new personality is born which envelops and includes the two beings" (Durkheim, 1975b/1911, p. 250). When this is not a fleeting event but instead becomes a stable and durable fact of relation—that is, in marriage—the profanation is undone and the two effectively become one for always. But if, on the contrary, the two, after the profanation and unification, again separate to reclaim their individual identities and reject the new being, then the profanation remains. Hence, Durkheim concludes, the immorality of free unions, which have no firm social bond to undergird them and break apart at the merest trouble. It is the recognition of the profound moral bond of the sexual unification in marriage and the creation of the new being that transcends the two original entities that make two divorced spouses who encounter one another after their divorce feel so viscerally uncomfortable. They recognize the awkward, unnatural strangeness of attempting to meet one another now as sacred, separate beings when each already fully knows the most profound mystery of the other.

Origins of the Incest Taboo

In a lengthy article of some 70 pages first published in the *Année,* Durkheim took on the question of the origin of the incest taboo. He begins with a statement about research methodology in sociology that would later be famously recapitulated in his book on religion. The study of an institution requires, he argues, "trac[ing] it as nearly as possible to its origin" (Durkheim, 1963/1898, p. 13). The point of origin of a social object, in other words, marks its entire development and trajectory, even if we do not at first recognize the specifics of this effect. With respect to the prohibition of sexual contact between those of close blood familial relations, it is the law of exogamy that we find at the origin (Durkheim, 1963/1898, p. 15). Exogamy is, in traditional anthropological language, the principle by which sexual relations between members of one clan are forbidden and clan members are required to take sexual mates from clans that are not their own. The clan is a kind of social group of considerable importance for anthropology, consisting of individuals who understand themselves to be relatives by virtue of one single mode of identification: "[T]hey are bearers of the same totem" (Durkheim, 1963/1898, p. 15).

The **law of exogamy** generally means no sexual contact at all between members of the same totem group, although Durkheim notes that some evidence suggests there are clan societies in which only marital sexual relations are prohibited (Durkheim, 1963/1898, pp. 16, 17). The punishment of the transgression of the rule of exogamy is sometimes repressive, with serious sanctions invoked up to and including death, and sometimes "natural"; in this latter case, it is understood that nothing explicit need be done to the guilty parties as they will be punished by the powers present in the natural order of the world itself (Durkheim, 1963/1898, p. 18). Often in clan societies, it is the case that rules that are taken with the most seriousness are the ones that are left to such "natural" punishment (Durkheim, 1963/1898, p. 19). The law of exogamy is generally considered one of these most serious laws, and transgression of it is seen as among the most "abominable" actions possible in these clans (Durkheim, 1963/1898, p. 19). Durkheim claims the law is of an absolute universality in clan society; there are no examples of such societies that do not practice it (Durkheim, 1963/1898, p. 25).

The central question to which Durkheim now turns is the cause of this universal rule. There have been other explanatory efforts, and he spends some time describing and then criticizing them. J. F. McLennan argued that the common practice of infanticide of female children leads to a deficit of females and hence a requirement to seek wives outside the clan (Durkheim, 1963/1898, pp. 54–55). Sir John Lubbock suggested that clan women are seen as the collective property of the clan, and so men of the clan are desirous of an exogamous woman over whom they alone can exercise sexual ownership (Durkheim, 1963/1898, p. 55). Herbert Spencer argued that exogamy arises from the love of war and pillage in these clan societies; brides here are yet another form of the spoils of war (Durkheim, 1963/1898, p. 57). Lewis Henry Morgan provided yet another attempt at an explanation, somewhat more convincing than the first three, all of which Durkheim quickly rejects. Morgan argued that the clans had already recognized the genetic risks of consanguineal couples mating and rejected it for this reason (Durkheim, 1963/1898, p. 60). But Durkheim shows that the law of exogamy cannot be based on an understanding of genetic problems stemming from mating of closely biologically related couples because clan identity, and hence the rule of exogamy, is based not on actual consanguinity but on totem identity, and there has always been "an enormous amount of fiction" in the basic clan belief of descent from a common ancestor (Durkheim, 1963/1898, p. 65). It is known, Durkheim notes, that totem identity can be adopted for reasons not having to do with familial lineage. Clan members are frequently recruited by a kind of adoption. Prisoners of war who are not killed are thus made members of the clan, and even whole defeated clans or parts thereof can be adopted in as members of the clan victorious in war. The rule of exogamy as practiced in clan societies does permit marriages of couples who are closely related biologically, as in matrilineal systems a clan member can marry the offspring of his maternal uncle, who are his first cousins, because the matrilineal system places them in another clan within the same larger social grouping, the phratry (Durkheim, 1963/1898, p. 66).

The true explanation for the rule of exogamy and the prohibition on incest, according to Durkheim, has to do with religiously based sentiments about contagion of the sacred with profane things. Cultural **taboos** (the word is Polynesian, but the concept behind it is universal for Durkheim) are "ritualistic prohibitions" designed to avoid the dangerous results of a thing in which there resides a "supernatural principle" coming into contact with something profane (Durkheim, 1963/1898, p. 70). The primitive man believes that energy is contagious, and magical, sacred energy cannot be trifled with by "mediocre" receptacles that cannot withstand the energy, literally, under pain of death (Durkheim, 1963/1898, p. 71).

So where is the supernatural principle to be found in the men and women of the clan that makes sexual congress between them a sacrilege? The answer lies in a general power located in women, and the specific way in which this power expresses itself within the clan. Menstruation is a phenomenon that, in many primitive societies, serves to place women into an isolated, dangerous position *vis-à-vis* males of the group (Durkheim, 1963/1898, p. 72).

Among many primitive peoples, women who are menstruating are socially removed from mundane circulation with others in the group. It is not just that men cannot have sex with them during that time, although this is certainly true. They are also not to be touched or spoken to, and in some groups they are placed on hammocks for the duration of their period, in order that they be suspended "between Heaven and Earth" and thereby not pollute the ground on which the other members of the society walk and sleep (Durkheim, 1963/1898, p. 74).

But this is not the entire explanation of the rule of exogamy. The taboo on menstruating women is compounded by religious beliefs concerning blood and its relation to the clan. The members of the clan understand themselves to be related to one another in kinship through their relation to a totem, which is usually an animal or plant that is seen to be the repository of a powerful magic force known as the totemic principle. (Durkheim later returned to the analysis of totemism at great length in his last book, *The Elementary Forms of Religious Life*.) The totemic principle, the magic force that unites the clan members and literally gives them life, is understood to inhabit the blood of the clan members themselves, which makes it a sacred entity. Spilling the blood—that is, any loss of blood by a clan member in a wound, illness, or otherwise—is seen as "the god . . . spilling over" (Durkheim, 1963/1898, p. 89), a potentially tremendously serious transgression. Blood is a central element of menstruation, and, because this spilt blood is emitted from the vagina, the general taboo on spilling clan blood is connected to sexual relations specifically, which charges them up still more with religious potency (Durkheim, 1963/1898, pp. 85–86). So the clan women literally emit the blood of the totemic principle through their vaginas, which makes them sexually untouchable by men of the same totemic principle. Women of other clans, however, are not connected in this way to the blood of the totem, and so they can be procured as mates (Durkheim, 1963/1898, p. 90).

The consequences of the rule of exogamy in totemic societies have profoundly affected our own modern conceptions of the functions of family and the realm of sexual practice. The rule of exogamy forbade sexual relations between relatives, and this pushed sex outside of the familial circle and led us to develop "sentiments of kinship" dramatically in opposition to all sexual impulse and desire (Durkheim, 1963/1898, pp. 108–109). Even today, we see the conjugal functions and the kinship functions as fundamentally opposed to one another, and we react spontaneously with horror and disgust when anyone dares to bring them too closely together (Durkheim, 1963/1898, p. 100). The familial realm, Durkheim argues, is and has always been tinged with religious power, and we understand the realm of the family as the realm of duty and selfless dedication to the collectivity. Sex, on the other hand, is a realm of freedom and the pursuit of individual pleasure and conquest (Durkheim, 1963/1898, p. 101). Marriage and the family are connected in essential ways, it is true, but Durkheim presents them also as firmly separated precisely by the historic emergence of the rule of exogamy. This totemic prohibition on marriage to close relatives meant that marriage and sex came to be associated with the exotic and the passionate, that which was not known and already intimately one's own, the opposite of the morally centered and orderly relationship to close kin (Durkheim, 1963/1898, p. 109). Sex thus comes to be seen as the sphere of the arts, music, and poetry, all the dangerous and creative forces, while the realm of the family is that of order and morality. The marital institution is the ingenious cultural solution to the need to regulate and exercise control over the wild, creative sexual function. It requires us, as it did the primitive clan member, to go outside of the ranks of close kin to seek a mate and to restrict sexual congress to that exotic mate sought outside the family circle while dedicating oneself self-lessly and morally to the offspring thereby produced.

The explicit rule of exogamy is now gone. If we take clan as a primitive translation of just about any modern identity-based social grouping above the family (ethnic group, class group, religious group, nation), the vast majority of us find mates within our "clans"—that is, we marry those who share our ethnic, class, religious, and national identities. Yet the incest taboo, a structural descendant of the original rule of exogamy, lives on. We are unaware of the historical and social reasons for its evolution, but we none-theless obey it without fail, and we feel moral terror when it is challenged. This is an example of an important sociological phenomenon for Durkheim: Given practices in the past produce a whole way of life around them, and some elements of that way of life can survive for a long time after the original practices have disappeared (Durkheim, 1963/1898, p. 113).

Durkheim's Work in the Cause of the War

In the early days after the commencement of the war, a manifesto supporting the German war effort appeared, invoking the spirits of Goethe, Beethoven, and Kant, and signed by nearly a hundred prominent German intellectuals. Durkheim's reaction was immediate. He helped organize a response manifesto from universities across France in November of 1914, in which the German intellectuals who had signed their manifesto were accused of uncritically subordinating their intellectual faculties to Prussian militarism (Fournier, 2007, p. 852). He was instrumental in organizing a committee of the most prestigious Parisian intellectual figures, including the philosopher

Henri Bergson and historians Charles Andler and Ernest Lavisse, to publish propaganda efforts for the Allied cause. Under the aegis of this committee, Durkheim wrote a large amount of material to contribute to the French war effort and, in so doing, drew upon his life's work as a student of morality and politics.

The Roots of the War in German Aggression

Who Wanted War? (*Qui a voulu la guerre?*), which was coauthored with the historian of Germany Ernest Denis (1915), is a more or less objective, relatively bloodless account of the events leading up to the war. The question of the title is bluntly answered by systematic exposition of the facts showing German culpability. From German complicity in the saber-rattling Austrian ultimatum to Serbia in the wake of the assassination of Archduke Ferdinand to the German declarations of war against Russia and France despite efforts by both the latter nations to avoid such an end, Durkheim and Denis construct a determined brief demonstrating Germany's instigation of the conflict, notwithstanding German efforts to blame Russia for the provocation.

The tone was different in Durkheim's second propaganda effort, *Germany Over All* (*L'Allemagne au-dessus de tout*). Here, the German nationalist historian and political writer of the 19th century Heinrich von Treitschke, who died in 1896 but was still widely read in nationalist circles in his country of birth and author of a multivolume history of the German 19th century, became a cipher for the spirit of the entire German nation. Treitschke, who had taken up the role of propagandist in the 1870 Franco-Prussian war that so affected Durkheim in his youth, is seen here as indicative of the thinking of all of Germany. Thoroughly suffused with the militant nationalist mentality dominant in his age, "friend of Bismarck and great admirer of William II," he was "one of first and most impetuous apostles of imperialist politics" (Durkheim, 1915, p. 5).

Durkheim describes this **German mentality** as a kind of religion of the almighty State, the "highest in the series of human collectivities," which is to recognize no power above itself (Durkheim, 1915, p. 23). Civil society is subordinate to it. This vision of the State sees treaties with other States as binding only so long as the German State desires to be restricted by them, and only so long as it can realize its interests through them. The will of the German people must subordinate any agreement with another State that does not meet those conditions (Durkheim, 1915, p. 9). Morality is a mere tool for the State to use in getting its interests realized. Treitschke's Machiavellianism is naked, and his sense that dissimulation can be useful in political affairs is transparent. But even this feigned morality is entertained only in relations with other "civilized" nations. When it comes to relations with the "uncivilized" world, the German mentality is unabashedly brutal. In relations with, for example, Africa or Asia, European principles of *Realpolitik* are to be replaced with unadulterated force, for "there, he who does not know how to terrorize is lost" (Durkheim, 1915, p. 25). International tribunals have, in this view, no power whatsoever to adjudicate between States, as States are seen as the highest sovereign authority, above which no international superior power is imaginable. War is thus "the only form of trial" that can be recognized as valid by the German people (Durkheim, 1915, pp. 10–11).

The capacity to wage war is for Treitschke the defining characteristic of a State, and those small, weak States without appreciable military might are laughable at best. War is the exalted state in which individuals are tied together into a collective mission over and above themselves and the dismal "reign of materialism" and conflict of individual interests that characterizes periods of peace (Durkheim, 1915, pp. 12, 32). The Army is the "State incarnated" and military power is the sole means of evaluating a State's efficacy (Durkheim, 1915, p. 14). The State's only duty to its citizens is to be strong, externally as well as with respect to its own citizens, and to expand as much as possible at the expense of its rivals. The individual, on the other hand, owes his entire allegiance to the State and thus has the central duty to the State of obedience. Thus, Durkheim writes, do we arrive at the "famous formula that the German learns to repeat from his earliest infancy: *Deutschland über alles*" (Durkheim, 1915, p. 23). The ideal political leader of such a State must be driven by a massive ambition and a realist intelligence that immunizes him against quaint moralizing. The role of the leader is to dominate both his fellow citizens and foreign States (Durkheim, 1915, pp. 33–34).

Durkheim then explains how the events leading up to the outbreak of the war can be explained by this German mentality. The violation of Belgian neutrality is an obvious matter for a German State that simply does not recognize the existence of other States unless they present a capable military threat. The trampling on the conventions of The Hague is completely consistent with the idea that a sovereign State need only honor international treaties so long as it desires to do so (Durkheim, 1915, pp. 36–37). The war waged by the Germans is "systematically inhumane," in keeping with the Treitschke-derived cultural mentality of the Germans (Durkheim, 1915, p. 38).

In his description of this German mentality, Durkheim implicitly defends the vision he had articulated in much of his life's work of a national polity that must be centered on a collective moral project in which the rising universal sacred object of rational societies, the human person, should be understood as protected by rights that exceed any one State. In rejecting Treitschke's appeal to a crude power politics, Durkheim recalls his refusal at the national level of political platforms based on crude self-interest and power. A moral politics requires a collective recognition of the human rights of all and thus a commitment to an international political structure in which merely national interests are no more permitted to win the day than individual interests are at the level of any given society. So while Durkheim's political sociology is consistent with Treitschke's on the principle that some collective entity above the individual must be the focus of his striving and work, he radically parts company with the German mentality on the details. For Durkheim, the individual submits himself to family, to occupational group, to nation not simply to enable the victory of one collectivity over another but because the vibrancy of a moral, collective life is a requirement for the individual's well-being, and the well-being of the human individual person is the single moral principle that unites all collectivities into a single unity, humanity as a whole. This latter collectively trumps all national collectivities for Durkheim, and its unity is created not by mere will to power but by the shared moral commitment to the human person.

Reading these pages makes it impossible to respond with anything more than laughter at the charge, leveled by some critics in the 1930s, that Durkheim's politics could reasonably be understood as sympathetic to fascism. The German mentality described herein is a hypernationalist Statism that sees the individual as a nonentity and posits war as the health of the State, and it is accordingly the obligation of the individual to pay the wages of the State with his life. These are precisely the central tenets of fascism, and Durkheim utterly and categorically opposes them all.

In the book's final chapter, Durkheim invokes another set of his earlier theoretical categories in describing the deficiencies of the German mentality. It is, he argues, not individual Germans who are stricken by "moral perversion"; Treitschke himself seems to have had a "character of high nobility" (Durkheim, 1915, p. 41). Individual German soldiers who commit atrocities on the battlefield may well be dutiful, honest, and loyal men, but "the mental system we have just studied is not made for private life and the everyday [but] for public life, and above all for the state of war" (Durkheim, 1915, pp. 41–42). Once war is declared, the perfectly normal, humane German is immediately made to adhere to the tenets of this collective consciousness, which scatters "all ideas and feelings contrary to it and masters wills" (Durkheim, 1915, p. 42). The formerly civilized German individual then becomes, in the grip of this fervent set of collective beliefs, capable of justifying and even committing atrocities.

It is, in other words, not a matter of individual consciousnesses that is of concern here. It is rather a state of the collective consciousness that produces the evil effects Durkheim condemns. The sense of will manifested in the German mentality is "morbid" precisely because it has not been subjected to the healthy constraint required for moral human voluntarism. There are, in healthy human collectivities, accepted limits on human action, some originating in the physical world, but some too coming from the moral realm, and the German mentality has evolved in such a way as to escape these necessary restrictions. It is ultimately, then, a social pathology from which the Germans suffer, and historians and sociologists will one day investigate its causes (Durkheim, 1915, p. 46). There may be sick characters who are able, because of their "neurosis," to briefly achieve formidable things and even to seem superhuman, but inevitably they exhaust themselves as they run up against reality, for the will unchecked cannot sustain itself (Durkheim, 1915, p. 46). In this classification of the German mentality, Durkheim invokes the thesis of *Suicide* on anomie and its concomitant discontents.

To Win the War: "Letters to the French People"

This collection of short essays exhorted the French public to a sustained, temperate, and unrelenting moral effort in the face of the horrible burdens and suffering of war. Of a total collection of 12 "letters" of approximately 10 to 15 pages each, Durkheim was author or coauthor of four and apparently worked substantially on the editing and revision of others. Three of the letters in which Durkheim had a hand addressed the details of the resources of the French military and its allies in Turkey, Bulgaria, Belgium, Serbia, and Montenegro, along with the military situations in the various fronts in which these forces were occupied. Others described the state of the Russian and British forces and the situation of the German military and its allies.

The central goal in these letters was to reassure the French reader about the Allied war effort, which was "in full progress" (Durkheim & Lavisse, 1992/1916, p. 94). In the introductory letter of the book, written by Durkheim and titled "Patience, effort, confidence," Durkheim preached the moral, collective values of his life's work. In order to win the war, he argued passionately, the French and their allies must have "an unbreakable will" and must fight against impatience, blind, lazy confidence, and depression (Durkheim & Lavisse, 1992/1916, pp. 24, 25). An ascetic demeanor would be necessary on the part of all in order to channel the economic resources to the war effort (Durkheim & Lavisse, 1992/1916, p. 27). While German chances for success depended on a lightning victory, which had eluded them, the Allies would need the morally central qualities of tenacity and patience to outlast them (Durkheim & Lavisse, 1992/1916, p. 167). The appeal to a selfless, collective service to something beyond the individual and the material, something ultimately sacred, suffuses the text: "We are all called to actively participate in the war, each in his manner" (Durkheim & Lavisse, 1992/1916, p. 27). The French are reminded, in their hour of distress, to recall the struggles of those with still less in the way of resources and still greater suffering to bear: "We cannot believe less than [Belgium, Serbia, and Montenegro] in the future of our cause, nor feel less vividly than them the humiliating indignity of a German peace. If, then, in certain moments of weakness, it comes to pass that we let ourselves fall into doubt and discouragement, let us think of the Serbs and the Belgians!" (Durkheim & Lavisse, 1992/1916, p. 165).

Conclusion

As we have seen, virtually the entirety of Durkheim's work during his lifetime can be seen as an inquiry into the nature of moral structure and representations. The completion of the two major studies on morality and marriage and the family that he was contemplating at his life's end would doubtless have given us two more classic texts for the canon in sociology. The practically oriented texts he produced as part of the French war effort were themselves deeply immersed in the sociology of morality. Here, however, the task was not simply to analyze the emergence of moral structures and describe the effects of various changes in them but to incite his fellow countrymen to a morally vigorous response to the outrage of the German aggression. Even in the midst of the stress and strain of the national war effort, Durkheim was developing and practically utilizing the moral theory and sociological knowledge he had spent his entire life studying and acquiring.

A few questions

- Was Durkheim's wartime activism consistent with his moral theory and moral sociology?
- How prevalent is the phenomenon Durkheim described as "the German mentality," which he applied directly to Germany here but which in principle could be used in a more abstract way to describe national cultural character generally?
- Why is Durkheim's sociology of the family so widely mischaracterized, misunderstood, and unappreciated in contemporary intellectual circles?

- Have Durkheim's arguments concerning the sacredness of sexuality and the sacrosanct status of the marital institution simply been left behind by the times? What have been the consequences of continued cultural movement on these topics in the direction Durkheim criticized in his lifetime?
- Could a feminist perspective on marriage, sexuality, and the family be made compatible with Durkheim's view, or are the two simply too mutually contradictory?

8

Further Readings

The amount written on Durkheim's work is voluminous, not only because of his status in the discipline but also simply because we are now almost a century from his death in 1917 and commentators have had a long time to write. Important functionalist strands in both mid-20th-century American sociology (in the work of Talcott Parsons and Robert Merton) and British anthropology (E. E. Evans-Pritchard and A. R. Radcliffe-Brown) were hugely indebted to his work, though they picked and chose among his ideas. Although functionalism is, despite the contentions of some of its critics, not dead, much of the early interpretive effort with respect to Durkheim's work has been left behind by a wave of new scholarship that began roughly 30 to 35 years ago, and it is on this later work that this chapter will focus. In France, the United States, and the UK, several generations of scholars have been working in recent decades to advance our knowledge of Durkheim's work and life and the applicability of his thought to the world we live in today.

Other Writings by Durkheim

Durkheim was an incredibly prolific writer, and although I have discussed a good deal of his output in this book, inevitably a good deal has passed without commentary. In addition to the four book-length studies published in his lifetime and the numerous lecture courses and lengthy essays published as books posthumously—that is, the core material discussed in the previous chapters—Durkheim wrote a vast amount of material for the *Année sociologique,* much of which remains unpublished in reliable English translation. I have discussed some of the most important of this material—for example, the essays he published there on incest, religious phenomena, and primitive classification—but there is much more. Victor Karady produced a three-volume collection in the mid-1970s of much of the most important of that *Année* material not already available in book form. Most of what I have discussed beyond the books and the course lectures can also be found there. Several volumes in English contain some of the material in the Karady volumes: These include *Emile Durkheim: On Institutional Analysis* (edited by Mark Traugott, 1994); *Durkheim: Essays on Morals and Education* (edited by W. S. F. Pickering, 1979); *Durkheim on Religion* (edited by W. S. F. Pickering); *Emile Durkheim: On Morality and Society* (edited by Robert Bellah); and the W. D. Halls translation of *The Rules*, which also contains a selection of Durkheim's other writings on method in sociology. Another book containing some of this material, *Emile Durkheim: Contributions to l'Année sociologique,* exists, but the quality of the translations is somewhat suspect.

Many of Durkheim's private papers were lost, presumably during the Vichy period when prominent Jewish figures and their descendants suffered significantly. Durkheim's colleague Maurice Halbwachs perished in a concentration camp, and his nephew Marcel Mauss, one of the most celebrated French intellectuals before the war, was forced to wear the infamous "yellow badge" in Vichy France near the end of his life as a public demonstration of his "non-French" identity. Some of the material from Durkheim's teaching not present in his own papers has been gathered from the notes of students and published as books. Such is the case for an early course he gave to *lycée* students at Sens in introductory philosophy while in his 20s, and for one of the last courses he gave in Paris before the start of the war, from 1913 to 1914, on the philosophy of pragmatism (Durkheim, 1983/1955).

Pragmatism, that American philosophical phenomenon of the early 20th century characterized by the work of John Dewey, William James, and Charles Sanders Peirce, had achieved significant acclaim in France, largely owing to the partisan position of Durkheim's old schoolmate, Henri Bergson, and Durkheim felt a need to address some of what he saw as its failings. The central aspect of pragmatism he addressed in the course on the subject was its epistemological position. Although he finds a significant point of commonality with the pragmatists in their insistence on seeing knowledge as inevitably connected to human life, rather than existing in some Platonic ideal realm outside of experience, Durkheim sees the pragmatist theory of truth, in which, in simplified form, the true is defined as that which is useful, as ultimately irrational, antisociological, and dangerous. Durkheimian sociology acknowledges that human life and consciousness shape our knowledge of the world fundamentally, but, as we saw in Chapter 6, they do so in ways that can be mapped sociologically, and these processes are rational and restricted by reality—that is, they are imposed on us even against our will and preference. In the most radical forms of pragmatism—for example, in William James's insistence that the key to the study of religion is mystical experience, which is true to the mystic however the scientific onlooker might consider it—pragmatism falls into an individualist and subjectivist fantasy about truth that is separable from the impingement of the real world.

Intellectual Biographies of Durkheim

There are at the time of this writing two major intellectual biographies of Durkheim. Steven Lukes (1985/1973) produced the first (*Emile Durkheim: His Life and Work, A Historical and Critical Study*) in 1973, and it was for many years the unchallenged primary source. It contains one of the most extensive extant bibliographies and several useful appendices that list Durkheim's lecture courses over his years at both Bordeaux and Paris, as well as the record of his comments on the doctoral theses of students. The recent publication in French of a nearly 1,000-page biographical study by Marcel Fournier (*Emile Durkheim*) now challenges Lukes's previously unrivaled position as the most comprehensive biography of Durkheim. Fournier consulted a great deal of archival material, including volumes of correspondence, that was unavailable to Lukes, in order to sketch Durkheim's public and private lives in fascinating detail. An English translation of Fournier's biography was published in 2012. Fournier's chapter in *The Cambridge Companion to Durkheim* points in summary form to many of the key themes he treats at length in the biography.

A great deal of Durkheim's correspondence has also been pulled out of the archives and presented to the public, at least those who read French. This is a wonderful resource that allows the student to see Durkheim's work being produced in the context of a life and the social environment surrounding it. Philippe Besnard and Marcel Fournier edited a collection of Durkheim's letters to his nephew Mauss from 1893 to his death (*Lettres à Marcel Mauss*); these letters provide a rich context for the fuller understanding of many of Durkheim's major writings and especially of the development of the *Année sociologique* project. Besnard also published a smaller collection of letters from Durkheim to Henri Hubert, another of the central players on the *Année sociologique* team and the coauthor of several of Mauss's most important works. In addition to the *Année sociologique* details, these letters provide great insights into Durkheim's involvement in the Dreyfus Affair.

The Historical and Social Context of Durkheim's Work and the *Année Sociologique*

As we saw in Chapter 2, it is arguably the case that one cannot fully under-stand Durkheim's work without noting how much of it was done for the *Année sociologique* and in collaboration with his colleagues there. Especially in France, but increasingly elsewhere as well, there is a growing literature that looks closely at Durkheim's work from within the contextual frames of both the *Année sociologique* and the larger intellectual field in France at the turn of the 19th century. A monumental study in this area is the edited vol-ume, *The Sociological Domain: The Durkheimians and the Founding of French Sociology*, compiled by Philippe Besnard. It carefully sketches the collective nature of work in the Durkheimian school, with Durkheim as the leader who nonetheless relied heavily on the collaboration of others (includ-ing especially, in addition to Mauss and Hubert, Paul Fauconnet, Georges Simiand, and Maurice Halbwachs). There is much in the book to satisfy an intellectual historian, but the general thrust of the chapters is more in the way of a sociological study of the Durkheimian research team as it emerged in the 1890s. Besnard's introductory essay describes the entire team over the entirety of its first edition (from 1898 to 1913), even graphically represent-ing the members' areas of contribution and the strength of various networks in the team. Other chapters look at the Durkheimian efforts to secure uni-versity positions for members of the team and various intellectual disputes and debates they engaged in with philosophers, historians, and other social scientists of the period. There are also a number of letters between Durkheim and various founding members of the *Année* team that reveal fascinating details of the origins of the journal. This is an invaluable resource into the emergence of probably the first true sociological research team in the world.

Terry Clark's 1973 book, *Prophets and Patrons: The French University System and the Emergence of the Social Sciences*, places Durkheimian sociol-ogy in the emerging field of French social science, where competitors were omnipresent. Clark takes an even more explicitly sociological approach than the Besnard book in trying to understand the success Durkheim had, in his lifetime, at establishing sociology in the French university system and broader intellectual world. He characterizes the Parisian intellectual world in Durkheim's day as a binary system of opposing types of intellectuals and their ideas: On the one hand, there are *cartesians,* thinkers sympathetic with scientific method and supportive politically of authority, order, and estab-lished institutions, while on the other are arrayed *spontaneists,* whose ideas are characterized more by aesthetic than scientific standards and who react against established political order. The Durkheimians were, according to Clark, fundamentally cartesians in this mapping.

In *Durkheim and the Jews of France,* Ivan Strenski situates Durkheim with respect to religious debates and divisions of the day in France. He argues that Durkheim was an intellectual ally of a conservative Judaism typified by the French Indologist Sylvain Lévi, a friend of the Durkheim family and one of Marcel Mauss's teachers, and that Durkheim's conception of religion, focused as it was on ritual and the social and public elements of religion, can be seen in this variety of Judaism. Durkheim's own father, as we noted in the first chapter, was a practicing Jew of the same conservative stripe as Lévi, so Durkheim did not need to go far to study the form.

In *Godless Intellectuals? The Intellectual Pursuit of the Sacred Reinvented* (Riley, 2010), I investigate the Durkheimian interest in religion as an important element in the existential meaning-making project for Durkheim himself. This complicates the traditional, dominant perspective of Durkheim as an unproblematically secular intellectual by arguing that intellectual life and collective intellectual labor itself became a sacred object for Durkheim.

We might also consider in this section a recent book by Susan Stedman Jones, *Durkheim Reconsidered.* It offers an effort at a significant reinterpretation of the core thrust of Durkheim's sociology, and much of the argumentative punch of the book comes from the sustained attempt to situate Durkheim accurately in his intellectual and political milieu. One of the most important intellectual influences, too frequently overlooked, is the neo-Kantian philosophy of Charles Renouvier, who provided Durkheim an outline of a philosophical project dedicated to a nonpositivist, critical scientific method and a republican politics based on a conception of the free individual.

Three "Life Works" Dedicated to the Study of Durkheim

In the sea of material on Durkheim produced over the last few decades, a significant body of work has been produced by three writers (Philippe Besnard, Edward Tiryakian, and W. S. F. Pickering) who have devoted a great deal of their own intellectual careers to the effort to clarify, expand, and apply the conceptual apparatus developed by Durkheim. Given Durkheim's influence in his native France and the English-speaking intellectual worlds in the UK and the United States, it is fitting that, of these three scholars of Durkheim, one is French, one British, and one American.

Philippe Besnard

The late Philippe Besnard (1942–2003) was one of the most important contemporary historians of Durkheimian sociology and also a practicing sociologist who generally worked from a basically Durkheimian perspective. Over more than a quarter century, he edited and published previously unknown works by Durkheim and his *Année sociologique* colleagues, including volumes of their correspondence, and served as a focal point for a number of important edited volumes and special journal issues that featured some of the most expert contemporary commentary on Durkheim's work and explored the emergence of the Durkheimian school. He was the impulse in 1976 behind the creation of a still-existing journal, *Durkheimian Studies/Études durkheimiennes,* devoted to Durkheim's thought and its legacy. He also did much to defend Durkheim's thought from commentators who launched misguided attacks without the benefit of adequate knowledge of the material.

Beyond these achievements, he wrote several other books and many journal articles dedicated to aspects of Durkheim's thought. Perhaps the most important of the books is *Études durkheimiennes.* Compiled just before Besnard's premature death, it contains much of his most important work on Durkheim and the *Année* group. It ranges widely, including seven chapters exploring various aspects of the research in *Suicide* (among which can be found an examination of the incomplete and sometimes contradictory consideration in the book of the effects of marriage on women), four that discuss *The Division of Labor,* and a selection of Besnard's many writings on the Durkheimian school. In an earlier book, *L'anomie, ses usages et ses fonctions dans la discipline sociologique depuis Durkheim,* Besnard (1987b) undertook a systematic examination of the concept, anomie, frequently understood (in Besnard's view, mistakenly so) as the central concept in Durkheim's sociology. He traces the concept in both American and French sociological domains, demonstrating the fragility and instability of its definition and its ultimately limited utility. His argument, in brief, is that anomie was a conceptual tool Durkheim used seriously for only a brief period, and this when he himself was undergoing a set of experiences (the deaths of several family members, occupational stress) that approximated an anomic state. Social integration, rather than moral regulation, is the key Durkheimian category in Besnard's view.

Edward Tiryakian

Edward Tiryakian (1929–) has written a great deal on Durkheim dating back more than a half century. His *Sociologism and Existentialism: Two*

Perspectives on the Individual and Society (1962) finds significant common intellectual territory in Durkheim's thought and the existentialism of the mid 20th century, including a relativistic perspective on truth, an emphasis on transcendence, and a sense that modernity has brought with it a deep moral crisis that we have not solved. Much more recently (2009), *For Durkheim: Essays in Historical and Cultural Sociology* brings together many of his journal articles and book chapters on Durkheim from the past 35 years. Among these are the following:

- "From Durkheim to Managua" uses the conceptual framework of *The Elementary Forms* to discuss numerous revolutions of the late 1970s and early 1980s. The coming to power of the Sandinistas in Nicaragua, the Khomeini-led Islamists in Iran, the EDSA in the Philippines, and the triumph of Polish *Solidarność* were in Tiryakian's view all powerfully driven by the same cultural effervescence Durkheim carefully analyzed in Australian totemism.

- "Durkheim, Solidarity, and September 11" looks at the solidarity, in the United States and globally, produced by the September 11, 2001, terrorist attacks on New York City and Washington, D.C., in relation to Durkheim's categories of collective effervescence and mechanical solidarity. This latter phenomenon, as Durkheim suggested, does not disappear in modernity, and 9/11 demonstrated this.

- "Sexual Anomie, Social Structure, Societal Change" draws attention to a phenomenon that has only become more exacerbated in the nearly 30 years since it was originally written. Durkheim long ago pointed to the fact that shifts in the social structure that undid the gendered division of labor would almost inevitably have consequences in the realm of marriage, the family, sexual relations, and gender roles. Tiryakian uses Durkheim's framework as the base from which to discuss what that situation looks like: increased deregulation of the marital institution, growing rejection of traditional female roles (including those related to childrearing) by women, and the rise of an androgynous gender standard.

W. S. F. Pickering

W. S. F. Pickering (1922–), in addition to currently serving as coeditor at the journal *Durkheimian Studies,* has had a hand over the last 40 years in whole shelves of material in English on Durkheim and the Durkheimian school. In addition to the numerous volumes of translations of Durkheim's work he has supervised over the years (some noted above), he has directed a number of edited volumes with new material investigating Durkheimian lines of thought and written many books of his own that do the same. *Durkheim's Sociology of Religion: Themes and Theories* (1984), published more than a quarter century ago, remains one of the most sustained explications of the argument of *The Elementary Forms* available. In the edited collection *Durkheim and Representations,* Pickering's introduction and two chapters present Durkheim's philosophical construction and defense of the notion of collective representations as formidable and complex. While the English tradition on the more philosophical elements of Durkheim's late thought has often characterized it as unconvincing and sloppy, Pickering presents a coherent if limited defense. (Among the other chapters of the book, David Bloor's is of particular interest, as it ties Durkheim's sociology of knowledge to contemporary perspectives in the social construction of scientific knowledge.) Still more recently, *Suffering and Evil: The Durkheimian Legacy* (with Massimo Rosati, 2008) examines Durkheim's engagement with evil and points out some of the ways in which his thought here may be useful to understanding contemporary phenomena such as genocides and terrorism.

The Division of Labor in Society Today

At the centennial of the publication of Durkheim's first book, two important publications, one in English and one in French, took stock of Durkheim's argument and its influence over the past century. *Division de travail social: La thèse de Durkheim un siècle après* (edited by Philippe Besnard, Massimo Borlandi, and W. Paul Vogt, 1993) offered interpretive efforts to explore the major themes of Durkheim's classic (for example, law, the individual, social pathology), investigations of the influences on Durkheim's argument in *Division of Labor* (for example, Comte, Spencer), and explorations of the reception of the text in various national contexts. Some of the most prominent English-speaking commentators on Durkheim's work—for example, W. S. F. Pickering and William Watts Miller—also count among the contributors to this volume. Edward Tiryakian directed a special edition of the American journal *Sociological Forum* in 1994 entitled "Durkheim Lives!" that included a range of contemporary utilizations of conceptual elements from *The Division of Labor,* as well as a reprint of a classic review of the English translation of the book by Robert Merton in 1933. Tiryakian's introduction of the issue ("Revisiting Sociology's First Classic: *The Division of Labor in Society* and Its Actuality") presents a case for a return of mechanical solidarity in the renewed vigor of ethnic and national identities as well as other problems of political division at the turn of the 20th century into the 21st.

In a compelling chapter in *The Cambridge Companion to Durkheim* (Alexander & Smith, 2005), David Grusky and Gabriela Galescu argue that Durkheim's framework for understanding social class is superior to that of Marx and Weber because contemporary class identities are better understood with Durkheim's theory. Both Marx and Weber posited that class identity in the future would center on national and international working-class identity and organization based primarily on large trade unions and working class–based political parties, i.e., macro-class groups. Yet when we look around the globe at how individuals actually think of the class groups to which they belong, we see that Durkheimian micro-class identity based on more local, small-scale occupational trade groups organized by specific job types and with only a vague if any sense of a broad, generic working class identity are much more common. Hence, we hear "I am a house painter," or "I am a plumber" much more frequently than "I am a member of the Worker's Party" or "I am a member of the international working class, which struggles united against the ruling classes."

The Rules of Sociological Method Today

While many contemporary sociologists would probably see *The Rules* as a flawed effort, there is a range of opinion on precisely *how* flawed it is and what, if anything, is still useful there. Some suggest it is wholly unsalvageable, while others have offered a contextualized argument for its utility, and still others see it as an important first step in the establishment of a truly scientific sociological research paradigm.

The most recent translation of *The Rules,* by W. D. Halls, contains an informative introductory essay by Steven Lukes that acknowledges the limits of the book while carefully explaining what Durkheim intended it to do. This translation also contains some interesting short texts, including the transcript of a fascinating discussion between Durkheim and Charles Seignobos on explanation in sociology and history. In *On Durkheim's Rules of Sociological Method,* Mike Gane (1988) ably defends Durkheim's effort, showing how the various criticisms of the book generally fail to accurately understand the argument and often contradict one another. In *The Development of Durkheim's Social Realism,* Robert Alun Jones (1999) argues that the position articulated in *The Rules* was an evolutionary product of Durkheim's intellectual development, and his student experience in Germany was one of the central sites of the origin of his later theoretical position. Warren Schmaus (*Durkheim's Philosophy of Science and the Sociology of Knowledge: Creating an Intellectual Niche,* 1994) is one of the relatively few to argue strenuously for the vision of *The Rules* in nearly its integrity and to endeavor to read the entirety of Durkheim's mature work as defined and directed by the methodological principles of that text. Schmaus is a philosopher, and his attempts to root his work as a philosopher of science in a sociology of knowledge fall short of the mark, but this is one of the few recent works to argue strongly in defense of Durkheim's case without qualifying the argument by reference to Durkheim's strategic goals in writing it, and for that reason alone it is worth consideration.

In French, there is an edited collection celebrating the centennial of the publication of *The Rules* (*La sociologie et sa méthode: Les Règles de Durkheim, un siècle après,* edited by Massimo Borlandi and Laurent Mucchielli, 1995) that places the book in its historical and social context, emphasizing Durkheim's intellectual strategy of positioning himself and the new discipline of sociology with respect to more established academic adversaries such as philosophy and psychology. Several chapters in the book examine the reception of the book in a number of countries.

Suicide Today

A good deal of the response to *Suicide* has consisted of criticism of the study's methodology and its data. Even the 1930 study of his *Année* colleague Maurice Halbwachs, *The Causes of Suicide,* which was characterized in the book's preface by Marcel Mauss as essentially part "of the same inquiry, conducted in the same spirit" as Durkheim's book, pointed out serious shortcomings of the statistical reasoning of *Suicide*. Later, Jack Douglas (1967), in *The Social Meanings of Suicide,* questioned the reliability of the official suicide statistics that are virtually the entirety of Durkheim's data. Some criticism has been leveled at Durkheim's categories as well. Whitney Pope (1976), in *Durkheim's* Suicide: *A Classic Analyzed,* controversially argues that anomic and egotistical suicide are not substantively distinct from one another, and therefore that regulation and integration (the two major independent variables in Durkheim's study) are actually only one variable.

Yet, although it is generally acknowledged (as Durkheim himself would have been the first to admit) that scientific research has over the past century left a good deal of Durkheim's work on this topic dated, there is still much to indicate that the book remains an important and compelling piece of sociological research and not just a "classic" to be read for historical reasons only. Several recent edited collections attest to the wide range of contemporary work inspired by Durkheim's study. *Émile Durkheim:* Le suicide *One Hundred Years Later* (edited by David Lester, a psychologist, 1994) is interdisciplinary and makes some effort to bring Durkheim's sociological approach to suicide and more psychologically based research on the topic into conversation while also demonstrating how well some of the relationships Durkheim presents (e.g., between marital/familial status and suicide rates) have held up in subsequent research. The book also contains a translation of Durkheim's important early essay on suicide, "Suicide et natalité," which was discussed in Chapter 4. *Durkheim's* Suicide, *A Century of Research and Debate* (edited by W. S. F. Pickering and Geoffrey Walford, 2000) offers chapters extending Durkheim's analysis as well as a good deal of material describing the reception of the book in various countries. In one standout contribution to that volume, Christie Davies and Mark Neal show that the two categories of suicide that Durkheim passed over most briefly, altruistic and fatalistic suicide, can be found commonly in some contemporary social strata—for example, in young rural Chinese women. A volume in French (Massimo Borlandi and Mohammed Cherkaoui, *Le Suicide: Un siècle après Durkheim*, 2000) brings together three groups of essays that examine the data sources on which Durkheim drew, the reception of the book in France and elsewhere, and subsequent research that builds on Durkheim's analysis.

The Elementary Forms of Religious Life Today

It is probably fair to say that at the time of this writing, Durkheim's work on religion and the sociology of knowledge is attracting the most vibrant attention from contemporary scholars. In the wake of the **cultural turn** and with the rapid rise of **cultural sociology** over the past several decades, a large body of work has emerged that puts Durkheim's thought on religion and knowledge to work on a range of phenomena in the contemporary world. It is a telling fact that nearly half of the chapters in Jeffrey Alexander and Philip Smith's *The Cambridge Companion to Durkheim* (2005) discuss material and/or utilize concepts presented in Durkheim's final book. In an earlier work (*Durkheimian Sociology: Cultural Studies*), Alexander (1988), in a vigorous introduction to a wide-ranging collection, made one of the first efforts to resituate the meaning of Durkheim's intellectual legacy with respect to the cultural turn in the human sciences. Chapters in the book ranged from reading Durkheim as a theorist of cultural revolution to applying some of his insights to mass-mediated phenomena that did not exist in his day, all centrally drawing from the arguments and perspectives in *The Elementary Forms.*

As we saw above, W. S. F. Pickering and Edward Tiryakian have both written a great deal over the past few decades on *The Elementary Forms.* Willie Watts Miller (*A Durkheimian Quest: Solidarity and the Sacred*, 2012) has more recently presented an interpretation of Durkheim's final book as an articulation of a theory of what he calls "total aesthetics." In this vision, Durkheim, in his theorizing of the role of collective effervescence, mimetic rite, and commemorative rite, was constructing an explanation of the workings of art forms ranging from classical dance to the contemporary rave. Donald Nielsen (*Three Faces of God: Society, Religion, and the Categories of the Totality in the Philosophy of Émile Durkheim*, 1999) presents Durkheim's book on religion as an effort to respond to the philosophical problem of the category of totality. In Nielsen's reading, Durkheim reduced religion to the social and equated society with God as a strategy for integrating traditional religious thinking and emerging social-scientific theory into a single, holistic field of knowledge. In *The New Durkheim* (2006), Ivan Strenski, a scholar of religion, presents some of his numerous journal article interventions on Durkheim's milieu and influences, as well as a chapter that uses Durkheimian sociology of religion to examine suicide terrorism.

Ann Rawls (*Epistemology and Practice: Durkheim's* The Elementary Forms of Religious Life, 2009) takes up the argument in *The Elementary Forms* in a manner that puts her in opposition to the culturalists. She argues that Durkheim there makes a case for the primacy of practices over beliefs and that his vision in *The Elementary Forms* is consistent with that present in his earlier work.

Durkheim's Educational Thought Today

Most of the best recent work examining Durkheim's thought on education and its relationship to sociology is in French. *Durkheim, sociologue de l'éducation* (edited by François Cardi and Joëlle Plantier, 1993) is an enlightening collection of essays that examine Durkheim's educational writings to find evidence of his political perspective, his theory of pedagogy, and his thoughts on religion and morality. Several pieces examine Durkheim's thoughts on the teaching of sociology at the *lycée* and university levels. Jean-Claude Filloux (*Durkheim et l'éducation*, 1994) summarizes what is useful for the contemporary teacher or pedagogical theorist in Durkheim's thought on the subject. The second half of the book consists of excerpts from Durkheim on a wide range of themes (e.g., "The Teaching of History," "The Authority of the Teacher"). In English, *Durkheim and Modern Education* (edited by Geoffrey Walford and W. S. F. Pickering, 1998) puts Durkheim into conversation with other central thinkers on education (e.g., the philosopher John Dewey and the psychologist Lawrence Kohlberg) and evaluates his educational theory by looking to schooling systems in a number of differing national contexts (e.g., the United States, the UK, and Japan). In an article from a French journal written in English ("Realism and Religion: Some Reflections on Durkheim's *L'Évolution pédagogique en France*"), Robert Alun Jones (1990) discerns a tight relationship between Durkheim's pedagogical realism and the concept of the social fact as a thing that is laid out in *The Rules*.

Durkheim's Thought on Politics and Socialism Today

There now exists a sizable body of interpretive work showing the importance of politics and socialism in Durkheim's intellectual development and career. Jean-Claude Filloux (*Durkheim et le socialisme*, 1977) interprets Durkheim's "original project" as political and socialist, if in terms that require some decoding. Durkheim's vision of socialist politics is, as we saw in Chapter 3, critical of the Marxian framework of class struggle and centers instead on a Saint-Simonian perspective in which solidarity, meritocracy, individualism, and equality of opportunity are all reconciled. In *Durkheim et le politique,* Bernard Lacroix (1981) attempts a similarly holistic reading of the meaning of Durkheim's entire output, arguing that it constitutes an intellectual investigation of the political realm spurred by psychoanalytic complications involving his relationship to his father. Two books in English, Mike Gane's (1990) *The radical sociology of Durkheim and Mauss* and Frank Pearce's (1998) *The Radical Durkheim,* also make strong contributions to counter the long-lived falsehood of "Durkheim the conservative thinker." Gane's book shows the connections and divergences of Durkheimian sociology and socialist politics, in the process demonstrating that Durkheim's work is much more focused on conflict than has generally been acknowledged. Pearce shows how some of what are taken as marginal concepts in Durkheim's work (the forced division of labor, fatalistic suicide) can be read as the elements of a radical critique of some of the key elements of Western capitalism.

Durkheim's Thought on Morality and the Family Today

A number of contemporary readers have interpreted Durkheim as a communitarian who nonetheless enshrines the individual in a privileged position. Mark Cladis (*A Communitarian Defense of Liberalism: Émile Durkheim and Contemporary Social Theory*, 1992) reads his work as something of a middle way between classical liberalism and communitarianism. Willie Watts Miller (*Durkheim, Morals and Modernity*, 1996) evaluates Durkheim's oeuvre as a theoretical attempt to establish a secular ethic to navigate between the opposed extremisms of despotic authoritarianism and anarchic individualism. In both these books, an effort is made to interpret Durkheim's sociology as perfectly compatible with the contemporary Western liberal emphasis on individual freedom.

Robert Bellah (1973) is one of the most thoughtful interpreters of Durkheim, and his introduction to *Emile Durkheim: On Morality and Society* shows the deep moral tenor of the entirety of Durkheim's work. Bellah sketches Durkheim as a moral philosopher endeavoring to construct an intellectual program to contribute to social reform in the service of French republicanism. He uses one of his own conceptual terms, that of **civil religion** (a body of beliefs about national identity and history that draw on nondenominational religious themes and narratives), to describe the content of Durkheim's own beliefs.

That Durkheim wrote as much as he did on the family is a fact unknown to many English-speaking sociologists because so much of that work, in the form of book reviews and short pieces for the *Année,* remains untranslated. There is a relative dearth of informed commentary on Durkheim's work on the family in English. Mary Ann Lamanna's (2002) book, *Emile Durkheim on the Family,* is one of the few quality efforts in this area. In this rigorously fair analysis, Lamanna contextualizes his work historically, examines reasons for the frequent (seemingly willful) misunderstandings of this aspect of Durkheim's thought, and makes a strong case for the importance of his work on the family, all while still, as a feminist, disagreeing with some of the elements of his analysis. Jean Elisabeth Pedersen ("Something Mysterious: Sex Education, Victorian Morality, and Durkheim's Comparative Sociology," 1998) makes a nuanced examination of Durkheim's position in a debate concerning sexual education that was discussed in Chapter 3. Superficial and ideologically dogmatic readings of Durkheim here see him as a conservative, but Pedersen aptly demonstrates that his insistence on seeing the case for or against sex education as a question of cultural politics and not biology makes him something more complex. The cultural historian Christophe Charle ("Le beau marriage d'Émile Durkheim," 1984) looks carefully at the ways in which the sociology of Durkheim's own family (e.g., the neat division of labor between him and his wife, the cultural and economic capital that came from his entry into the Dreyfus family) constitutes a chief element in the production of his own work.

Durkheimian Studies/*Études durkheimiennes*

This journal was created in 1977 by Philippe Besnard, who had by the mid-1970s established himself as the leading interpreter of Durkheim in his generation, in 1977. It was based in Paris, at the Maison des Sciences de l'Homme, for a decade until the funding source dried up. In 1987, Robert Alun Jones at the University of Illinois, Urbana-Champagne, took over the project, subsequently passing the torch to the British Centre for Durkheimian Studies at the Institute of Social and Cultural Anthropology of Oxford University in 1994. This journal bearing Durkheim's name remains there today, dedicated to publishing, in English and French, interpretive readings of Durkheim's work and new research that takes it as a starting point. The journal's trajectory since its founding is appropriate, indicating the tremendous influence of Durkheimian thought in all three (France, United States, and UK) of these national intellectual cultures.

Conclusion

The evidence presented above, and much that I could not include, shows precisely how vibrant Durkheim's legacy is today. As we home in on the date marking the centennial of his death, his work has never seemed more relevant. Whether we look to the near-collapse of the Western economy in the wake of neoliberal legislation designed to remove any moral discipline and regulation from the system, or to the explosive cultural debates over the massive changes in the family and marriage over the past 40 years, or to the invigorated face of religion and other forms of cultural collective effervescence around the globe, Durkheim remains a thinker that all serious students of contemporary society and culture must read and reread.

A few questions

- What does the fact that we can still profitably read Durkheim tell us about how sociological knowledge advances?
- Do you think Durkheim's work will still be relevant in 2050?
- Why is *The Rules of Sociological Method* so frequently seen critically? Is the vision of sociology Durkheim presents there still viable?
- What national differences can be seen in how Durkheim is interpreted in France, the UK, and the United States?
- What can intellectual biographies tell us about the work of a thinker like Durkheim that traditional textual interpretation cannot?

Glossary

A priorism Theory of the categories of human knowledge that sees them as given by human nature.

Altruistic suicide Type of suicide caused by excessive social integration; it is typical of less advanced forms of society and expected by Durkheim to shrink in modernity.

Animism Primitive form of religion based on a belief in spiritual entities, originally the double of dreams, then souls that are freed from the body at death. This form of religion eventually becomes focused on mortuary cults to the spirits of deceased ancestors.

Anomic division of labor Abnormal condition in which there is insufficient regulation of the relationships between the various elements of the division of labor.

Anomic suicide An act of self-destruction caused by insufficient moral regulation; it is seen by Durkheim as one of the two rising kinds of suicide in modernity.

Asceticism The central element of the negative cult, illustrated in the sufferings the religious undergo to attain the purified state necessary for interaction with the sacred.

Attachment to groups One of the three central elements of education, intended as a means to curb egoism in the child.

Authority An external moral power to which we are obedient and that sets up a system of rules to which we subordinate ourselves.

Autonomy One of the three central elements of education, which describes the individual's willing submission to educational authority.

241

Blood covenant   A primitive form of contract involving members of two groups not related by kinship bonds and therefore requiring the pledge of blood to solidify the contract.

Bureaucratic division of labor   The abnormal form wherein individual effort is not given appropriate scope and the various elements of the division of labor are not effectively coordinated.

Churinga   In central Australian aboriginal totemic groups, a wooden or stone object understood to possess magical powers that are derived from the image of the totem it bears.

Civil religion   A body of beliefs about national identity and history that draw on nondenominational religious themes and narratives.

Classificatory systems   Forms of organization of phenomena in the world and related concepts that are collectively produced by human groups as a kind of epistemological parallel to the structure of the group itself.

Collective consciousness   The set of beliefs that is shared by all or nearly all of the members of any given society.

Collective effervescence   Ecstatic emotion produced by members of a religious group engaged in intense ritual action focused on some religious symbol.

Collective representations   Collections of ideas and symbols, often found in myth, legend, and religion, shared by members of a social group and used by the group to express its relationships with the world.

Communism   Primitive, utopian form of socialism in which all production and consumption are regulated.

Concomitant variation   According to John Stuart Mill, the study of cause and effect wherein any phenomenon that varies whenever another phenomenon varies is recognized as either a cause or an effect of the other, or it is seen as connected to it through some fact of causation.

Conjugal family   The typical modern familial form, consisting of the husband, wife, and their unmarried children.

Contract theory (or social contract theory)   The philosophical view of the origins of human society based solely in the willed agreements of individuals pursuing their own individual self-interest.

Corroboree   Intense collective religious celebration in Australian aboriginal totemism.

Cult of the human person   A secular republican quasi-religion that pointed to the human person as an abstract concept and to its uniquely human characteristics (reason, creativity, moral concern for others, ability to transcend merely biological desires and needs) as its sacred object.

Cultural relativism   The perspective that no one moral system can be posited as optimal for all human societies throughout the history of humankind and thus that no civilization's accomplishments are inherently superior to those of others.

Cultural sociology   The sociological perspective that sees culture as at least potentially autonomous from social structure.

Cultural turn   The increased interest in culture as a relatively independently acting aspect of human society in the human sciences over the past several decades.

Democracy   The form of modern political organization in which the State elites periodically change rather than remain static, as in monarchies.

Discipline   One of the three elements of education, consisting of the imposition of limits on the will based on adherence to rules and authority.

Division of labor   The specialization of tasks and functions existing in any society, more complex and differentiated in some than in others.

Dreyfus Affair   A central point of political and cultural debate in Third Republic France. French Army captain Alfred Dreyfus was prosecuted and found guilty of a treasonous act that there was no real evidence he had committed. France's public figures and intellectuals divided up into opposing sides: conservative supporters of the Army and the Church against republicans who adhered to the abstract principles of the French Republic and reverence for the Republic's sacred entity, the individual.

Dynamic or moral density   The level of intensity and frequency of interaction among individuals in a population.

École Normale Supérieure   The prestigious postsecondary institution in Paris that trained all those who would enter the secondary and postsecondary teaching profession in France.

Egoistic suicide   An act of self-destruction caused by insufficient social integration.

Empiricism   The philosophical view that human knowledge derives entirely from experience; typified by David Hume.

Fatalistic suicide   An act of self-destruction caused by excessive moral regulation.

Forced division of labor   The abnormal form in which there is pronounced inequality of opportunity and some workers feel trapped in positions below what they feel they deserve.

Free union   The form of sexual relationship that exists outside legal sanction; concubinage.

Functions (and functionalism)   The relations between activities of an organism (organic or social) and specific needs of that organism. Functionalism is the view of society that concentrates on functions as its central elements.

Gemeinschaft   According to Ferdinand Tönnies, a form of social relations based on intimacy, tradition, and organicism. Usually translated as "community."

German mentality   The aggressive, militant view of the State as an ultimate power and of violent force as the ultimate arbiter of human relations, discernible in the German writer Heinrich von Treitschke and, according to Durkheim, in the entire German people during World War I.

Gesellschaft   According to Ferdinand Tönnies, a form of social relations based on purely egoistic and economic goals. Usually translated, somewhat inadequately, as "society."

Guilds   Trade organizations that came into existence in the time of the Roman Empire, then reemerged in a different form in medieval Europe before being dismantled with the rise of the Industrial and French Revolutions. They united all the members of a particular trade or craft into a single body and pursued numerous goals in their interests.

Homo duplex   The idea that the human individual is in fact two beings united in one, the one purely individual and ultimately biological, the other having to do with the presence in the individual of the social groups of which she is a member.

Imitation   In the thought of Gabriel Tarde, the large-scale mimicry of established patterns of behavior that spreads over wide expanses of the human world.

Impure sacred   The blasphemous; sacred things that inspire horror.

Indirect experimentation   The comparative method in sociological research.

Innovation   In the thought of Gabriel Tarde, the explosive and unpredictable spontaneous divergence from the established pattern of doing things.

Institutions   Well-established and relatively long-lived social facts.

Intichiuma   Ceremony of Australian aboriginal tribal peoples designed to ensure the reproduction of the totem.

"J'accuse" letter of Émile Zola   A major element in the intellectual debate over the Dreyfus Affair. In this letter, published on the front page of a prominent Paris newspaper, Zola denounced the French military and the government for their unjust prosecution of Army captain Alfred Dreyfus and accused the establishment of anti-Jewish prejudice that struck at the very heart of republican France.

Just contract   A contractual form that takes into account the status of knowledge and coercion of the two parties and declares a contract null and void if one or the other party has been misled or forced to act; the future direction of contract law, according to Durkheim.

Law of exogamy   The prohibition of sexual contact between members of the same totem group in primitive social organizations.

Law of Three Stages (in Saint-Simon and Comte)   A theory of history that sees human society moving through three progressive stages (feudal/juridical/socialist in Saint-Simon; theological/metaphysical/positivist in Comte).

Lumpenproletariat   The term used by Marx to describe the reactionary peasantry and the urban underclasses who were frequently mobilized politically in a cynical fashion by reactionary leaders such as the Emperor Louis-Napoléon.

Mana   The idea of force as expressed in primitive societies as a magical energy inhering in certain parts of the world.

Mechanical solidarity   Form of solidarity typical of primitive societies, in which individuals are generally much like one another and their moral relations are based fundamentally on religion and deeply held moral beliefs.

Methodological individualism   The theoretical principle that society is nothing more than the sum of individual dispositions and actions.

Mill's Methods   The five types of inductive reasoning in scientific research that were presented by John Stuart Mill in *A System of Logic*.

Mimetic rites   Aspects of the positive cult that consist of worshippers imitating the totem entity and thereby (in their view) demonstrating their relationship to it.

Mimicry (in suicide)   The phenomenon of individuals learning of the actions of previous suicides and copying their act.

Moieties   Subdivision of primitive tribal societies; moieties are further divided into separate clans that often have specific, structured relations to one another.

Moral education   The training of youth with the goal of their moral integration into society.

Moral individualism   The variety of individualism championed by Durkheim, which emphasized the cult of the abstract human person.

Moral regulation   The action by which a social group sets boundaries to the actions of individuals in pursuit of their desires.

Morale laïque   "Secular morality"; an invention of the Third Republic that was intended specifically to refer to the ethical precepts and system taught in the public school system.

Naturism   The theory that early religion was based in worship of natural phenomena.

Negative cult   Aspects of a religious rite that involve ascetic preparation of the worshipper so that he is in a proper state to contact the sacred.

Negative solidarity   The form of solidarity that consists solely in marking the boundaries between individuals and defining relationships between persons and property.

Nominalism (in study of human groups)   The view that each society is an incomparable, unique entity.

Normal and pathological   Respectively, the typical, average type of a given phenomenon and any type of that same phenomenon that is atypical, abnormal, and deviant.

Organic solidarity   Form of solidarity typical of modern societies, in which individuals are differentiated from one another and the bonds that unite them have to do with contractual relations and mutual interdependence.

Paris Commune   In the wake of the French defeat at the hands of Prussia in 1871, the revolutionary "state" that existed in Paris for several months early in the year before it was brutally crushed by French troops.

Pedagogy   The theory of education, as opposed to its practice.

Phratries   A category of hierarchical organization of primitive societies consisting of numerous groups of related clans taken together.

Piacular rites   Religious rites oriented to death and the dead, often involving suffering on the part of mourners.

Positive cult   Aspects of religious ritual that actually bring worshippers into contact with the sacred, including sacrifice, mimetic rites, and commemorative rites.

Positive solidarity   The form of solidarity that directly contributes to the integration of members of the society. It consists of two types: mechanical and organic.

Positivism   The view that all knowledge must be demonstrable through empirical evidence available to sensory experience, and that therefore all deductive reasoning is flawed.

Pragmatism   The American philosophical phenomenon of the early 20th century characterized by John Dewey, William James, and Charles Sanders Peirce, critically addressed by Durkheim in a late lecture course.

Profane   That which is mundane and not inhabited by sacred energy.

Professional ethics   Moral rules that apply to individuals based on their particular place in the division of labor.

Property right   Legal codes delineating relations of individuals to property, which originated in religious beliefs.

Pure sacred   The holy or the venerated; sacred things that inspire respect and reverence.

Race   An amorphous category of identity that Durkheim describes as virtually indistinguishable from "ethnicity" or "nationality."

Real contract   A form of exchange in which the obligation to complete the agreed-upon exchange is contained in the actual handing over of the first thing in the exchange.

Real rights   Rights that do not help to form social bonds but rather mark the boundaries between people and, in general, establish the relation between persons and property.

Realism (in study of human groups)   The view that all distinctions of type in human societies are arbitrary and that humanity as a whole is the only real group.

Representative or commemorative rites   Religious rites that reenact some supposed act of importance in the mythic past of a group; their effect is to revitalize the group's sense of collective identity.

Right of contract   Legal mechanism by which relation of exchange is established between two parties, which, like property right, originated in religious beliefs.

Sacred   A quality adhering to certain things and concepts that requires its separation and protection from the everyday world; sacred things are believed to be receptacles of great power.

Sacrifice   A religious rite that consists of a communal repast in which the god and the worshipper become one flesh and create a bond of kinship between them. It is at once an act of communion and offering.

Social constructionism   The view that phenomena in the human world have the meanings they have because of the values and beliefs of given societies, not because of any inherent moral qualities they have. Thus, what is a crime in one society might be perfectly acceptable in another.

Social current   The powerful forces that move individuals acting collectively in ways that are beyond their individual control—for example, in crowd situations.

Social fact   A way of acting, thinking, and feeling defined by two characteristics of its action on humans: its externality to the individual consciousness and its coerciveness.

Social integration   The action by which a social group provides individual members of the group with a sense of well-being and protection against excessive egoism.

Social solidarity   The moral force that brings individuals together into a collective life, binding them beyond their merely individual interests and desires.

Social species   Discrete social groups that are united by their immersion in the same social facts and collective representations.

Social type   A given kind of society at a given stage in its development.

Socialism   The economic organization of society in which all economic functions are connected to the directing and conscious centers of society.

Solidarism   The dominant political ideology of the early years of the Third Republic, which advocated a form of social democracy seen as a middle way between extremist collectivism (on both the right and the left) and liberal economic individualism of an asocial variety.

State   The collection of officials who work out formal representations of the collectivity and act on its behalf.

Taboo   A Polynesian term indicating the status of a thing as consecrated and therefore to be set apart from other, mundane things.

Totem   An entity in the animal or plant world, and sometimes an inanimate natural thing or phenomenon (e.g., a stone or a star), that in totemic societies is treated religiously as the progenitor of the social group.

Totemism   A social and religious system based on divisions of human groups into clans that are conceived as members of a common family.

Value judgments   Statements that allude to external things in a manner that attributes to them an objective character independent of one's individual feelings—for example, stating that a certain painting has high artistic quality.

References

Alexander, J. (Ed.). (1988). *Durkheimian sociology: Cultural studies*. New York: Cambridge University Press.

Alexander, J., & Smith, P. (Eds.). (2005). *The Cambridge companion to Durkheim*. New York: Cambridge University Press.

Bellah, R. (Ed.). (1973). *Emile Durkheim: On morality and society*. Chicago: University of Chicago Press.

Bellah, R., et al. (1985). *Habits of the heart*. Berkeley: University of California Press.

Besnard, P. (1983). *The sociological domain: The Durkheimians and the founding of French sociology*. Paris and Cambridge: Éditions de la Maison des Sciences de l'Homme and Cambridge University Press.

Besnard, P. (Ed.). (1987a). Lettres de Emile Durkheim à Henri Hubert. *Revue française de sociologie, 38*, 483–534.

Besnard, P. (1987b). *L'anomie, ses usages et ses fonctions dans la discipline sociologique depuis Durkheim*. Paris: Presses Universitaires de France.

Besnard, P. (2003). Études *durkheimiennes*. Geneva: Librairie Droz.

Besnard, P. (2004). En suivant ma pente: de Bud Powell. *Revue française de sociologie, Revue européenne des sciences sociales, XLII*(129), 385–401.

Besnard, P., Borlandi, M., & Vogt, P. (Eds.). (1993). *Division de travail social: La thèse de Durkheim un siècle après*. Paris: Presses Universitaires de France.

Borlandi, M., & Cherkaoui, M. (Eds.). (2000). *Le* Suicide*, un siecle après Durkheim*. Paris: Presses Universitaires de France.

Borlandi, M., & Mucchielli, L. (Eds.). (1995). *La sociologie et sa méthode. Les Règles de Durkheim, un siècle après*. Paris: Harmattan, 1995.

Cardi, F., & Plantier, J. (Eds.). (1993). *Durkheim, sociologue de l'éducation: Journées d'étude 15–16 octobre 1992*. Paris: L'Harmattan.

Charle, C. (1984). Le beau marriage d'Émile Durkheim. *Actes de la recherche en sciences sociales, 55*, 45–49.

Cladis, M. (1992). *A communitarian defense of liberalism: Emile Durkheim and contemporary social theory*. Stanford, CA: Stanford University Press.

Cladis, M. (2005). Beyond solidarity? Durkheim and twenty-first-century democracy in a global age. In J. Alexander & P. Smith (Eds.), *The Cambridge companion to Durkheim* (pp. 383–409). Cambridge, MA: Cambridge University Press.

Clark, T. (1973). *Prophets and patrons: The French university and the emergence of the social sciences*. New York: Harvard University Press.

Davy, G. (1919). Emile Durkheim. *Annuaire de l'Association amicale des anciens élèves de l'École normale supérieure*.

Davy, G. (1960). Allocution. Commémoration du centenaire de la naissance d'Émile Durkheim. *Annales de l'Université de Paris, 30*(1), 16–22.

Davy, G. (1995). Emile Durkheim: L'Homme. In P. Hamilton (Ed.), *Emile Durkheim: Critical assessments* (pp. 87–99). London: Routledge. (Original work published in 1919)

Douglas, J. (1967). *The social meanings of suicide*. Princeton, NJ: Princeton University Press.

Durkheim, É. (1887). Nécrologie d'Hommay. In *Victor Hommay: Hommage à une chère mémoire* (pp. 13–21). Bordeaux.

Durkheim, É. (1898). Preface. *Année sociologique, 1*, i–vii.

Durkheim, É. (1915). *L'Allemange au-dessus de tout: La mentalité allemande et la guerre*. Paris: Armand Colin.

Durkheim, É. (1953). *Sociology and philosophy*. (D. F. Pocock, Trans.). Glencoe, IL: Free Press. (Original work published in 1924)

Durkheim, É. (1956). *Education and sociology*. (S. Fox, Trans.). Glencoe, IL: Free Press. (Original work published in 1922)

Durkheim, É. (1960). *Montesquieu and Rousseau: Forerunners of sociology*. Ann Arbor: University of Michigan Press.

Durkheim, É. (1961). *Moral education*. (E. Wilson & H. Schnurer, Trans.). Glencoe, IL: Free Press. (Original work published in 1925)

Durkheim, É. (1962). *Socialism*. (C. Sattler, Trans.). New York: Collier. (Original work published in 1928)

Durkheim, É. (1963). *Incest: The nature and origin of the taboo*. (E. Sagarin, Trans.). New York: Lyle Stuart Inc. (Original work published in 1898)

Durkheim, É. (1969). De la définition des phénomènes religieux. In É. Durkheim, *Journal sociologique* (pp. 140–165). Paris: PUF. (Original work published in 1898)

Durkheim, É. (1973). Individualism and the intellectuals. In R. Bellah (Ed.), *Emile Durkheim on morality and society* (pp. 43–57). Chicago: University of Chicago Press. (Original work published in 1898)

Durkheim, É. (1975a). Le rôle des grands hommes dans l'histoire. In É. Durkheim, *Textes. 1. Éléments d'une théorie sociale* (pp. 409–417). Paris: Éditions de Minuit. (Original work published in 1883)

Durkheim, É. (1975b). Débat sur l'education sexuelle. In É. Durkheim, *Textes. 2. Religion, morale, anomie* (pp. 241–251). Paris: Éditions de Minuit. (Original work published in 1911)

Durkheim, É. (1975c). La science positive de la morale en Allemagne. In É. Durkheim, *Textes. 1. Éléments d'une théorie sociale* (pp. 267–343). Paris: Éditions de Minuit. (Original work published in 1887)

Durkheim, É. (1975d). Origine du mariage dans l'espèce humaine d'après Westermarck. In É. Durkheim, *Textes. 3. Fonctions sociales et institutions* (pp. 70–92). Paris: Éditions de Minuit. (Original work published in 1895)

Durkheim, É. (1977). *The evolution of educational thought: Lectures on the formation and development of secondary education in France.* London: Routledge & Kegan Paul. (Original work published in 1938)

Durkheim, É. (1978a). Review of Antonio Labriola. In M. Traugott (Ed.), *Emile Durkheim on institutional analysis* (pp. 123–130). Chicago: University of Chicago Press. (Original work published in 1897)

Durkheim, É. (1978b). Socialisme et science sociale. In M. Traugott (Ed.), *Emile Durkheim on institutional analysis* (pp. 131–138). Chicago: University of Chicago Press. (Original work published in 1897)

Durkheim, É. (1978c). Introduction to *La Morale*. In M. Traugott (Ed.), *Emile Durkheim on institutional analysis* (pp. 191–202). Chicago: University of Chicago Press. (Original work published in 1920)

Durkheim, É. (1978d). Review of Marianne Weber. In M. Traugott (Ed.), *Emile Durkheim on institutional analysis* (pp. 139–144). Chicago: University of Chicago Press. (Original work published in 1906–1909)

Durkheim, É. (1978e). The conjugal family. In M. Traugott (Ed.), *Emile Durkheim on institutional analysis* (pp. 229–239). Chicago: University of Chicago Press. (Original work published in 1892)

Durkheim, É. (1978f). Divorce by mutual consent. In M. Traugott (Ed.), *Emile Durkheim on institutional analysis* (pp. 240–252). Chicago: University of Chicago Press. (Original work published in 1906)

Durkheim, É. (1982). *The rules of sociological method and selected texts on sociology and its method.* (W. D. Halls, Trans.). New York: Free Press. (Original work published in 1895)

Durkheim, É. (1983). *Pragmatism and sociology.* (J. C. Whitehouse, Trans.). New York: Cambridge University Press. (Original work published in 1955)

Durkheim, É. (1984). *The division of labor in society.* (W. D. Halls, Trans.). New York: Free Press. (Original work published in 1893)

Durkheim, É. (1992). *Professional ethics and civic morals.* (C. Brookfield, Trans.). London: Routledge. (Original work published in 1950)

Durkheim, É. (1994). Suicide and the birth rate, a study in moral statistics. In L. David (Ed.), *Émile Durkheim: Le suicide one hundred years later* (pp. 115–132). Philadelphia: Charles Press. (Original work published in 1888)

Durkheim, É. (1995). *The elementary forms of religious life.* (K. Fields, Trans.). New York: Free Press. (Original work published in 1912)

Durkheim, É. (1998). *Lettres à Marcel Mauss.* P. Besnard. & M. Fournier (Eds.). Paris: Presses Universitaires de France.

Durkheim, É. (2006). *On suicide.* (R. Buss, Trans.). New York: Penguin. (Original work published in 1897)

Durkheim, É., & Denis, E. (1915). *Qui a voulu la guerre? Les origines de la guerre d'après les documents diplomatiques.* Paris: Armand Colin.

Durkheim, É., & Lavisse, E. (1992). *Lettres à tous les français.* Paris: Armand Colin. (Original work published in 1916)

Durkheim, É., & Mauss, M. (1963). *Primitive classification.* (R. Needham, Trans.). Chicago: University of Chicago Press. (Original work published in 1903)

Filloux, J.-C. (1977). *Durkheim et le socialisme*. Geneva: Librairie Droz.

Filloux, J.-C. (1994). *Durkheim et l'éducation*. Paris: PUF.

Fournier, M. (2007). *Emile Durkheim*. Paris: Fayard.

Gane, M. (1988). *On Durkheim's rules of sociological method*. London: Routledge.

Gane, M. (1990). *The radical sociology of Durkheim and Mauss*. London: Routledge.

Greenberg, L. M. (1976). Bergson and Durkheim as sons and assimilators: The early years. *French Historical Studies, 9*(4), 619–634.

Halbwachs, M. (1930). *Les causes du suicide*. Paris: Librairie Felix Alcan.

Hayward, J. E. S. (1961). The official social philosophy of the Third Republic: Léon Bourgeois and solidarism. *International Review of Social History, 6*, 19–48.

Héran, Jean-Michel. (1989). De *La Cité antique* à la sociologie des institutions. *Revue de synthèse, 4*(3–4), 363–390.

Johnson, B. (1994). Commentary on suicide and the birth rate, a study in moral statistics. In D. Lester (Ed.), *Émile Durkheim: Le suicide one hundred years later* (pp. 133–204). Philadelphia: Charles Press.

Jones, R. A. (1986). *Emile Durkheim: An introduction to four major works*. Thousand Oaks, CA: Sage.

Jones, R. A. (1990). Realism and religion: Some reflections on Durkheim's *L'evolution pédagogique en France. Archive des sciences sociales des religions, 69*, 69–89.

Jones, R. A. (1999). *The development of Durkheim's social realism*. New York: Cambridge University Press.

Jones, S. S. (2001). *Durkheim reconsidered*. London: Polity.

Lacroix, B. (1981). *Durkheim et le politique*. Paris: Presses de la Fondation Nationale des Sciences Politiques, Presses de l'Université de Montréal.

Lamanna, M. A. (2002). *Emile Durkheim on the family*. Thousand Oaks, CA: Sage.

Lester, D. (Ed.). (1994). *Emile Durkheim, le suicide: One hundred years later*. Philadelphia, PA: Charles Press.

Lukes, S. (1985). *Emile Durkheim: His life and work, a historical and critical study*. Stanford, CA: Stanford University Press. (Original work published in 1973)

Mauss, M. (1925). In memoriam. L'œuvre inédite de Durkheim et de ses collaborateurs. *Année sociologique, n.s.*(I), 8–29.

Mauss, M. (1979). L'œuvre de Mauss par lui-même. *Revue française de sociologie, 20*(1), 209–220.

Miller, W. W. (1996). *Durkheim, morals and modernity*. Montréal: McGill-Queen's University Press.

Miller, W. W. (2012). *A Durkheimian quest: Solidarity and the sacred*. London: Berghahn Books.

Nielsen, D. (1999). *Three faces of God: Society, religion and the categories of totality in the philosophy of Emile Durkheim*. Albany: State University of New York Press.

Nisbet, R. (1966). *The sociological tradition*. New York: Basic Books.

Nisbet, R. (1974). *The sociology of Emile Durkheim*. New York: Oxford University Press.

Nisbet, R. (1976). *Sociology as an art form*. London: Oxford University Press.

Parsons, T. (1937). *The structure of social action*. New York: Free Press.

Pearce, F. (1998). *The radical Durkheim*. London: Unwin Hyman.

Pedersen, J. E. (1998). Something mysterious: Sex education, Victorian morality, and Durkheim's comparative sociology. *Journal of the History of the Behavioral Sciences, 34*(2), 135–151.

Pickering, M. (2006 and 2009). *Auguste Comte: An intellectual biography*, volumes I, II, and III. Cambridge, UK: Cambridge University Press.

Pickering, W. S. F. (Ed.). (1979). *Durkheim: Essays on morals and education*. London: Routledge & Kegan Paul.

Pickering, W. S. F. (1984). *Durkheim's sociology of religion: Themes and theories*. London: Routledge & Kegan Paul.

Pickering, W. S. F. (Ed.). (2000). *Durkheim and representations*. London: Routledge.

Pickering, W. S. F., & Rosati, M. (2008). *Suffering and evil: The Durkheimian legacy*. New York: Berghahn.

Pickering, W. S. F., & Wolford, G. (Eds.). (2000). *Durkheim's* Suicide: *A century of research and debate*. London: Routledge.

Pope, W. (1976). *Durkheim's* Suicide: *A classic analyzed*. Chicago: University of Chicago Press.

Rawls, A. (2009). *Epistemology and practice: Durkheim's* The elementary forms of religious life. New York: Cambridge University Press.

Riley, A. (2010). *Godless intellectuals? The intellectual reinvention of the sacred*. New York: Berghahn.

Schmauss, W. (1994). *Durkheim's philosophy of science and the sociology of knowledge: Creating an intellectual niche*. Chicago: University of Chicago Press.

Stock-Morton, P. (1988). *Moral education for a secular society: The development of morale laïque in nineteenth-century France*. Albany: State University of New York Press.

Strenski, I. (1997). *Durkheim and the Jews of France*. Chicago: University of Chicago Press.

Strenski, I. (2006). *The new Durkheim*. New Brunswick, NJ: Rutgers University Press.

Tiryakian, E. (1962). *Sociologism and existentialism: Two perspectives on the individual and society*. Englewood Cliffs, NJ: Prentice Hall.

Tiryakian, E. (2009). *For Durkheim: Essays in historical and cultural sociology*. Burlington, VT: Ashgate.

Traugott, M. (Ed.). (1994). *Emile Durkheim: On institutional analysis*. Chicago: University of Chicago Press.

Walford, G., & Pickering, W. S. F. (1998). *Durkheim and modern education*. London: Routledge.

Weber, E. (2004). *Questioning Judaism: Interviews by Elisabeth Weber* (R. Bowlby, Trans.). Palo Alto, CA: Stanford University Press.

Weisz, G. (1983). *The emergence of modern universities in France, 1863–1914*. Princeton, NJ: Princeton University.

Index

About the Author

Alexander Riley has written a good deal on Durkheim and from a fundamentally Durkheimian perspective on various topics over the past 15 years. These writings include his doctoral thesis at the University of California, San Diego ("In Pursuit of the Sacred: The Durkheimian Sociologists of Religion and the Modern Intellectual") and several of his books (*Godless Intellectuals? The Intellectual Pursuit of the Sacred Reinvented; Impure Play: Sacredness, Transgression, and the Tragic in Popular Culture;* and the forthcoming *Angel Patriots in the Sky: The Crash of United Flight 93 and the Myth of America*). He is spending the academic year 2013 through 2014 in Paris on a Fulbright Research Grant, along with his wife, Esmeralda; their daughter, Valeria; and the family cat.

⑤SAGE research**methods**

The essential online tool for researchers from the world's leading methods publisher

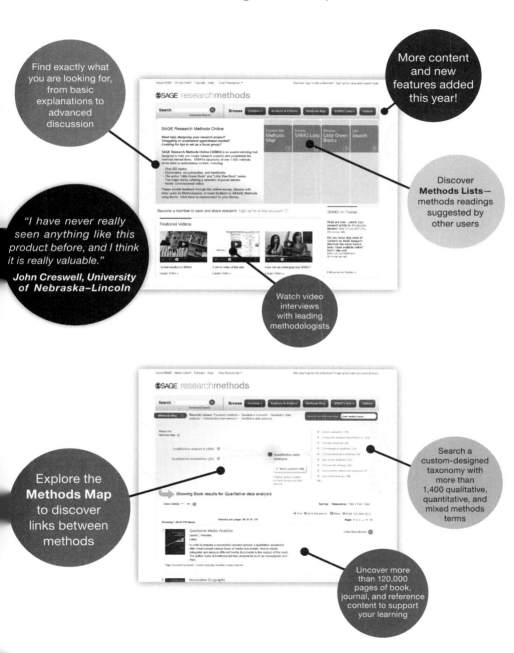

Find exactly what you are looking for, from basic explanations to advanced discussion

More content and new features added this year!

"I have never really seen anything like this product before, and I think it is really valuable."
John Creswell, University of Nebraska–Lincoln

Discover **Methods Lists**— methods readings suggested by other users

Watch video interviews with leading methodologists

Explore the **Methods Map** to discover links between methods

Search a custom-designed taxonomy with more than 1,400 qualitative, quantitative, and mixed methods terms

Uncover more than 120,000 pages of book, journal, and reference content to support your learning

Find out more at
www.sageresearchmethods.com